CORNSILK

Growing up Green

Jane Belton Glazer

Press-22
Portland, Oregon

Copyright © 2006 by Jane Belton Glazer
ISBN 978-0-942382-12-9

Press-22
4828 Southeast Hawthorne Boulevard
Portland, Oregon 97215

CORNSILK

My heartfelt gratitude to wonderful friends who so generously encouraged me to finish this book: Hilary Bacon, Annie Callan, Andrea Carlile, Robin Cody, Sandra Dorr, Martha Gies, Pamela Glenn, John Laursen, Judith Montgomery, and, of course, Howard. To all of you who helped me hoe the weeds from these long rows of memory, I send my love and, if I could, a freshly steamed ear of sweet corn, dripping with butter.

In memory of my parents

MERRILL JESSE BELTON   XELA CHANTRY BELTON
1896–1986   1898–1974

and of my brother

ROBERT RIED BELTON
1923–1992

Contents

Looking Back
PAGE 1

Our Stories
PAGE 9

Letting Go
PAGE 265

Looking Back

Prologue

Anyone who has ever shucked an ear of fresh corn knows why the satiny fiber between the husk and those milky rows of teeth is called "cornsilk." Shiny as a girl's hair in the sun, so blond, so soft, so flyaway that it clings to the cob, it seems loath to be separated. Electrostatic, as if bewitched by brushing, it is as hard to get off the hand as shrink-wrap. Like wet rice noodles, it glues itself to the kitchen sink, the counter tops, the stove. Even after a newspaper is wrapped around the torn-off husks and wedged into the garbage can, even after the steamer is washed and put away, a few threads of cornsilk stick to the dishtowel.

And so it is with memory. This book is written in stop-time, to reflect on the days that fly away like cornsilk, yet cling to the heart. The impressions left over from childhood remain vivid, not always literal, but true to the perception of that time, an ear of corn stripped of its husk with a few threads still clinging.

To grow up green in Iowa is to know the land and the things that grow there, the changes the seasons bring to Osage oranges, wild roses, oats, barley, hay. Deep in the woods, we know where black walnuts and hickory trees grew, where to pick honeysuckle, wild violets, hearts-ease. It is to know the sky, the clouds that are driven by winds and weather, the flat blue slate of unrelenting sun, the opacity of oncoming snow.

And it is to know corn, the planting of seed corn, the way it grows, the ripening tassels, the harvesting, the husking, the taste of sweet corn, the recipe for fritters, the rustle of dried stocks still in the field in October, the hulling of popcorn for winter Sunday nights.

In the ways of the wider world, though, we children were green as spring grass.

The Promise

When a flash of memory takes me by surprise, triggered by a sight, a smell, or something I've read, I am a child again, running naked through the rows of greening corn, playing hide and seek with my brother. As dusk begins to cool the heat of an Iowa summer day, we strip off our clothes, curl our bare feet into the sun-warmed dirt, and run whooping, as if sprung free of earth, through the long blades of rustling cornstalks.

We lived then in a rich and precious time of innocence, roughly between the two World Wars, nearly eighty years ago. The freedom to explore both the close-in world of home and barn and pasture with animals—their skins, their tongues, their smells—and the opened-out world of a child's imagination was ours. Clouds drew pictures for us, the creek was a mighty river, and we, forever together, rode the wings of the wind. Like unfettered savages, we measured time by the way the seasons turned, felt the world on the soles of our feet or through the flannel lining of our winter galoshes. Trust and freedom were our birthright, a life more of the spirit than of matter, of the wonder of small things, leaf color or snowflake, of being read to, talked to, listened to. It was a world before television or antibiotics, where our images were gleaned either from our own observations or experience—the fury of a blizzard, the nut gathering of autumn, the death of a playmate—

or from stories read to us or overheard from the unhurried talk around the table.

Long after we were grown, my brother Bob and I toyed with the idea of writing a book together, a collection of stories about those long-ago first years of our childhood so intimately shared, mostly on the land. Of course, the places and the people we grew up with would have changed, if in fact we had not conjured them from memory in the first place. But the smell of the prairie, the sniff of blooming crab-apples, the pinched nostrils in a cold snap, and the freedom of summer under the wide arc of a blue and cloudless sky, these, in the small brick town in the Midwest that had shaped our earliest years—these were indelibly ours.

As adults, our lives having deepened and widened since the years of being "young sprouts," as our father called us, we longed to work on something together. Our professional lives, medicine and education respectively, had netted each of us life experience and a sense of confidence. We shared a liberal view of the world and a love of travel, study, and learning new languages. He had a hilarious and dry sense of humor, contagious as impetigo. We could laugh uproariously, cry with indignation at the injustices of life. So we thought the time had come to pool our memories, to write them down, for our children or our siblings if for no one else. We welcomed a creative challenge.

I was two years younger than he, and had been thrown into his brotherly care since the day our twin sisters were born when I was three, he five years old. Now, as adults, whenever we looked back, we molded our memories into a larger-than-life adventure.

So, we began to plan. We wanted to meet back in Redfield, Iowa, he from Washington, D.C., and I from Portland, Oregon, to revisit the setting that had shaped our lives so strongly, that still informed our memories vividly. Busy months passed. Neither of us made reservations; neither of us started noting down our childhood recollections.

And then it was too late. Bob learned he had maybe two months to live, maybe two weeks. He had come to Portland at Christmastime, already jaundiced and ill. Being an internist, he knew the days were numbered. So, precipitously, we flew back to Washington together, knowing what faced him, what we had to face together. On the plane, sitting beside each other, something would occur to him, and out of his jacket pocket would come the piece of paper and a pen, and he would jot it down. Then, replacing the list in his pocket, we would continue our conversation.

"I'm damned sorry about this, Jane. All our plans. On hold for now, I guess. Sorry to let you down. Guess you'll have to write the stories yourself." He paused, took a deep breath.

"We've become a part of history, you know. Can you believe how different the world is from what we once thought it'd be? . . . Janie, promise me something will you? You'll go ahead and write them on your own, okay?"

"Someday I will," I said, partly to put his mind at ease, partly to stop talking. I yawned so widely my jaw cracked. "But now, we've got a lot of other stuff to think about."

And out came the list. Bob wrote down, "Pick up shirts from laundry."

Mother always used to say, as we went outside to play, "Keep an eye on Janie, Bob; take care of her." Now, fate had turned the tables; it was my turn to take care.

Our Stories

December Surprise

Two great south-running rivers, the Mississippi and the Missouri, border the state, and its land is meshed with smaller waterways. Rivers, creeks, and ravines hold the secret of its rich soil and dense woodlands, abundant wildlife, migratory-bird flyways, its nut-bearing, sheltering trees. Among the earliest Americans to live here, one tribe gave the state its name. Iowa, the word itself, sounds to me the way it looks. The letter "I" stands high as the clouds, and the letter "O" is the open and waiting earth below them. "W" forms the hills and valleys, and "A" ends with a sigh of peace, amen. Fanciful, yes, yet it conjures up the hills rolling toward the horizon, covered now with tidy cornrows, evenly spaced as far as the eye can see.

But having lived the first years of my life in this heart of the heartland, I know that the cultivated, idyllic beauty of the tilled land comes at a high cost of labor and the impermanence of luck. For the weather sweeps across that prairie land dramatically, and the blue sky can become mustard yellow with impending wind storm or tornado, lint gray with rain, or charcoal black, pregnant with snow. We lived on the land with an eye cocked for weather. The narrow county road that leads out of small-town Redfield winds across a bridge that spans the middle fork of the Raccoon River, doglegs left to the white clapboard farmhouse we called home, set in the amplitude of space.

Inside that house, our family of four enjoyed the fruits of work, the taste of home-grown food, the comfort of a big dog, and the courage to face whatever risks fate had in mind. We lived on what was called the "Ficken" farm, the name carried down from the first owner. Just a mile or so out of town, the farm had enough room for Daddy's herd of shorthorn cattle to pasture, Mother's flower and vegetable garden, an oak-sprinkled large front yard, and several obligatory fields of corn. A screened-in front porch with a swing kept us cool in summer, and Daddy shoveled snow off the sidewalk out to the garage so we didn't slip in winter.

With winter came the silver days, the cold air turning rain to ice, the driveway a glaring mirror. Snow refused to melt. Everything shone in the winter sun, wan but lovely above the stone-cold world. Across the backyard ice, a bird, trying to land where breadcrumbs had been thrown, slipped and slid like a child on a newly waxed floor. The sky was filled with slatey clouds. After dusk, which came sooner as December crept along, the glint of the moon was silver on the bare-branched trees, and, as it grew full, would pour in through our windows like daylight. At age three, I would get up out of bed, dragging my comforter around my shoulders to marvel at the starry sky, the nakedness of the shivering, leafless trees, and to watch for the little ice feathers that started to form along the edges of the glass.

"Bobby," I whispered to my older brother, "come here. Someday I'm going to paint a picture like this."

He would get out of bed and come over to the window, but he wouldn't stay long. "It is too cold to be beautiful," he said, hopping back underneath the covers.

Jack Frost came in the night to paint on the glass, and those pictures, Mother told us, were like Siberia. We saw feathers and trees and icicles all tied together with spider webs of silk, silver and sparkling as tinsel. The big front lawn of the Ficken farm was like a new white sheet of drawing paper spread out over the ground.

After many days of deep freeze, a howling blizzard driven against the window so loud with wind that we weren't allowed outdoors, it gradually warmed up a little bit. Mother gave in to Bobby's pleading to let us go outside. We put on our heavy snowsuits that zipped up the front and our buckle-up galoshes. We pulled a chair up to reach and take down our own hats and mittens from the closet shelf. Whoever made our woolen mittens had also knitted hats to match with little pompoms on the top. A long string of yarn attached to our mittens went up one sleeve, over our necks and down the other sleeve, so we wouldn't lose one in the snow. Bobby's were blue, mine red.

Our snowball tracks scribbled across the paper lawn toward our snowman. Since we needed three balls, one for his body, one for his belly and one for his head, we rolled and rolled them around the lawn, watching each of the three get big enough to use. Some winters the snow stayed sticky enough long enough to make several snowmen before they began to melt.

Daddy let us use his plaid scarf around Snowy's neck and gave us a big carrot out of the root cellar for a nose. I buttoned the pieces of coal down his vest, turning my mittens black.

We made ice caves in the frozen drifts piled up against the garage, and wore ourselves out playing fox-and-geese, or making snow angels in every empty stretch of snow. Icicles hung down from the edge of the house like vampire's teeth, and we knocked them off with a long stick. When we came in, we took off all our stuff on the back porch and put the wet clothes, even our long socks, on a wooden drying rack by the kitchen stove where they smelled like wet dogs.

On one of Mother's blank recipe cards, Bobby made a little calendar to cross off the days until his birthday, December 18, 1928, when he would be five years old. He drew a big circle around the eighteenth and the twenty-fifth with our red Crayola.

The air was crisp with suspense, with the mystery of waiting. Our parents, too, were waiting: a new baby was to be born. They talked about the date Mother would go to the hospital, about who would come to take her place while she was in Des Moines. She let us feel the baby inside her stomach, kicking, very much alive. I sensed something of the risk and drama of these weeks without yet knowing that she had lost her firstborn little girl.

As soon as school let out for the Christmas holidays, Grandma Chantry arrived from town. My mother's mother, Ella Clementine Chantry, whom we both called "Gango," a name Bobby called her when he was just learning to talk, was a school teacher, a working widow who taught mathematics in the Des Moines public-school system. She was a witty, proud, industrious woman. Against a backdrop of carpet beaters, flat irons, curtain stretchers, and pickle crocks, she emerges from her busy widow's life in Des Moines as the liveliest person in my girlhood. She always spent part of the summer, and Christmas and Easter holidays with us, helping Mother with the canning or the sewing of school clothes in the fall.

Rocking in our porch swing on summer evenings, she recited long poems to us from memory, like Whittier's "Snowbound." We thought it would be exciting to be snowbound, but she was always kind of sad when she said it out loud. Her voice would match the rhythm of the porch swing as she pushed it back and forth with her pointy black shoes, and she would look far away, like she expected to see somebody.

And while in life's long afternoon,
Where cool and long the shadows grow,
I walk to meet the night that soon
Shall shape and shadow overflow,

> *I cannot feel that thou art far,*
> *Since near at need the angels are.*

I wondered how you could "walk to meet the night" which would be all around you anyway, but that angels were near made me sit very still, in case I might scare them away.

Gango had another favorite that she said she knew only parts of, a very mysterious story about somebody in a far-off land named Sohrab who got up early and sneaked into an old man's tent, "when the first gray of morning filled the east and the fog rose." I could just see him, this man with the funny name, slipping silently around before anyone else was out of bed, out there in the desert where nomads lived. Gango could cast a spell with her poems and her singing, making a place or a person seem real, even if they sometimes flew around the sky on a rug.

Hymns were her favorite. She would raise her voice when she sang and sometimes Mother or Daddy would sing along with her. They all liked "The Old Rugged Cross," and as I listened, I felt sorry for Jesus who died hanging on one of those with nails pounded into his hands. "On a hill far away stands an old rugged cross," she'd sing, and I could see it up there silhouetted against the sky.

> *So I'll cherish the old rugged cross,*
> *Till my trophies at last I lay down,*
> *I will cling to the old rugged cross,*
> *And exchange it some day for a crown.*

Most of her favorite ones were sad, like "God Will Take Care of You." Even if you died, she told us, He would see that you got fed and had a warm bed. But I liked the happy ones best, like "Jesus Wants Me for a Sunbeam." Barely humming, drowsy and soft, she sang about how Jesus was always in the garden by the roses, and you were never alone.

And He walks with me, and He talks with me
And He tells me that I am his own.
And the Joy we share as we tarry there,
No other has ever known.

I was glad I was one of His own, and Bobby, too, and Mother and Daddy, and probably Frieda, if they allowed dogs in heaven. Obviously they had roses up there.

When we all joined in to belt out, "Mine eyes have seen the glory of the coming of the Lord, He has trampled out the vineyard where the grapes of wrath are stored," we sounded like the revival tent put up in Mr. Van Deventer's pasture.

Sometimes, bending over the dishes or folding clothes, Gango would burst into snippets of World War I songs: "How ya gonna keep 'em down on the farm, after they've seen Paree," or "K-k-k-katie, beautiful Katie, you're the only g-g-g-girl that I adore, When the m-m-m-moon shines, Over the cowshed, I'll be waiting at the k-k-k-kitchen door." She had been in love with a soldier who was killed in France in that war, and once when we visited her, she unwrapped from some yellowing tissue paper the gas mask that had belonged to this boy.

"Why does it have such big eye holes?" I asked her.

She didn't answer me, but just wrapped it up again.

We thought of Gango as a part of winter, somehow, maybe because she always brought the yummy pickled peaches and hardtack candy to us when it was cold.

Mother's holiday specialty was divinity with chopped black walnuts in it, dropped on a cookie sheet in little mounds like macaroons. Just thinking about it made your teeth wet. This year, she promised us we could help stuff the dates with fondant. She put just a drop of green food color and two drops of wintergreen flavoring in one batch, a drop of red and peppermint flavoring in another, and left one just plain white, Daddy's favorite. We took the pits out of the dates and opened them up like little books on a sheet of waxed paper. Then we put the pits in our mouths and rolled them around in there to get the last of the good taste before spitting them out.

Some of the fondant got made into little balls to squash with nuts, usually on the white ones, because otherwise they'd look so plain. Mother wiped her hands on her apron and put her arm around Bobby's shoulder, cooing to him,

"Like this, Bobby. Put the almond in the middle of the ball and push it down. See?" And he would do it just the way she wanted, smiling up at her.

"Can I do it, too?" I asked Mother.

"Just watch Bobby, and do it the same way."

I got tired of always having to copy my brother, but Mother thought he was perfect, I guess. Inside my heart, I knew I could do it even better than he could, could make little designs around the nut, even, make them special. But I rarely got the chance to prove it.

At Thanksgiving, Daddy had brought us empty cigar boxes from Mr. Diddy's drugstore, and we had cut out and pasted scraps of colored magazine pictures on the lids. By now the shellac would be dry enough to fill. Each of us had made two boxes, one for Auntie Bing and Uncle Keith, one for Uncle George and Auntie Oreen, and two more we could decide after we were all through. We lined the boxes with waxed paper, folded to fit exactly, then packed them with squares of fudge and toffee, fondant dates and divinity, sneaking bites of crumbs as we worked.

But Christmas was more than candy, even if that was the best part. We got to make Christmas garlands to decorate the tree. Three or four days before Daddy brought the tree in on its crisscross wooden stand, we worked to make long paper chains out of the colored paper from our rainbow tablets. We cut out strips and stuck the loops together with flour paste.

"You're not s'posed to let it squish out, Janie. When it dries it turns all white and looks messy." Bob told me how everything should be done. I knew how to do it, just my fingers didn't always work right. Once it made me so mad I yanked my chain out of his hands and it broke.

"Muuuuutherrrr," he yelled, tattling on me.

"Janie, dear, Bobby just wanted to help you. . . ."

"I don't *need* any help!" I snapped back at her.

"Don't you be impudent, or I'll slap your big, ugly face!" she said, never liking to be sassed. But she made me cry. I didn't care about impudent, but I didn't want to be ugly. I bit my lip, and Bobby turned sweet.

"I'll fix it," he said. "Your chain'll stick together with just a little glue. But where it's too much, we'll pretend its snow, okay?" With the new baby coming, Mother was fat and crankier than usual, and it was hard for her to breathe.

We spent hours stringing long strands of cranberries and of popcorn, sometimes both of them on the same string. Mother popped the corn we'd helped to shell, those little sharp kernels of the dried popcorn cobs that made the fat part of our palms red and sore. Daddy helped us thread the needle even though he had to hold the needle up to the light to see the hole where the thread went in.

"If you get stuck with the needle," he advised, "just pretend the bloody popcorn is a cranberry, okay?" He was fun to talk with sometimes.

"I used to do this when I was a kid. My brothers, Uncle Howard and Uncle Walter, would eat so much of the popcorn the strings never got long enough to go all the way around the tree."

"Didn't *you* ever eat any, Daddy?"

"Well, now, would I do a thing like that?" he said, his eyes pretending to be shocked at such a question. He made us laugh, sitting on the braided rug in our warm house, the smell of the tree and the promise of candy around us like a halo.

"How could you ride a trike in the snow—if Santa *did* bring you one?" Daddy asked Bobby, knowing that was his dearest wish for Christmas.

"I'd make a snow plow in the front with cardboard, like the cowcatcher on a train." I thought Bobby was a genius! And to me, Daddy said, "I guess we don't have enough sidewalk to roller skate on, do we?"

"We could go back and forth," I said, thinking it wasn't too late for Santa.

"No doll this year, honey. We'll have a real live doll around here, soon, so we won't ask Santa for another Clementine, will we?"

Clementine was my precious baby doll. The day Gango told us her whole name—Ella Clementine Cowden Chantry—I named my dolly her middle name, Clementine. When I told them how I planned to baptize her, Mother burst out singing, "Oh, my darlin', oh, my darlin', oh, my darlin' Clementine. . . ." I thought it was a beautiful name, like a silver bell, ringing. My dolly had a little flannel nightie just like mine, even the lace around the neck Mother had sewed for her.

That year Gango came to be with us, wearing her red dress with a funny belt down below her waist, as if it was going to drop off soon. She brought us a big tin of colorful hardtack to put in our stockings. It was loopy, the way honey comes out of the jar. We said if we could melt it and stretch it out flat, it would make a good road for our toy cars. Multicolored, it would be prettier as a hair ribbon, I thought. But it was brittle and hard, not chewy like taffy. You had to break off bits of it to fit in your mouth, and it lasted a long time. Mother loved the licorice ones best, even if they were as gray as the barn cats. We tried to get some of every different kind. Some of it we hid, only to find that if we hid it in our dresser, it would stick to our underwear, or to the paper liners in the drawers. My favorite was the red, transparent loop. It was cinnamon, and smelled as good as it tasted.

Four more days before Bobby's birthday, he woke up to a loud knocking. He reached over and pulled at my pajama sleeve, "Listen, Janie. Did you hear someone on the porch?" Both of us piled out of bed to peer down the stairway. Maybe Santa Claus had lost his way in the storm and come to ask directions. Maybe he was going to deliver a secret one of us could catch a glimpse of. We stood there, ears cocked, listening. Shivering in our attic room, a raw space with rafters that could give you splinters, we heard the knocking again.

"Is it your birthday, yet?" I whispered from the top of the stairs, not wanting to be heard.

Bobby turned around, put one hand on his hip and said in an exasperated voice, "No, silly. I told you it wouldn't be till after Sunday."

"Is it getting nearly Christmas?"

"That doesn't come till *after* my birthday," he hissed.

"Well, what day *is* it, then?"

"I haven't looked yet."

We heard Daddy open the door and then, high and kind of loud, the voice of Auntie Oreen, Mother's only sister. She came in, stomping her shoes on the little rug by the door, a huge bunch of red roses all over her arms.

"Oh, Merrill! I am *so* excited, so happy for you, honey! I just can't believe it. Where are they? How is Xela? Oh, Merrill, it just isn't fair. I want a baby so badly, and now you've got two!" She spilled the armful of roses into Daddy's arms and headed for their bedroom.

"Two? What does she mean? Two what?"

"I think she means babies," Bobby said.

"Let's go downstairs."

"It's too cold. Let's wait. Let's go back to bed till Daddy calls us."

"Let's play having a baby," I suggested.

"Okay. You get pregnant with Clementine, and come to see me." So, caught up in the make-believe and ignoring the chill, I stuffed my dolly inside my panties so I looked fat like Mother. Bobby sat up very straight and serious in one of our chairs with his back to me, having turned another chair around to be the door, pretending to be the doctor. I waddled over to it and knocked, which made both of us giggle.

"Who's there?"

"Is this the doctor's office?"

"Yes it is. What do you want?"

"I am going to have a baby and I need help getting it born."

"Well, come in. What is your name?"

I hesitated, wanting to make up a new name, but I couldn't think of one. "I am Mrs. Merrill Belton."

"How long have you been pregnant? I see your stomach is very huge."

"I think about a year, but I'm not sure."

"Well, you lie down here, and I'll see what I can do," Doctor Bob said.

I pushed the backwards chair away and walked over to the front of him, lay down on the floor and began to breathe hard. Bobby pushed on my stomach several times until I cried "ouch," and made him stop because he was pushing too hard.

"How do you know that's the way to do it?" I pleaded.

"Because little pigs come out of the sow's pee hole. And lambs squeeze out between the ewe's legs, too, so people can't be very much different."

He reached up under my nightie, then, and pulled Clementine out of the panties I wore to keep warmer. Then, he put her in my arms, as we imagined it would be, stroking her head and tucking her arms in close to her body.

"Now, you're s'posed to get her to suck on your breasts for milk," Bobby said.

"I don't have any breasts," I complained.

"Well, I guess the baby will die then," he said, and tossed my doll into the corner. The game was over.

We snuggled back in under our bed covers, spooning as we did on cold nights, shivering until the warmth of the pieced woolen comforters quieted our skinny bodies.

"Keep your hands on your *own* pajamas; they're freezing!" Bobby warned. Lucky for us both, our Dr. Denton pajamas had feet.

Of course, we didn't sleep this morning. We were too curious. We whispered about the bustle downstairs. Mother had told us she would be going to the hospital in Des Moines to bring back a new brother or sister for us. Maybe if she stayed at home, she'd get to see it sooner. But what was Auntie Oreen doing here? Was Mother all right?

We heard Daddy's footsteps on the stair. He came into our bedroom, looking tired.

"What are you kids doing in the same bed?"

"We're warmer like this," Bobby answered.

He came and sat down on the side of the bed.

"I've got some great news for you two," he said. It didn't sound at all like a Christmas secret. "You have *two* new baby sisters downstairs, can you believe that? Last night, on the way into Des Moines, we got as far as the bridge and Mother said, 'Turn back home! Now!' She thought the baby was going to be born in a hurry. So we did. I called Dr. Mormon and he came out as soon as he could, but when he skidded his Dodge into the driveway, Frieda began to bark and bark."

"I heard her barking, Daddy," I said, "but I thought she was chasing away a fox."

"No sir. She was keeping the doctor from getting out of his car. By the time he finally got her to quiet down and come on into the house, it was too late. I had delivered both those babies by myself! Two little girls, can you believe it? He's gone now, and your Auntie Oreen is here with Mother."

"Is this their birthday, then?"

"Yes it is, honey. December fourteenth. A real red-letter day!" He was getting kind of silly.

"Can we see them? Can we see Mother, too?"

"Yes, you can. Get up, now, and put on your robes and slippers and come on downstairs. But remember. Be quiet! Your mother has been through an ordeal, and she needs to sleep." He smiled, reached over and patted our heads. Then, he went back downstairs.

We got up, scurried around to put on our Indian-blanket bathrobes with the twisty rope belts and our sheepskin bunny slippers, the warm ones that had rabbit ears with two red shoe-button eyes on the face. Sometimes we raced each other to see who could get dressed faster, but this morning, neither of us wasted any time. We scampered down the stairs, quiet as mice. The door to Mother's bedroom was closed. We stopped, stood outside until Daddy came out. He closed the door behind him and came over to the bottom stair step.

"Come here," he said, sitting down on the stair. We snuggled into his welcoming arms so close we could smell his breath. I thought maybe he was sick. He smoothed down our hair with those wide, warm hands that could do everything.

"I shut the door to keep it warm in the bedroom," he said. "Little babies need to be warm. But Mother's kinda tired, so we won't stay long, okay? You'll get to see your new little baby sisters."

It was dark in the room. Mother lay in her single bed, one of a handsome pair of mahogany beds with Jenny Lind spooling and posts at four corners. Over her lay one of the trousseau quilts she had made before they were married, appliquéd red and green tulips on a white background. Around the edges twined a border with a vine made of green bias tape. On her bedside table was a tall vase with all the roses Auntie 'Reen had brought sticking straight up. Our four Hudson's Bay blankets hung over the windows, two gray and two red ones with their black stripes on the ends, tucked up there and secured with clothespins on the curtain rod. Daddy did that to keep out the cold.

Mother reached out one of her arms for each of us, and we took hold of her like two baby possums.

"Darlings," she said, "My Bobby. Dear Janie. What a Christmas present, isn't it? Come around the bed. Take a peek at the two little dollies. They're your new baby sisters, one for each of you."

We did what we were told, very quietly, awed by it all, the realization just beginning to dawn on us. There between our parents' beds, propped up on two chairs facing each other, was the bottom drawer of their built-in bureau. The bassinet was over against the wall between the windows, and this drawer had been hurriedly pressed into service.

There they were. So tiny. Those two little heads, one covered with black hair, and the other one almost bald, were our first glimpse of brand new babies. They were wrapped in flannel blankets, all wrinkled and red, their little hands like dead birds' feet, their claws curled up.

They didn't look like much fun to us. Too little. We kept looking at each other, as if for reassurance.

"What are we gonna call 'em?" I asked.

"Merilyn, named after your Daddy, Merrill, and MaryLou, for the little dark-haired one," she told us.

While I was engrossed, marveling at such little people, Bob was preoccupied with the closet door, left open just enough to show something bright and shining. His interest in the babies waned. I just looked and looked and looked, not really knowing what to say or do. Mother's eyes closed. I reached over to feel those little pink hands. Such tiny nails.

"Don't touch, Janie," Daddy said. I yanked my hand back. Then, he took us by the hand and led us out, closing the door behind him. He said he had put the oatmeal on the back of the stove, that we could have breakfast in a little while, to go back upstairs and put on our clothes.

Once upstairs, Bob said, "Guess what I saw!"

"Is this a riddle?"

"No. Really. Inside their closet is my red trike!"

"How do you know?"

"I saw it in there. The door was open, and I saw it. Honestly. Isn't that wonderful? When Christmas comes, I'm gonna drive shingle nails into the wheels so I can ride up and down in the snow and ice and not slip."

"Maybe when the twins grow a little bigger, they can ride on the back."

"You can be first," Bobby said, already pairing us as the survivors of this most tumultuous event in our lives. Tender and sweet sometimes, it was as if he could know what I was going to say next, what my feelings were. "We'll be the 'big twins,'" I said, and he said, "Okay."

"MaryLou and Merilyn," we chanted. Dumb names, we thought,

much preferring the simpler sound of our own. "Merry" and "Merry" we nicknamed them, this close to Christmas, but still thought "Bobby" and "Janie" took first place. Certainly we were thrown into each other's arms from that day on.

Instead of our individual names, we were suddenly "the older children," and for both of us, the closest "other" each of us had for the busy years that lay ahead. Maybe the closest other we ever had. I gave Bob the piece of fudge I'd sneaked from our candy making, and he broke it in half for me. Neither of us knew then how instinctively compassionate we would become, displaced by two at once and forever bereft of our parents' undivided love. For years my vivid memory of Mother was her nursing the twins, one at a time, in the rocking chair kept in the kitchen by the stove.

"How's my favorite Jersey cow?" Daddy would say, fondling her huge breasts at nursing time.

"Merrill, please!" she would say, pulling away from his tenderness, not wanting us to witness anything intimate. They parceled out their affection to the children, but rarely let the world see loving overtures pass between them.

The next bath night after the twins were born, nobody remembered we were soaking in the tub. They were all huddled around the two new babies. Our hands and feet were wrinkled up like the inside of a chicken gizzard and we were bored.

"Two more girls," Bobby said. He had hoped for a brother.

"It'll be fun," I said, "like having two baby dolls to dress up. But they're awfully little, like baby birds. How fast do they grow?"

"I don't know. But I'm the only one of us now who has a penis," he said, thrusting his skinny bottom up out of the water. "See. If you play with it, it'll get bigger."

What magic! I reached over to take hold of that little bud and, sure enough, it grew like a corn stalk, taller and harder.

How long we stayed in that tub, the water cooling, our shoulders shivering, I can't even guess, for the overriding discovery of what made boys so different from girls moved into my consciousness forever. Bob wasn't curious about me, and neither was I, really. I just washed where my legs came together, but I sure didn't have anything quite as exciting as a penis or its little bag of marbles down there.

"Can you pull it all back inside of you, like the cat does?" I wanted to know.

"No. Besides, I don't want to," he told me. His penis was little again and looked like a shriveled up carrot when Daddy suddenly burst into the bathroom.

"Sorry, kids. Are you freezing to death? We got so busy I forgot it was already past your bedtime." We had forgotten how cold the big white porcelain bathtub could get when the water cooled down, or how chilly the black and white tile floor was on our feet. So we were glad to see Daddy with a big bath towel over his arm. He dried us one at a time, hard, to make us stop shivering. He rubbed us down until our skin was pink and warm and we slipped into our warm Dr. Denton sleepers and hustled upstairs.

On the way up, I asked Daddy, "Can we take one of the babies to sleep with us?"

"Not yet, Janie. When they are older, maybe. What if you rolled over in your sleep and squashed her?"

I hadn't thought of that. They must be treated very carefully, I guessed, or they might break.

The Flies of Summer

For me, Iowa is hot as a skillet and buzzing with flies. The sun is merciless in July and August when the corn ripens and the tar in the road joints melts enough to chew. In our childhood, tar was the country version of bubble gum. Bob taught me to scoop up a wad on the end of stick and to chew just a little bit at a time. But it never bubbled, and it was bitter tasting. It stuck to the bottoms of our bare feet, to our fingers, probably to our teeth. Kerosene took it off our skin, but I think, with much spitting, it just wore off our teeth. It was a filthy substitute for gum, but easier than finding and prying off old wads from the bottoms of chairs, a habit both of us admitted to.

In the heat, I smell and feel the hot earth, the torture of walking on the gravel in the long driveway up from the road. We mince and hunch along that pebbly path like grasshoppers with broken wings, lifting one foot after the other off the searing rocks in a quick two-step dance. The brittle grass, stiff and brown as field stubble, is hardly better. By the end of summer, the calluses we develop make it almost bearable. By then, it is time for the annual trip into Des Moines to buy the too-big Buster Brown shoes with scuff-resistant reinforced toes. Our feet wedged under a big X-ray machine, we press our eyes to a viewer like a stereopticon and see our very own bones, toes and all. One pair of shoes, my father hopes, will last us through the school year.

We brown like molasses taffy those hot summer days under a cloudless sky, unrelentingly blue for weeks on end. Lazy dog days along the Middle Raccoon River, we build our miniature towns on the bank, pick the flowers of weeds for pretend weddings or funerals or an out-of-season May Day basket. The straps of our homemade seersucker overalls fasten in front with two big buttons as shimmery as seashells, leaving tan marks on our shoulders, for we rarely wear a shirt beneath them, or for that matter, underwear. Bobby and I find things to do in the shade, stringing buttons from Mother's button box into exotic necklaces, making mudpies with chopped acorn frosting inside the garage, or trying to force-feed spit-moistened oatmeal to the baby guinea pigs in their pen under the trees.

From this climate, sizzling in summer, freezing the horse trough solid in winter, our parents make a life. Through the drought years, the Dust Bowl, the Great Depression, they never have enough money. How they stick it out, raising children through blizzards, hailstones as big as snowballs, the scorching drought that shrivels the corn and causes their prize shorthorn cattle to line up along the fence and bawl for water, through the snowbound winters, we can hardly appreciate, being young. They cope. They work hard, long hours of the day through the week. In the evenings, they read until the book falls to the floor and their eyes will not stay open. On the weekends, they take us to Sunday school. But life is not without joy, for they laugh easily and often. Sometimes they cry.

───◆───

Our privy at the edge of the orchard had a half-moon in the door for ventilation—and for letting in the flies. When it was sweltering in there, too hot to breathe, the door could be propped open with a handmade doorstop, the result of our winter make-work project. We folded each leaf in an old Montgomery Ward catalog from the top of the page to the center in a diagonal fold. Then, we folded the fold in half toward the center spine, and that began to take shape and fatten into a doorstop. Ugly past believing, that conical, recycled book was a source of great pride for me, who had done most of the work! We heard a lot about idle hands, idle minds, those long, snowbound winters. There were prizes for such contests as who could put all the states in the right puzzle place first, poems we memorized from *A Child's Garden of Verses*, and tinsel Christmas decorations we cut out and pasted to cardboard, made from the foil of cigarette packets found along the roadside in the summer. The challenge of finding new ways to use old things delighted all of us. The catalog was our pride and joy.

The flies of summer drove my mother nearly mad. She hated bugs of all kinds, jumped when the big June bugs bumped against the screens. Mosquitoes could ruin our picnics, and ants, she said, were a sign of a dirty house. But flies were her nemesis. She draped a napkin over the sugar bowl to keep them from crawling around the rim. Their tacky little feet carried disease and infection, she felt, and she swatted at them with a killer's instinct, her jaw clenched. No relief could rid our hot kitchen of flies, and they were worse when she had the wood stove stoked to keep the canner boiling long enough to sterilize the blue Bell jars full of home-slaughtered beef.

Drawn by the cut raw meat, the blood on the butcher's block, and the boiling chunks of meat in the cast iron pots, carnivorous hordes of flies swarmed into our house. Our back door opened onto an unscreened porch just a stone's throw from the barnyard, breeding ground for these voracious insects. More than once, I remember Mother sitting down on a kitchen chair in the midst of her steamy work, fanning her flame-red face with a dishtowel, crying. Once, when I put my arms around her for comfort, she said, "God never sends you a task He doesn't think you can handle, honey." She wiped her eyes on her apron hem and carried on.

Almost unendurable heat came from the constant canning. Vegetables seemed to ripen all at the same time, beans, tomatoes, beets, carrots. No fresh breeze in the middle of a late-summer day rescued her from that stifling task, necessary for wintering over her family.

When she was fed up enough with the heat and the flies, her exhaustion turned to rage. Then, the dishtowels were pressed into service for what we came to call "the great round-up."

"Bobby," she yelled, or "Janie, come help me!" We knew, from the tone of her voice, that she had reached the limit of her endurance. From the yard where we were practicing to join the circus like Toby Tyler, doing headstands on the broad, nearly flat back of our big white workhorse, Doll, we hurried inside.

She handed each of us a white, flour-sack dishtowel. With one of us on each side of her like gatekeepers at a rodeo, Mother strode into the arena with her two huge dishtowels turning like sails of a windmill. We followed her lead. Starting at the far end of the kitchen, she began to gyrate them, whipping faster and faster like a cowboy twirling his lariat, and we did the same, loving the game as if we were lashing our ponies into a gallop. We three were a crew, driving those flies across the kitchen to the back door, which Mother had kicked open with her foot to let out the herd of flies. If enough had managed to elude our frenzied attack, we repeated our performance until the only ones remaining were the black carcasses sticking to the curlicues of flypaper hanging from the ceiling, or those writhing on the flat, gelatinous sheets of sticky papers along the window sills. She grabbed a flyswatter from the nail by the door, and went into a final swatting frenzy with the few who failed to exit.

We all caught our breath for a while, then, thankful for a brief respite from the maddening buzz. She would feel accomplished, would lavish praise on our cooperative effort, maybe reward us with a rare little piece of hardtack candy she kept in a small tin box on the cupboard shelf.

The lack of money, the blistering weather, the sheer endurance of first picking the ripe fruits and vegetables, preparing them for canning, keeping the stove hot enough to sterilize the jars, filling them, lifting them out of the scalding water in the deep enamel canner, left her bone-tired and quiet.

How often I think of her life, how her lovely face leathered and lined in that parched landscape, how her nail-bitten hands got callused, working at wringing clothes, braiding rugs, snapping beans, hoeing weeds, fighting dirt. Her once-graceful legs were gnarled with varicose veins from each successive pregnancy. She became apologetic about her thickened body, gave up wearing the pretty clothes that no longer fit. In defiance, she adhered to her standards of cleanliness and beauty, planting delphinium, tulips, oriental poppies, and prize irises, airing woolens in summer breezes, bleaching her dishtowels a dazzling white. In spite of her efforts, though, like water in *The Sorcerer's Apprentice*, the flies flowed on forever. Mother gave us an unforgettable example of creative forbearance, but the cost was high. Summer heat, the plague of flies, and a scarcity of cash drove our parents to the brink of endurance.

When Mother canned, Daddy would put down the *Wallace's Farmer* he was reading, to savor the fruits of her exhausting effort. He would stand up and walk into the kitchen where it was his job to tighten the lids when the hot jars emerged from the steaming water, a bath towel looped over both hands to protect him from being scalded. Magenta jars of berry jam and strawberry sunshine preserves lined up on racks on the painted gate-leg table, alongside the canned peaches which we'd eat in the coming months, spicy with cloves and cinnamon, and covered with thick cream.

"Beautiful, Zee. Beautiful! Makes my mouth water. Do we have to wait for winter?"

"Absolutely! I'm going to count them, see that they all get down to the root cellar!" But she loved his praise, and knew that she deserved it.

Now, antique stores line their shelves with blue Bell canning jars, hand-cranked clothes wringers, rusting big tongs for carrying blocks of ice to the insulated box, carpet beaters, flat irons that heated on the backs of stoves, wooden-handled potato mashers, and always, old flyswatters made of window screen. Six or seven decades later, these tools are history, as are the swarms of flies that buzz through our memory.

Our parents were different spirits who respected each other for the most part. But, when overwork or lack of money or moodiness surfaced, they made huge issues over petty details. Dad smelled like sweat and animals and dirt sometimes, and Mother hated that. He would track in on her just-mopped floor apparently oblivious of her work or her physical effort to maintain a clean and pretty home. She would set her jaw, lock her lips, and wipe up his footprints with jerky disgust.

He, fearful of disappointing her as provider, was penurious at times, holding her accountable for things he deemed extravagant. The silk yardage she made her own underwear out of could as well have been flour sacking, he thought. And she loved licorice whips, vanilla beans, pretty quad-A shoes for her slender feet. And when her rebellion was buried in reading a big book, he felt that time "doing nothing" was a slacking off of duties. She was immaculate and yet not tidy;

he was tidy to a fault but not overly disturbed by dirt. He was a farmer at heart, and she was a city girl.

Dad used to ask us, as we tried to scrape clean a pan bottom with a residue of scorched meat or burned sugar or stuck oatmeal, "Why do you think God gave you fingernails?" He used the heel of his hand to swipe away water from a wet counter top, for example. No sissy dishrag for him. Digging, gardening, planting, it was the *feel* of the earth, the tilth of the soil, that he enjoyed (not unlike Mother's fingers, making pie crust—it was the *feel* of it that told her when it was ready). It was the *feel* of a hammer and a nail that made a good carpenter, he contended. So I learned early from them to dig in, to touch, to know the feel of whatever was at hand, to utilize the natural gifts we were born with.

When we got holes in our shoes, Daddy would buy rubber soles at the IGA store. Always he took the worn-through shoe with him to match the size.

"Got any horseshoes this size, Hank?" he would tease. We were always tagging along on trips into town, and we didn't know Daddy was going to get horseshoes. At first, the idea of tacking iron hooves onto our Buster Browns was terrifying, but we caught onto the joke soon enough. After he selected just the pair of rubber soles needed, we took them home where he put the holey shoe up on his own iron shoe last, brought up from the basement. With a metal rasp, he roughed up the worn sole.

"This'll make the glue stick to the new soles better," he explained, as he always did when we were watching him work.

"Here, Bob. You try it. Bear down hard enough to rough it up, now."

"Can I have a turn?" I begged.

"No," Bob answered, "you aren't strong enough."

"Am too!"

"You could let your sister at least try," Daddy said, because he was always playing fair.

"She always butts into everything."

"Well, how else will she learn?"

"Okay. Just a little bit."

So I got to climb up on the chair and push the rasp over the old holey leather. But it was heavy and slipped off the edge.

"See," said Bobby.

"That's good enough, now. Time to put on the glue and stick the soles on tight. When they dry, we'll cut off the bit that sticks over the sides with my pocketknife. Should last you another little while."

"Phew." We wrinkled our noses as the rubber cement squirmed out of the metal tube. It made long threads, like the syrup for divinity when it reached what Mother called the hard-ball stage.

"Stay clear of this stuff, now," Daddy told us. "It could take your skin off if you aren't careful." I got down off the chair and moved away. I needed my skin.

With a C-clamp, he held the shoe firm until the glue on the sole dried. Later, before we went to bed, he pared off the edges with his pocketknife as he said he would.

"Now, you can hit the floor running in the morning; they're good as new!"

But sometimes, only a few days later, the sole might come unglued from our rough use. Then, loose, the sole flapped from the front of our shoe like a horse's lips, and Dad would have to do it all over again.

◆

Congenial people both, they spoke clearly and rarely raised their voices. But Bob and I both remember vividly the morning of our parents' big fight. We had never heard them shout at each other in anger.

They stood facing each other in the kitchen as we slid behind the stove early one cold morning. For whatever reason, Mother had threatened to leave Daddy, to take us both and go back to Des Moines to live with her mother. He was furious, raised his voice and shouted, "By God, you are not going to leave the place!"

"You can't stop me!" she yelled.

"Oh yes, I can. If you think you can just take the kids and walk out, you've got another think coming."

"I hate you and your stinking animals and your stinking friends," she hurled.

"*You* could never win a purple ribbon, that's for damn sure!"

The keys to their Model A hung by the back door, and he grabbed them. She tried to grab them back, and they tussled.

"You have no more right to the car than *I* do," she yelled, fighting like a trapped bear. We, forgotten behind the stove in the heat of their quarrel, were paralyzed. Our fronts were hot, our backs pressed against the wall, both of us terrified, afraid to move.

In the end, Dad wrestled the keys away from her, pushed open the backdoor screen, stomped outside and threw them down the well. "There! Now, you just try to get away!" he shouted as he charged back into the kitchen.

She began to cry angry tears, to stomp her feet in fury and frustration.

"Janie," Bobby whispered, "we'd better get dressed."

"Will you help me tie my shoes? I can't stoop over back here."

"Neither can I. Let's grab our clothes and go back upstairs."

"Will Mama be alright?" I worried.

"I dunno. Daddy's being mean."

We scampered out of the kitchen as quietly as we could, scared for our parents, afraid to stay.

An hour later, dressed, we found Daddy sitting alone on the back steps. Big tears rolled down his whiskery face, and he snuffed them up and blew his nose into a big, wet handkerchief. He was sorry he'd tossed the keys, for he had also trapped himself, but sorrier to see Mother so sad.

"But I love her," he told us.

We tried to console both of them in turn. Mother, sullen and seething, just ignored us, the tears streaming down her cheeks and the snot running out of the nose she didn't even bother to blow. She'd pull up the corner of her apron and swipe it away. For a long time she smoldered. Maybe they talked it out in private. Maybe it just wore them down after several days. Maybe it was never mentioned again. They rarely let their emotions get out of control, and maybe they needed to blow up just to let off steam, pressurized by hard work and no money.

Dad got a neighbor with a rope and flashlight and miraculously retrieved the keys from the well bottom. Long after we'd gone to bed, we puzzled about how they did it. Bob said he thought they tied a magnet to the end of the rope.

At any rate, he had an extra key made so each of them had one.

Mother never left.

There was no malice between them, but they covered deeper truths with wit and frivolous exchanges. It was a tactic they used to thaw the chill we sometimes sensed between them, to distract them from misunderstanding or an uncomfortable distance that could not otherwise be crossed. Mother's silent aloofness could create a palpable tension and, I suspected when I got old enough to analyze it, it was sexual, her fear of pregnancy and his virility. Her upbringing relegated sex to wifely duty, though she was capable of outrageous flirtation. She had lost her father when she was only two, never had a brother, and learned from her mother the weapon of silence. Daddy's warmth was spontaneous. He would often put his arm around her, and she would shrug him off, saying "Oh, Merrill!" A kiss was only a "peck on the cheek." Neither of us ever remembers an example of intimate touching, something they must have saved for their bedroom, behind a locked door.

Still and through it all, Mother kept alive the fragile flame of hope she brought to her idealized image of wife and mother. At least she put on a brave face given their circumstances. The still-unreleased sadness of losing a firstborn baby began to whittle away romance. My guess is that she suffered from depression, long before such states of mind were acceptable. One time when she was crying, both of us nearly smothered her with our mystified concern until she said, with mock cheerfulness, "Thank you, darlings. I was just tired, but you make me feel a lot better, now." Farm life, even with a sporadic veterinarian's income, fell short of the picture Mother had had of marriage.

Dad never reneged on his unequivocal honesty that I know of, never told a lie, never gossiped, never shirked duty or need, and worked hard all his life. He taught us the meaning of frugality during those spare years when pennies were counted and cash flow was critical. He crusaded against waste of anything, even in our old outhouse with the cutout stars on the sides. When he reached the end of his rope, exhausted or hungry, his temper would flare, but he reined it in, usually with an apology.

"If you have to use the toilet paper roll, keep it to three sheets only. Or one page from Monkey Ward's catalog ought to do the trick. Your Grandma Belton taught me 'Waste not, want not,' and that applies to toilet paper, do you understand!"

"What if we have diarrhea?"

"Don't you be impudent, young lady. Use your own judgment in a case like that. Just try to make the toilet paper last, that's all." And we did, monitoring each other if we sat on adjacent holes in the outhouse, fearful the other one would tattle if we miscounted. We rarely did.

Mother was a Des-Moines-born beauty, a tall, thin girl who longed to go to Wellesley, who walked with the white-tennis-dress crowd along Grand Avenue, her head and her heart full of dreams. But her widowed mother's teaching salary was meager. A man who came to court Grandmother had, the story goes, a "crush" on her daughter, my mother, then an irresistible seventeen-year-old.

"He pulled me down on his lap every chance he got," Mother told me once. "I didn't trust him because he polished his fingernails. I avoided walking in front of him."

But it was he who offered to send Xela to Iowa State College in Ames, to pay her tuition and bus fare to and from college and home. That way, she would never be too far away from his lustful eyes. He bought her a new winter coat, opened a bank account in her name, and thereby ensured her gratitude if not her willingness to compromise her principles. When she told us about him, her face scrinched up and her head shook from side to side, a way of saying his kindness failed to endear her to him. "He wasn't the right one for my mother, either," she said.

In college, young Xela Chantry majored in home economics and pledged a sorority, Pi Beta Phi, where she met her best friend for life, Rachel Garst, whom we always called "Auntie Bing." In the spring of her sophomore year, she met my father, a handsome young veterinarian with a shock of wavy black hair and dark, seductive eyes. He was finishing his final year at Iowa State, and already knew what lay immediately ahead. It was 1918, and Europe was being torn apart by war.

We were curious about them, how they met and where, and never tired of hearing their stories. Daddy still teased Mother about the time his fraternity, Kappa Sigma, invited her sorority for a picnic. The girls were to bring the food. It was the first time he met young Xela Chantry. She had been assigned to make the chicken gravy, but having added too much flour, served a solid glob of gravy that set up like aspic. She, now a superb cook, always denied it, saying he exaggerated. But he had fallen in love with her regal beauty, her quick wit, her gray-green eyes and raven hair. That summer she took a job as the "schoolmarm" of a small country school for the following fall, and Dad joined the army and went off to Texas.

Drafted into the United States Cavalry in 1918, as were most animal husbandry graduates in those war years, Dad was sent to Lubbock, Texas, to an army post for gathering horses and mules, destined for the Allied troops in Europe. Both the mules, pack animals for supplies and ammunition, and the horses, mounts for the cavalry, were shipped by train across the United States to Canada and thence to Nova Scotia. From Halifax, they were sent by sea to ports in France and England. The chosen animals were inspected, fed, and accompanied by a qualified veterinarian all along the line to their destination. The rail route of the animal boxcars heading for Toronto ran through Omaha, Nebraska, about 150 miles from Des Moines.

It was too close for Daddy not to get to Des Moines, to try to surprise his sweetheart. He left a subordinate in charge of the mules and took a short leave to visit Mother, joining the train again further up the line. Smitten all over again, he asked if she'd marry him after the war, proffering his fraternity pin in lieu of an engagement ring.

But another man was also in love with Mother. A suave and handsome blonde, blue-eyed urbanite who was, she told me more than once, "a wonderful dancer," maybe the one she should have married.

But Grandmother Chantry convinced her that Merrill Belton was the more stable man who would give her healthy babies and be true to her forever. (Bobby and I always thought Gango and Daddy loved each other.) Mother accepted Dad's fraternity pin and promised to wait.

She used to say it was his uniform that seduced her, but that was a cover-up, for she was a sensuous woman who had been attracted to him even before his years of cavalry service. A portrait of Mother at twenty leaves little doubt about what bewitched Daddy. They were married on April Fool's day in 1920, running away to Omaha, Nebraska, to save Grandma Chantry the expense of a wedding. Auntie Bing and Uncle Keith Merrill, best friends from their college days, stood up with them.

Years later, Mother told me an unbelievable detail of their wedding night. She was a virgin and was both excited and apprehensive about sex. Her period came early, and not wanting Daddy to know, she sat in a pan of cold water, hoping to stanch the flow. It didn't work, and she said he was such a considerate and patient bridegroom that he was willing to wait.

Both articulate, both quick-witted, they overcame the hurdles with the leap of humor. We loved their banter.

Daddy, brown as a walnut from having worked days in the sun, fixing fences, butchering, haying, caring for animals, usually lined out the day's tasks over breakfast.

"What's your plan for today, Merrill? Going to sit on the porch and twiddle your thumbs, are you?" Mother teased.

"You're exactly right, Zee, while you shop for champagne and caviar!"

Whose Little Darling Are You?

Mother wanted Bob to be a doctor. "Like Daddy, but without the manure on your boots," she used to say. Married to a veterinarian, she nonetheless felt offended by the smell of animals, by the antiseptic on Dad's hands, by dog hairs in the house, or by small animals stretched out on the kitchen counter for surgical procedures. She thought it unclean somehow. The way she screwed up her nose when she talked about Dad's work always made me uncomfortable, certain it would hurt him whom I was forever trying to shield. But the idea of a doctor, a man in a white coat working in pristine conditions, appealed to her more. Her son, she hoped, would prefer the more sanitized version of medicine.

Dad's dearest dream for me was that I become a nurse. Around our house, many discussions revolved around the best medical procedures or the best-known home remedies: warm salt tied in the corner of a handkerchief and held on an earache; analgesic balm under a wool flannel poultice for sore throat; Iodex rubbed into a sprain or aching muscle; breathing the steam from eucalyptus oil in boiling water under a tent sheet draped across the warming oven on top of the stove, for loosening up chest congestion or clogged sinuses. Dad removed splinters and swabbed on red mercurochrome. Mother mixed castor oil in orange juice and fixed us milk toast. No doubt more than once they wished for professional advice. But living where we did, with as little ready cash as we had, they didn't often get it. As for my becoming a nurse, already I'd helped to care for my twin sisters constantly, and I must have craved more attention for myself. Servitude made me grind my teeth. Medicine was Bob's calling; nursing would *not* be mine.

Bobby and Mother were thick as thieves. He would do anything she told him, and vice versa. On top of the piano was an eight-by-ten portrait of Bob in a middy shirt, about age three, taken by a professional photographer in Des Moines. He was angelically dimpled and clear-eyed, not a hair out of place. I could just hear it, "Smile for Mama." And, of course, he did. None of the rest of us had our picture taken. Maybe they could never afford another professional portrait, another silver frame, who knows. He smiled down on us from up there like the picture of Jesus on our Sunday-school wall, holy perfection. I always hated that picture of my brother. It was phony. He never really looked like that.

But he did "show promise," as people were fond of pronouncing over children. Our family never had enough money to save up for college tuition. But we did have a taste for education. Mother and Dad, both alumni of Iowa State Agricultural College, as it was then called, surrounded us with books. They instilled in us the values of their place and time: the Golden Rule, the Ten Commandments, cleanliness, hard work, frugality, and faith. As I look back, the strongest one, avid readers that they were, was a reverence and a hunger for knowledge.

Thick dark hair framed Mother's patrician nose and clear, blue eyes. Tall for that time—she was five-ten—she commanded attention with her mere presence, and, Dad bragged, often to her embarrassment, that she had won a beauty contest for homecoming queen at Iowa State. One of Mother's many gifts was a sense of harmony, of space, and of color. Within her means, she dressed tastefully. Too, the rooms in our house were simple but lovely, the hooked or braided rugs of her own making, the upholstery, such as it was, complemented with pillows whose colors picked up the threads in the fabric.

She was the queen of our home and of our lives, honest, intelligent, generous, sometimes impatient or imperious, lacking the warmth we often craved. She had never known her father—Orren Chantry—who died of consumption when she was barely two, and her busy mother was an engine of activity. As the older daughter, she learned to cope early, to take pride in her work.

Once married, she devoted her life to the ideals instilled in her by a home-economics major, and she strove to be the best at whatever she undertook.

"Where do you want me to hang this picture, Zee?" Daddy asked her once.

"I'm not sure yet. How about in the space to the left of the bookcase?"

"That'll put it too close to the fireplace, I think." he countered.

"But it balances that side of the room," Mother began, her way of persuading him.

"If the paint melts from the heat, there goes your balance," Dad argued.

"It won't melt," Mother insisted, "and that's the only place it really looks right."

So that's where he drove the nail, measuring the exact center of the available space with a yardstick.

They each gravitated toward their opposite-gender child. So Bob was Mother's. She taught him to read early, to use the colors in the Crayola box in gradations of shades and tints. As surely as a potter molds clay, she shaped him and pointed him toward his ultimate profession.

But she did not limit her ambition for her children to Bob. In those days, gender roles were fairly rigid, and so she taught me those things she thought would turn me into the ideal wife and mother.

She loved flowers and the first pussy willows of spring thrilled her. A fresh bouquet of narcissus or anemones, even miniature containers with violets or snowbells, would suddenly appear to change the mood of the house, replacing the vase of dried Japanese lanterns covered with dust by the end of winter. Mother taught both of us so many subtle things about beauty while we were very young, small enough to stand so our chins were barely even with the dining-room table. She had taken a class in *ikebana* from an Iowa City artist living temporarily in Redfield. We could sense her delight as she placed flowers in her best blue bowl.

"See, children," she would demonstrate, "Japanese people use flowers to suggest something else. The tall one stands for heaven...." As she spoke, she snipped a tall stem and stuck in onto the frog in her lovely, shallow vase.

"And this next one," she cut a curved stem shorter, placed it next to heaven on the right, "stands for man. We are in the middle, do you see, halfway between Heaven and Earth?" Then she laid the last stem almost horizontally along the bottom, off-center but secure on the frog.

"There! Earth!" She stepped back, pleased with her effort, moved in close to add three or five spiked leaves to fill in the empty spaces.

"They always use odd numbers," she went on, she who had been reading *The Soong Sisters*, she who yearned for a world beyond the one she so fully inhabited. "One, three, or five. Now, don't you think that's pretty?" she asked us both.

"Yes, oh yes!" I said, as charmed with the idea that something could mean something else at the same time as I was with the delicate arrangement.

"Do boys ever make bouquets sometimes?" Bob asked her.

She put her arm around him. "Oh, honey, of course," she said. She didn't hug me, I remember, even though I had been the more attentive student. To this day, I work to make pleasing flower arrangements, shaped by those early lessons on form and proportion.

Daddy was *my* hero. He listened to my questions and honored my ideas. We were kindred in understanding, it seemed, needing only to catch the other's eye to grasp a situation. He touched, hugged, kissed goodnight, and tucked me in bed, with fatherly tenderness. I would play to his approval, trying to please him by cleaning my plate, polishing my shoes, ironing his shirts just so, and learning how to darn his socks. His soft, brown eyes and easy smile, his praise, were rewards enough. It was many years before I learned about the death of their first baby girl whom they had also named Jane, and I think his devotion to me was somehow doubled-up because of that loss.

Praise came to me easily from him. I think he identified with the other "brown-eyed Belton," as he called me. He let me follow him around the barn, feed the chickens, gather the eggs. Whenever he had a call from some farmer whose cow was bloated or whose pigs needed cholera vaccinations, he would let me come with him to make the call. Because I had practiced balance, could stand on one leg for a long, long time, he let me ride on the back of the harrow with Bobby and the big rocks he used to weight it.

"You smart enough not to get hurt, Janie?" he asked.

"Yes, Daddy. I'll be careful, honest I will."

"All right, then. You and Bob'll be a big help to break up these clods. Keep your eyes on the rocks, though. They could shift around and get your toes. Be careful." We contributed our puny weight on that flat harrow through clouds of dust, not caring about dirt. Our father trusted us to use common sense.

Bobby and I used to practice balance on the train rails along the spur that went by the brickyard, each of us daring the other to stay on the narrow rail. A fence with a horizontal board across the top stretched between the end of the back porch and the beginning of the pasture. Waiting for dinner or for Daddy to wash up, we used to walk along the top, keeping our balance with outstretched arms. I was better than Bobby was, and Dad would tell everyone I had the makings of a tightrope walker in the circus.

We played in the haymow, walked with him up to the high pasture to check the fence, gather pumpkins, count the new lambs. He trusted me not to get in the way, even to be helpful. If he ever checked up on my numbers or on my observations, I never knew it. He took my word at face value, and acted upon it. Out of that greatest gift of all, trust, he gave me confidence in myself, urging me every chance to be an accurate recorder and a keen observer of the world around us. Mostly he taught by his example.

Sometimes he was so cross it was scary. Once, during rhubarb season, Mother had dished up the beautiful pink sauce into our separate bowls. When MaryLou saw the stringy stuff, she reared back in her high chair, turned her face away and said, "I don' like rhubarb all time, all time, all time!"

"Just eat a little bit of it, honey," Mother cajoled.

Bobby bent over her ear and said, "If you don't eat it, you'll get a hard spanking from Daddy."

She began to howl. "Don' spank I, peez, peez!" she begged.

Daddy came to her rescue, calmed her down, ate her rhubarb himself. Then he asked, "Which one of you told MaryLou I would spank her if she didn't eat her rhubarb?"

Silence. "Did you hear me? Which one of you?" Neither of us said a word.

"Janie?"

"I didn't."

"Bobby?"

"I didn't."

"Okay. You will both just sit there until one of you tells me the truth."

A long time passed. We knew it was Bob, but he hated to be caught being a bully. MaryLou had cried and cried, heartbroken and afraid. She genuinely hated rhubarb and would clench her little hands into bitter fists at the mere sight of it. Finally, Bob confessed.

"Into the bathroom with you, young man. I will not tolerate a liar in this house," he said, his mouth like petrified wood. And Bob would be spanked with a few whacks with the razor strop while I, wishing I had taken the blame, would stand outside the bathroom door, pounding and yelling, "Stop, Daddy! Please, Daddy, stop!"

Too, in a voice of absolute command, he got us out of bed as surely as if a bomb had gone off. "All right, kids, hit the deck!" He admired the order of military discipline he had tasted as a young man. He had an orderly mind by nature. When he assumed the role of top sergeant, we had no choice but to obey him.

He stacked newspapers in the garage as evenly as if they were pleats in my skirt, three days' worth with the fold toward the back, the next three days with the folds toward the front, alternating them to make a flat stack. After they reached a mark he had made on the beam behind them, he would wrap them up with twine, tying the bundle down tightly, his big thumb securing the string while he looped it under and over the other way. The knot he tied never came undone and he carried them off to the trunk of his car by that intersection of secured twine.

Inside his top dresser drawer, he kept his handkerchiefs the same way, stacked as neatly. Fresh ones from the ironing board went on the bottom. Being the one who had ironed them, I asked him, "Why do you put them on the bottom?"

"To even the wear," he told me. "This way, they *all* get a chance!" he laughed. But the image of his dresser drawer was so different from Mother's dresser. Her underwear and socks and nightgowns all fell into the same drawer, which smelled of lavender, fresh and clean but never terribly tidy.

Daddy and I talked easily. We laughed at the same things and, I believed then, he knew all the answers—how to take out splinters, pull teeth, lace boots, gather eggs, currycomb cattle. I trusted him. He never told me a lie. He never reneged on a promise. His answers were crisp and accurate, and his care was demonstrated by his actions, rarely put into words.

Once, when one of my large front teeth began to wiggle, I showed it to him.

"Let me see." He moved it back and forth. "I think the tooth fairy will need a couple more days before she gets *that* one," he said. And he was right. On the day that it seemed ready to pull, it would not come out. It hurt. He kept trying to loosen it more.

"Can't we wait until it just falls out?" I wondered. So we did. The next day, it was almost out, and Daddy tried again.

"I've got a great idea," he told me, "if you can be brave enough."

"What?"

"Well, I'll tie a string around your tooth and tie the string to the doorknob. I'll hold you and you hang on, and then I'll slam the door when you're not looking. That should do it. Are you game?"

I said, "Yes," but I was scared.

"Don't worry, honey. I wouldn't do anything I thought would hurt you. That tooth is dying to come out of your mouth, and I think today is the day." And he tied the string tightly to the root of the tooth, held my forehead against his chest with his strong hand, and, as he promised, slammed the door. I could taste the blood, feel the hole in my mouth with my tongue, and I saw the string hanging on the doorknob with a tooth attached to it.

"That's a doozy," he said. "You're one brave little girl, Janie."

"Will the tooth fairy leave me thom more money?" I lisped.

"I'll bet she does. You look under your pillow in the morning and tell me what you find."

I cannot remember the cash payoff for that memorable operation, but I do remember it took forever for the new one to come back in. When it did, the edges were crimped like pinking shears, and it was a huge tooth that made me hold my lips over it when I smiled. It took ages for me to forget my self-consciousness on both counts, the hole in my smile and the big tooth that stuck out like a beacon, but I finally did. Daddy, for a long time, would tease me by asking if I had any loose teeth, to which I always let out a mock yowl, saying, "No, no!"

He put his hand on top of my head, mussing up my hair a little, and said, "You're my girl for sure."

Once, when Mother stayed in Des Moines with the little twins, and Bob and I were driving out to California with Dad to visit his mother, our Grandmother Belton, we stayed overnight in a motel. Toward morning, knowing Daddy would come into our room to waken us, I let out my braids and spread them out over the pillow like a halo. Then I closed my eyes and smiled as if in my sleep, thinking he would find me attractive and alluring, the way we'd seen seductive movie stars. I just loved my Dad, the first man in my life, and I think he knew it, for he said, "Get up and comb the snarls out of your hair, Janie, and be quick about it." What I expected, I had no idea, but I felt sad. Obviously he still loved Mother more than he did me. But I would still be his best pal.

Mother and Bob were psychically close, as Dad and I were, though none of the four of us ever stated such affinities. After the twins were born, and later, when the two younger boys came along, such pairing diminished. Each of us was so much a part of the whole, the distinctions ceased to matter. But those early years were as indelible as the stamp of a signet ring on hot wax.

Listening to the Lambs

My father built a lambing shed. Four low posts, not much taller than he was, supported timbers cut from the woods and laid across them, horizontally first, and then vertically. Other trees had been cut to fill out the roof support. Then, thickly thatched with straw, the roof was weighted down with stones or extra boards against the ravaging winds. Into the timbers, wherever they were strong enough, long nails had been hammered to hang up the lantern whenever extra light was needed. Three sides of the shed were open at the top, the fourth one backing against the wind, closed with rough-hewn boards. The wind could cut like broken glass, blowing close to the ground. It was sometimes hard to see in the chalk-white breath of a blizzard. Often the snow would drift up against that wall, filling in the chinks and adding warmth.

January and February in Iowa—months the lambs are born—can reach temperatures no newborn can survive outdoors. Dropping below zero, sometimes as much as ten to twenty degrees, the weather will freeze a wet lamb dropped on the frozen ground. Too, winter blizzards and deep snowdrifts disorient the livestock, and new mothers will desert their hapless infants to wander off, blinded by the weather. So, farmers with sheep expected to give birth during the lambing season, usually the first months of the year, build a place for the pregnant ewes to keep their lambs out of the cold, a nursery to keep them from freezing to death.

Banked along the boards at the base of the entire shed, straw, that great insulator, enclosed a space in which fenced pens separated the ewes, pregnant, newly delivered, or waiting. The expectant mothers were poor waddling creatures, their woolly bellies wide enough to force their four legs to support them like stiff chair legs. Nervous new mothers were attentive, nudging, licking, totally new-baby absorbed, while mothers of more than a week, their lambs already nursing, waited to go back out into the world.

If he heard restlessness among the penned sheep, regardless of the hour, my father rose up out of his warm bed to go out to the shed. He put layers of clothes on over his pajamas, pulled on his boots and his heavy coat, the collar standing upright to keep the biting cold off his neck and ears, and crunched out through the freezing weather, feeling responsible for them, needing to be where they were.

We had overheard him telling Mother over dinner that there had been a pack of wild dogs roaming the countryside, killing the sheep. So, when I heard a commotion in the lambing shed, I got out of bed, throwing the woolen comforter back over the flannel sheets to keep them warm while I was gone, and went down to their bedroom.

"Daddy, we heard the sheep baaing out in the shed," I whispered through a crack in the door, feeling like an important bearer of news.

I found him already out of bed, putting his sweater and woolen shirt on over his pajama tops. He answered, "I'm going out to see what's going on. You wanta come? Get on your warmest clothes, and make it snappy. I'll wait a minute, throw a chunk of wood in the stove. You'll stick close to me, understand?"

"Can Bobby come too?"

"Sure. But dress warmly, Janie, and come help me with the birth.

It'll be good practice for your nursing career. You can be my Fleecy Nightingale," he quipped. I was intrigued but hated the steaming blood and the smell, and felt sorry for the little wet babies with no blanket to wrap around them. I raced upstairs, shook Bobby. "Come on, quick, put on your snowsuit! Daddy said we could come out with him." And he did. We tagged along, following the lantern.

Dad was the midwife, the kerosene lantern his only light in the early dark of winter, checking up on the new births. Holding the lantern high over his head to locate the ewe who was about to deliver, he found the nail closest to her and hung up the light. It shed a pathetically small wigwam of warmth around the scene, as he freed his hands and set to work.

With a low, slow voice, he would try to calm her, stroking her wool back from her head to her tail. "You know, kids, she is a little bit scared, so I'm trying to make her relax. Then, her muscles will work better to help push the new little lamb out into the world."

"Does it hurt her, Daddy?"

"You bet it does, but it doesn't last long, and she'll have a lot to do, once it arrives. When she starts to lick it clean, she'll forget how much pain there was."

As he talked, both to the sheep and to us, he took hold of the little head that was sticking out her bottom and gently pulled on it. He would help a ewe expel her placenta, rub life into a cold, blue lamb, then support a first stand on wobbly legs or massage a stubborn udder. He knew animal nature and they sensed it, as animals do, both seeming to trust the other, to work together for their common good.

So I got to witness my first delivery. It was a hard one, Dad told me later, which had caused the ewe to strain and cry out, her head lolling back and her bleating tongue dry. That had agitated the others around her, and they were milling about, empathic and frantic the way animals can be. But our father, a veterinarian who could almost speak the language of animals, kept talking to her, urging her not to give up, rubbing her sides and soothing her tense body, her legs that kept dancing or twitching. She finally lay down on her side and Dad reached in, his big hand around the lamb's head, and pulled, ever so gently.

"Easy, girl," he crooned, "Easy does it. There, atta girl, keep trying. Here she comes! Easy, now. Yes. Yes!" And suddenly the little thing was out on the straw. We were a bit squeamish, huddled together in one corner of the straw bank, to see the blood, the sticky water, the little tiny, blue lamb no bigger than our teddy bear.

I thought Daddy was like Jesus, walking among his sheep, counting, watching their progress, helping the newborn lambs learn the art of nursing, the ewes the art of parenting. The bleating of labor, the maternal act of ownership, the gentle licking off of their newborn baby was a ritual of love he never tired of watching over. When they seemed less nervous and the flock had settled down, he said, "Okay, kids, back to bed!"

One day, probably in autumn, we were walking with Dad along the path through the woods, coming home from the upper pasture, when he heard the bark of a red fox. We had been looking at a tree that had been struck by lightning, as Dad explained why the deep, white scar corkscrewed down the trunk. He stopped talking suddenly and stiffened, alert as an animal whose ears prick up, and put his hand on my shoulder saying, "Shhhh, Janie! Listen. . . ." We both froze as the barking continued. He bent down to our height and whispered, almost inaudibly.

"That bark is ricocheting off the hill. It is a red fox, warning its mate. Stay still. He hasn't caught our scent. With luck, he'll run right past us."

I was electrified. Only Reynard the Fox in our bedtime story, or the fox and the grapes of *Aesop's Fables* lived in my imagination. I had never seen one. We hunkered there, I snuggled into his chest and knees, and waited. Bobby looked like he was playing statues, still as a stone.

And the fox came, beautiful tawny breath of grace like a furry ballerina, loping along the pasture road. And the fox saw us, caught by surprise, rare for a red fox, and slammed on the brakes. Dust rose in the road and the fox seemed suspended for a brief moment. Then he took off, yelping, his fluffy tail pulled straight behind him like a kite string in high wind.

My father sat down on the spongy grass of those Iowa woods and laughed and laughed and laughed. I had never seen him so totally abandoned to joy. He had outwitted a fox! He slapped his knee, was so tickled at having tricked the trickster that he blew his nose and wiped his eyes where pure delight had seeped into his sinuses. "Red devil," he said. "They're foxy alright."

He told us, then, as we walked on down the path, how clever foxes are, how they have been seen to run across the backs of a flock of sleeping sheep in order to ditch a dog in pursuit. The lanolin in sheep's wool camouflages the scent trail, and the frustrated dogs mill about the edge of the flock, stumped, trying to pick up the scent while the red fox runs free.

Both Bob and I inherited our father's love of nature's tricks, a fascination with the absurd and a close observation of the places where surprise takes place. We loved to recall for each other, mostly to test a similar memory, events like this one with the fox. We could even see the prickly grass we knelt in, even the lay of the land, even the kinds of tall trees in that part of our woods. And the color of the fox, that shiny auburn fur, the pointed ears, the tail that bushed out at the end, all of that remains. Even our father, in his old age, got a special delight in retelling the uniqueness of that experience.

Usually it would lead him into other stories of animal intelligence, an admiration, I am sure, that had led him to specialize in veterinary medicine in the first place. Certainly his German shepherd, Frieda, knew everything Dad wanted almost before he spoke a word. With her sharp ears cocked, her eyes riveted on his face, she would wait for the command she'd already suspected, and go out to round up the milk cows, or chase the chickens out of the vegetable garden.

Mules, Dad thought, were more intelligent than horses, and their refusal to work any harder or faster was an instinct to preserve their strength, to pace the work they had been harnessed to.

Nothing made him laugh so easily as watching the strategies of a mother squirrel protecting her babies from marauding birds, or from a stray cat climbing the tree trunk. Out of their tree and onto a rooftop, she might put her brood in the gutter and then try to decoy the assumed attacker, her tail raised and flicking as if to threaten the assailant with a whip.

Their nut storing in the autumn, along with the groundhog looking for his shadow on February second, were ways that Dad predicted the weather. "Animals are smarter than people," he insisted. If the squirrels began their gathering as soon as the nuts fell, that meant an early winter. If they waited for the hulls to dry, the winter would be late. For a trained scientist, he held more than a few bits of folk wisdom on which he relied.

The Cat's Paw

Our parents kept their best books on the upper shelves, but we could reach them if we stood on a dining-room chair. The big black-walnut corner cupboard stood next to a window in Daddy's study. Mother loved that big antique, kept her pattern books and other mysterious treasures behind the two doors that shut on the lower part. The light was natural in that little room off the dining room, and we could sit on one of Mother's braided rugs that ovaled in front of the return-air register. We liked to sit there in the space between the corner cupboard and Daddy's oak roll-top desk, looking at the books with pictures of things we'd never seen. In the year or so it took the twins to grow into real people, to waddle around on two legs in real little shoes, Bob and I learned a lot about animals from Dad's illustrated *Dictionary of Veterinary Medicine*.

Part of our outdoor play, the animals were there to examine, to satisfy our curiosities. Dad had staked his big white workhorse, Doll, for us to play on out in the front yard. Since our bedtime book was *Toby Tyler, or Ten Weeks with a Circus*, we practiced to be circus performers, leaning the ladder from the barn up against her side to climb on. Doing headstands on the back of this wide-backed and patient animal, we found out how the whole back of a horse shifts as its hindquarters move, then how to compensate for the shift. We watched the other horses slobber as they drank the filthy water in their big galvanized tank.

Taking turns, we rode the ram bareback down the hill to the creek, dragging him up again by a rope around his neck. Dad finally made us stop because the ram was getting harder and harder to catch. No small wonder. The little pink piglets, nursing the ravenous sow, we tried to pet, having helped to slop their mother by filling her trough. But she wouldn't let us near them. She swilled her food once we'd left her pen. I wondered why the bull's penis was so far from the sac that hung low between his legs, and Bobby told me it was because he couldn't "do it" if it was too far back. He didn't know why the rooster had a red comb on his head and the hens did not.

If people were made of two kinds, so must all the animals be. We made a pact to explore that curiosity, to prove or disprove the similarities. It started simply enough. We examined the barn cats. Sure enough, the boys had little sacks like acorns between their hind legs, and the girl cats did not. They had a double row of nipples up their bellies for nursing, like most animal mothers did. And the bull's penis hung down where his belly button ought to be, and always it had hair all around it. When he peed, the water dripped off the end of the hairs. The sack between his legs was big like a saggy balloon full of water. The ram was similarly equipped, his sack all woolly and soft, and the ewes were as tidy and neat as the cows were, only with less extra skin around their bottom hole.

The rooster was a puzzle. He hopped up on the backs of chickens and made a big flap with his wings and always a lot of noise. He could make the dust rise up in a cloud from the floor of the chicken pen while he was at it, but he didn't even have a penis that we could find. The poor hens had only one opening in their bodies out of which came all that poop and the eggs besides. That didn't seem a likely outlet for baby chicks.

"They grow inside the eggs, silly. They don't get born whole. They hatch out, don't you remember?" Yes, I did. So that was that.

Dad encouraged us to look inside his big, heavy book as much as we liked, and to study the illustrations. That taught us about their insides as well as their outsides, and since neither of us could read very well, the pictures answered our questions, or gave us some we hadn't known enough to ask. The light of afternoon came through the glass, haloing those years of learning from pictures, of establishing a love of books and their magic, the unveiling of mysteries we could neither name nor fathom.

The *Medical Dictionary* had illustrations of a cow cut open so we could see her insides; of a pig's head where we could see the tubes in it; of a heart whose four parts were crisscrossed with lines; and of various legs, all stretched across with muscles and nerves like rubber bands. Hard as it was for us to believe, all cows have four stomachs. That's why they're always chewing their cuds, trying to digest stuff in one or the other. One of our favorite sandwiches was made of cold sliced cow's tongue with mustard, but neither of us could believe how long it was in the picture. We got to watch Mother fixing various parts of chickens for supper, too, like hearts or tongues or gizzards or liver.

We spent hours in that corner by Daddy's big oak desk. It had a tiny keyhole at the bottom of the lid that rolled down like an accordion when he wasn't working there. On the wall above it was mounted, on a large shield of wood, the horns of a Texas longhorn bull about six feet from the tip of one horn to the tip of the other.

"Don'tcha think those big horns are kinda scary?" I asked Daddy once, when he was working there.

He looked up and laughed. "No, they don't scare me, especially since they aren't attached to a real animal any more! That bull must have been one giant son-of-a-gun!"

Inside the drawers he kept the records of his shorthorn herd, who was the father and who the mother of a newborn calf. He wrote on those lined papers with ink, all about when it was born, where the mother cow came from, who the bull was that made her pregnant, and what he'd paid for each animal.

We watched Daddy make a splint for a dog's leg, run over by a tractor, and he was always giving us baby rabbits or guinea pigs or bummer lambs to nurse with a bottle. If we lost one of the rubber nipples that fit over the end, we could get some new ones at the IGA store, from a box on the lower shelf. We had to look very carefully to get one that really fit, or the lamb would suck it right down its throat. He spoke the language of the little creatures of the world, and we wanted to learn it.

"If you pick a guinea pig up by the tail, its eyes will fall out," he told us. Since he always told the truth, we had to believe him.

"Why?"

"I don't know why. Go and see. Try it. See if I'm right."

Rather afraid that we would have to pick up the loosened eyes from their cages, we went out to the shed to test his theory. There, the guinea pigs lived in a big wire cage with a little cup where we put their food. Bob reached in to pick up one of them, and we found out that guinea pigs have no tails, so we couldn't experiment. We learned the lesson he wanted to teach us, never to forget it.

Nothing else in our large world, mostly empty, was as interesting as the animals around us, especially the way they got up on top of each other—the dogs, the cats, the cows, the sheep, the pigs, and the pigeons, even the birds that nested in the shed.

"Why are they always doing that, Mother, playing leap-frog?" I asked.

"They are making babies," she explained, "so there will be little calves and little pink piglets. Sometimes the mother sheep has twins, just like our baby girls."

"Do people do it, too?

"Yes, but in a different way. Will you bring me the eggbeater from the top drawer, honey," she said, changing the subject. She wasn't as satisfying as Daddy, because she was always changing the subject, while Daddy told us the answers. If he didn't know, then he'd ask us more questions until we finally got to the point.

We were relieved to learn that people did it differently, which came close to explaining our little sisters, "Merry-Lou" and "Merry-Lyn," as we nicknamed them. They were cute. We loved watching them crawl across the living room, lickety-split. 'Lyn would decide to go in a certain direction, look at MaryLou with her big blue eyes, and take the lead. MaryLou would follow or team up, like a pair of horses in the trace.

'Lou had a head of black, curly hair. She would pull out one hair at a time to tickle her nose with while she stuck her other thumb in her mouth, rolling over on her back to suck, suck, her eyes closed, moving into some baby space of her own. One whole side of her head was bald by the time Dad figured out a solution. He shaved her whole head, "clean as a whistle," as he put it. It must have been awful for her, though, to wake up one morning deprived of her springy curls. I held her in my arms, one of my hands on her poor whiskery head, feeling sorry for her, hoping she wouldn't catch cold. I thought it was mean of Daddy to cut off her hair and I offered her some tickling hairs from my own head, but she didn't want them.

Merilyn had soft brown hair as fine as tender new grass all over her head. Her eyes twinkled whenever she smiled, which was always. They were both adorable, everyone agreed. They had a language of their own. All of us tried to decode their messages, but no one ever could. They understood each other, that was clear. I can't tell you what the sounds meant, but it sounded like hilarious gibberish.

"Mmmuhtenga," Merilyn would say, or something like that.

MaryLou would imitate, "Mmmuhtenga," and off they would crawl, together like a miniature trick they were performing, headed for the toy box or their cribs where their beloved blankets hid. Endlessly fascinating as they were, they took up all our parents' time.

Except at bath time. We had a real bathroom in that house, one with a long tub that had four feet like those of lions. Mother laid out our clean pajamas while Daddy ran our bath water and we climbed into that warm place together, as usual. It was our swimming pool. We loved to splash, to wash each other's back, to brush the dirt from under our fingernails with a special brush that had bristles on both sides of it. To help get all ten of our toenails clean enough for inspection, we dug around the edges with either one of Mother's hairpins or a broken piece of broom straw.

"Don't be in such a hurry, Jane, or you'll hurt me," Bob complained.

"I'll just be as careful as you were with mine!" I said, always competitive.

We checked each other for belly lint and toe jam, even hair lice, because we'd heard about head lice making children bald. That would be too cold to bear, so it was wise to keep an eye out for any crawly thing. Luckily, we never found any of those.

No one ever minded the water splashed over the edge onto the black and white tiles; we could wipe it up with our towels after we got dry. Once a week, usually on a Saturday night, we got to bathe. Daddy usually dried us, rubbing the towel over our skin as though he were polishing shoes, until we begged him to stop. He would laugh at our pleas, saying the redness was a sign of being really clean. We were glad we didn't have to wear diapers like the twins had had to, because they used to stink.

"If they'd been boys," Bobby said, "I don't guess they'd smell so bad."

"There's no difference, silly," I argued. "Once the pee or the poop comes out, you can't tell whose it is."

"How do you know?"

"I just think so," I answered, lamely.

In those first two years of the twins' life, we lived on the Ficken farm, which had a huge front yard and pastures behind, a high field where corn grew, and places along the creek where the animals grazed. We were free to roam in the woods, play in the creek, hide in the barn. Bob was in charge of numerous adventures which he called his "scientific experiments." I was his cat's paw, his slave girl, his assistant, depending, the one who would execute his weird ideas.

"Let's take our tire pump and blow up the cat," he said one day, "then, when we let her loose, she'll squiggle around the yard like a balloon letting out air."

"Will it hurt her?"

"No. She may explode, pop like a balloon. But if we do it in the outhouse, we can clean it up and no one will know. Chances are, though, she'll just yowl 'till we let her loose. You get to hold her claws. Hold 'em tight. And I'll stick the hose up her bottom and pump in the air. When she swells up, I'll open the door and you throw her outside, okay?"

We did that. Not without hazard, however. At the first jet of air, she turned into a fury of resistance, but I held on tight. Bob was giggling like a madman, but pumping over and over. Finally, her front feet yanked free and she clawed my arm raw before Bob opened the door and I flung her out. We never saw that yellow cat again. Maybe she lived forever underneath the barn.

"Don't you dare tell anyone what we were doing, or I'll pump *you* up like the cat," he threatened.

"Look at my arm, Bobby. It's all bloody. And it hurts." I began to cry.

"Come on. Tell Mother one of the cats attacked you, but that's all. If she asks were you tormenting it, say no. She'll put mercurochrome on it and you'll get better. Don't you dare tell, Janie, I mean it!" So, I lied to Mother and she wrapped gauze around the wound with plenty of adhesive tape. It did heal, eventually.

In the barn at milking time, twice a day, the cows were locked into their stanchions. Sweet hay was forked down from the mow into the manger, and as they moved toward the delicious smell to plunge their faces into it, Dad would lock the stanchions around their necks. Two boards, a lot like pliers but much bigger, would snug up around their necks with enough room to allow them to keep eating. But they were scissored together at the top and held in place with a rope loop. After they'd been milked, they'd be released by tossing off the rope. The boards were shiny as satin where the necks of generations of cows had rubbed up and down as they ate. The little three-legged milking stools were shiny, too, but from the pants of the milkers. These were stored upside down on a wide board by the barn windows.

Once, when Dad was ready to carry the full pails up to the milk separator, he called out to us, lurking nearby as usual.

"Bob," he said, "You release the stanchions and drive the cows out, will you? Be sure to lock the barn door when the last one's gone. Can I count on you to do that?"

"Sure, Dad," he said in his best saint's voice. Bobby was seven and he thought he could do everything.

"Will you keep an eye on Janie, too?" he added.

"Okay."

Dad left. "Hey, I've got an idea," Bob said the minute our father was out of sight. "I broke off a long, skinny icicle from the roof and I want you to put it up the cow's bottom, just to see what she does. She can't get out of the stanchion. You have to be careful, though, because she may kick, so stand to one side. I'll hold her tail up and you shove it in, like the bull does."

He was excited, secure because the stanchion was still in place. But I was scared, though more scared of what he would do to punish me if I didn't do it. So I did, reaching up to where her opening was and twisting it in, my fingers sticking to the end of it. She reared up, arched her back and twisted from side to side like a bucking horse, expelling that ice-cold suppository onto the straw, along with a jet of liquid manure. I scurried up on the edge of the manger to escape her wild reaction, but Bob, backing off safely behind her, was laughing maniacally.

"Too cold, maybe. We'll try a carrot or a turnip next time."

"I'm not going to do it again," I yelled. Once was already too much for me. I thought it terribly unfair to the cow to keep her so she couldn't get away.

Other episodes, although not as naughty, were nevertheless life-threatening "scientific experiments." One day in early spring, Bob instructed me to shinny up the shed post to take the baby robins out of their nest. We could see their little mouths open whenever the mother bird arrived with something to eat, and Bobby thought the time was right. He had a plan to train the little birds as house pets. We always wanted a canary, or a parrot like Uncle Dave had, and, resourceful always, Bob hit on the unsuspecting robins.

"If you carry this bag up in your teeth so you can use your hands to climb, you can scoop the little birds into it, twist it shut, and toss it down to me. Then you can slide down and we'll take them up to our pigeon house where we can build them a cage."

"What will they eat?"

"Worms, silly."

"Where will the worms come from?"

"You'll dig them up and I'll feed them to the little birds. There are lots of worms in the garden." Another task. I was beginning to resent so many instructions, but resisting brought hideous consequences. He might not let me be a part of his ideas for fun anymore, if I didn't do my part.

So I shinnied up the pole. No sooner did I approach the nest than a swarm of birds circled around me and dove at my head with their sharp beaks. They pecked and pecked the part in my hair, chirping and cawing and carrying on. I couldn't let go of the pole for fear of falling. I couldn't shoo them away with one arm while I clung to the pole with the other, because what would I do with the bag, then? It hurt terribly, and my hair got all bloody. I dropped the bag, slid back down the pole in tears. Bobby was scared. He said he was sorry, he didn't know the birds would do that. He took me by the hand and we ran to the house.

"Just say the birds attacked you, okay? Don't tell Mother you were going to rob the nest." Mother was wonderful. She'd heard me crying and met us at the kitchen door.

"What happened?"

"The birds hurt Janie."

"Oh, honey," she cried, "come here and let me look. I'll wash your hair in warm water and we'll put salve on the little bird bites." She turned me onto my back up on the kitchen counter, held my head under the faucet and lathered my sticky hair clean with her best new-smelling glycerin soap.

Perhaps the scariest of all the adventures from that time was Bob's plan to create high drama on the roadside. Few cars drove by on that gravel in front of our house, and those that did drove slowly—Model

T's or Model A's. What would a driver do, Bob wondered, if he saw a dead girl lying in the middle of the road?

"I'll hide in the ditch where I can see it, and I'll tell you what happened, later. You pretend to be dead, just lie still in the road with your arms flung out like you'd been hit or something and when the car sees you, he'll slam on his brakes, stop, get out to see what happened. Then, you jump up and run toward me. He'll be mad at our joke, but together, we'll cut back through the pasture toward home, okay?"

"What if he doesn't stop?"

"He'll stop, don't worry," he-who-knew-everything said.

I went into the road by the curve below the driveway and lay down. I tried to imagine how being dead would look. I pulled my dress up over my knees and stuck one leg out like a broken stick, threw my arms out, and lolled my head over to one side. The road smelled like gray chalk and I'd just had my hair washed and didn't want to get it dirty.

So, for what seemed an interminable length of time, I lay in the itchy gravel, hoping the man we were going to fool would come along soon. Suddenly, we heard the sound of tires coming down the road.

"Lie still," Bob hissed from his hideout. "Keep your eyes shut!"

Sure enough, the car came around the corner, then slammed on the brakes and shimmied to a stop. A man in a black suit jumped out of the driver's seat and ran toward me.

"Now," Bob prompted.

I leapt up and ran toward him.

"You damn little bitch," he yelled, and took out after me. Terrified, I ran with every ounce of strength my five-year-old legs could muster, Bobby with me now, heading for the barbed-wire fence that edged the pasture. The man was panting and gaining ground.

"If I catch you kids, I'm gonna tan your hides, do you hear me? So help me God, I will. Tan your hides!" I had visions of us, covered with brown paint or something, for I had no idea what he planned to do.

Never before or since have I run so fast, so desperately fast, over hummocky grass and under the barbed-wire fence, praying that my clothes wouldn't get caught and stop me, having no idea then, what it meant to have one's hide tanned. Vaguely I knew it must be skinned and hung, like the groundhogs, skunks, and weasels we trapped, hung on shingles to dry on the side of the chicken house, then shipped off to the Shenandoah Fur Company for spending money—twenty-five, fifty, or seventy-five cents a pelt. And I believed he truly meant to kill us, huffing so close behind us we could almost feel his wolf breath. Would a human pelt bring him more than a dollar?

We wiggled through the fence and headed up through the tall weeds to safety. I got a little triangle tear on the hem of my skirt from where the barbed wire grabbed at me. The man in the suit did not come over the fence. He just kept yelling from where he was, threatening us further.

"I'm going to tell your folks what you've been up to, you little heathens, and they'll let you have it!"

When we realized he was no longer on our trail, we were winded, glad to sit down in the grass and catch our breath. Relieved to be alive, we watched him get back into his car and drive on. Bobby was more than rewarded for his first venture into horror.

That night I asked Daddy what it meant to tan a hide.

"They skin a cow and take off all the hair, then treat the skin with chemicals until it makes leather. That's called 'tanning.' Why do you want to know?"

"I heard a man say that the other day," I answered, deliberately vague, glad my precious skin was still mine, holding my insides inside. I told Bob I would never play dead again, no matter what he wanted to prove. I was beginning to get a mind of my own, to exercise some unexpected independence. I think he believed me, for he never put me in danger to such an extent after that.

Dad suspected something working between us, I think. "Getting tired of being the cat's paw?" he asked me.

"Why do they say 'cat's paw'?"

"Well, I think it's an English fable about cats and chestnuts. Once, when there were chestnuts roasting in a fireplace, one cat said to the other, 'Why don't you reach in and pull that chestnut out, and I'll share it with you?' The second cat, wanting to be friendly, put his paw into the fire to retrieve the hot nut, and d'ya know what happened? Sure. He got burned, all the hair singed off his hand and a big blister, I'll betcha. So when someone tells you to do something they don't want to do, and you do it, you're being the 'cat's paw,' do you understand, now?"

I did. I didn't want to get a bloody head ever again, and I didn't want to get kicked by the cow, or run over by a car. After all, I'd be six my next birthday.

A Doctor in the House

One day, Bobby and I were in the upper pasture near where Dad and a work crew were mowing hay. From the large gatepost at the corner of the field, we had been jumping barefoot into a pile of brittle corn stalks, cut and tossed there for making into silage. We scrambled up the gate to try again and again, competing as usual, this time to see who could jump the farthest. When something pierced the sole of my foot, I yelled out in pain. My brother, frightened, tried to wipe away the blood with cornhusks.

When Daddy arrived back from his work with the mower, he found me stretched out on a makeshift bed of fodder, being the patient, and Bob pacing up and down, playing doctor. Bobby must have felt somehow responsible, having egged me on to jump just one more time. Dad squeezed and squeezed my foot, trying to force the splinter out, or to cleanse the wound. He was determined and it hurt. I wanted him to be proud of me, so I tried to be brave.

"Let's get you home and clean this out," he told me. "You can ride on the mower seat if you'll promise to hold on. We'll go down slowly, honey. This'll be over before you can say 'Jack Robinson.'" We inched our way down the road that ran along the pasture edge and when we got to the barn, Dad carried me into the house.

In an old enamel pan on the kitchen floor, Mother poured boiling water laced with Epsom salts, and made me sit forward on a kitchen chair and soak it. As soon as I could bear the heat, I would put my foot almost in the water, feel the burn, and yank it up again, until I could grit my teeth and hold it on the surface for a while, finally putting it under. It was painful.

All the soaking in the world failed to dislodge the piece of dry corn stalk that had embedded itself in my right foot arch. Dad dug into the tender hole in my instep with tweezers. No luck. When the tears welled up in my eyes, Mother said, "Merrill, let's give this girl a rest for awhile. We can finish tomorrow. Can you sleep with your foot elevated, Janie?" she asked, her hand gentle on my shoulder.

"I've never tried it, but I can prop it up with pillows, I guess." And I did.

For all his admonishments about wearing shoes, for all his squeezing, the cornhusk did not come out. A piece about half an inch wide and nearly an inch long worked its way in deeper and deeper, and my foot began to fester and swell. It hurt terribly. After awhile, even my bedroom slipper no longer fit, and I awakened one night crying. My foot was so red, so swollen, so raging with infection it would have to be lanced, they said. The build-up of pus had stretched the skin shiny, made my toes look like little pig sausages. I realized, from the behavior of my parents, that some critical moment had arrived. Suddenly, it had become urgent and they came to a quick decision. Dad was a veterinarian, so *he* had the instruments. There was no emergency room, then, no hospital in small town Redfield, Iowa, and no money to call a doctor out from Des Moines. He would perform the operation on his daughter's foot—on the ironing board.

Before the advent of antibiotics, disinfecting was taken very seriously. Mother washed my foot several times, rinsing it in the kitchen sink, in a bowl full of scalding hot water and iodine. It smelled like sheep-dip and turned my foot yellow. The hot washcloth on that tender flesh was almost unendurable. I bit into my lip, winced with each application.

Bobby just stood around, looking sad. He took hold of my hand and said he was really, really sorry. "It won't be so bad, Janie. Daddy will open your foot up like a watermelon and let all the seeds out," he said. He promised me it would feel better, and I trusted him.

Mother had called Mrs. Van Deventer, our bosomy neighbor who was once a nurse, to please come over to help, to keep an eye on the twins while all this was going on. She wore a white top like the butcher's smock over her flowery dress and smelled like our butterfly bush. She had what my mother said were piano legs. At first we thought she meant made out of wood. But no. The more we looked, the plainer it became; they tapered down from her knees to her feet, feet sure enough like the little brass boxes on the Straights' grand piano legs. Mrs. Van Deventer minced along in shoes that looked like little pigs' trotters, too small for the rest of her body. But she was nice to us. She didn't have any kids, but she loved to can things and had once won first prize for her green-tomato preserves at the county fair.

She promised me my foot would feel better, once it was over. Rubbing her fat fingers through my hair, Mrs. Van Deventer said, "I'll give you a nickel, honey, if you don't cry."

Mother looked worried, covering the ironing-board operating table set up in the kitchen with a clean, white sheet. She said my foot would feel better soon, she was sure of it.

On the wood stove, metal instruments out of Daddy's pigskin satchel boiled in the shallow cake pan: heavy tweezers with long, pointy tongs, some squares of gauze, and a little sharp knife. Dad would know how. Hadn't he let me watch him cut open the cow's belly, bloated from eating green apples? And after that stinking explosion burst from her stomach, didn't the cow get better, get up on her feet again, walk back to the barn? She got flat again, too, like tar bubbles we'd pop in the road on hot days. They all promised me it would feel better, and I believed them.

Stepping up on a chair seat, I crawled onto the ironing board and lay down on my back. Dad sat at the end, under our best floor lamp he'd moved in from the living room. Mrs. Van Deventer took my hand in one of hers, and with the other, began to smooth my forehead, messing up my bangs.

"Try to count the flowers in the wallpaper border, honey," Mother said, "and don't be afraid. Daddy loves you and wouldn't hurt you if he didn't think it would make you feel better."

And then, a pain like fire cut through my foot. The two women kept talking to me, trying to distract me until the quick lancing was over. With a sharp intake of breath, I bit my lip, scrunching up my face to keep from crying. Pus spurted out, then kept oozing. Daddy put both hands around my split-open right foot and squeezed gently but with increasing pressure. Bobby stood by like a medical assistant, a little sick-looking, but trying to be strong. He kept saying, "Don't cry, Janie, don't cry!"

And then, suddenly, it was over. The putrefied, half-inch-wide splinter had exploded out in all that pus. Dad held it up like a trophy.

"There!" He let out a huge sigh and straightened up. "By God, we got it! Look at that whopper! You're a brave girl, Janie, you held so still I could see exactly what to do!"

I remember actually feeling as if some tight rubber band had been cut from my foot. Being the center of attention, the star attraction, with everyone looking on, was a rare and delicious sensation. Then Daddy poured iodine on the cut and it stung and turned my skin yellow. When I began to breathe more normally, even to smile, Mrs. Van

Deventer bent over to look closely at my eyes, halfway hoping, I thought, to find some tears at the corners, at least. But there were none. She had to fork over the nickel.

Daddy finished cleaning the wound, swabbing it with little pieces of cloth, pouring some more stingy stuff on it. He wrapped a long piece of gauze around and around my foot, then taped it together with his roll of Johnson & Johnson adhesive tape. He put one of his white socks over the bandage ever so carefully. Then, while everyone else was talking, he eased Bobby's right bedroom slipper onto my foot. My own wasn't big enough for the swelling or the miles of gauze around it.

"I told Daddy he could use my slipper," Bobby said, proud to be a part of this medical team.

"Thank you, Bobby," I told him, all pathos in my weak and wounded voice.

I couldn't put any weight on that foot for days and was cared for like an invalid by Mother and Daddy and Bob. In his Red Flyer wagon, equipped with a big pillow in a clean pillowcase, my brother, all caring and solicitude, pulled me around outdoors, bumping down the one step in the sidewalk near the back door, and out to the garage and back.

"Would you like to ride down the driveway to the road, Janie, or is it too bumpy?" he asked me, sensing even at his young age how bored a patient can get, bedridden, housebound, or immobile.

"It's not too bumpy. If I lie down and keep my foot up in the air, it won't hurt. Let's do it."

And we did. But only once. The gravel was harder to pull the wagon over than the sidewalk was. So, my turn to be solicitous, I said I preferred to stay on the smooth flat walk. We managed to get into the garage where I could slide out of the wagon and sit on the cement to play, to make mudpies for our make-believe "bakery" or cut out paper dolls.

My foot began to heal and I could hobble, then hop around on my strong left foot, pretending to be a circus performer who had lost one leg. One day, after Bob's teacher had called and talked to Mother, I was allowed to go to school with Bobby as his visitor, his "show-and-tell" prize.

"We have a special guest today," the teacher told the class, looking straight at me. "Bobby brought his little sister, who is just recovering from an operation on her foot. Bobby, would you like to introduce Janie and tell the class about why she is wearing a slipper?"

I was afraid to look at anyone, afraid of what Bobby would say, afraid to have to show off my ugly big foot to the other kids. I just kept looking at the map of the United States that hung up by the flag, wishing I could be in Wisconsin or somewhere else. I stared out the window, ran my pointer fingernail around the letters scratched into the desktop, and wanted to disappear like Alice in Wonderland.

Bobby stood up. "Well," he said, "you can guess who my sister is. She's sitting right here. She's Janie, and she has only been trying to walk on her sore foot for a couple of days. How it happened was she jumped off a fencepost into a pile of dry cornstalks and got a huge splinter stuck in her foot. It swelled up like a balloon and hurt until she cried."

Please don't let him tell them *everything*, I prayed. But he went on. "Then our dad put her up on the ironing board, took a huge knife and sliced it open. It was gruesome, the blood and stinky stuff oozed out all over the room. . . ."

"Not *all* over," I whispered. He didn't pay any attention to me, feeling good about being the one to tell the class this experience, blowing it up into high drama.

"And out popped the cornstalk. It was huge, about this big," and he showed about how big with his thumb and forefinger. "She didn't even cry and got a nickel for being so brave. I pulled her around in our wagon for a long time, but it feels better now, doesn't it, Janie?"

"Yes," I said, embarrassed to be asked in front of everybody.

"Can you put your foot up on the desk, honey," the teacher said, "so we can see how painful it must have been?"

So I did, pulling my dress down between my legs so nobody could see my underwear. Everyone got up and came to see my slipper-shod foot, but there wasn't anything to see, so I think they were disappointed.

"You can sit down now, Bobby," she told him. "Who else has something to share with the class, today?" she said, moving the attention away from both of us.

That night at supper, I told about my day at school, how Bobby had made me feel like a sideshow at a carnival, but that I enjoyed it finally, and would like to go again.

"No," Bobby said, "not unless you get another operation." That I didn't want. The pain finally went away, the swelling went down all the way, and I could wear my own shoes again. The scar remains visible on the instep of my right foot, still.

The Bucket Brigade

It was dusk, the time of day Grandma Chantry, if she was with us, would always announce as "night beginning to lower." A natural hush fell over this hour, just after dinner, our bodies full, the day's work finished, the evening ahead full of possibilities before bedtime, maybe reading, maybe playing a game of tiddly-winks or pick-up-sticks, maybe a bath. On this night, we had just finished supper with a treat, a rich egg custard Mother had made for dessert in little individual ramekins, and it was my turn to "red up the table," as we called moving all the dirty dishes from the table to the sink counter. I tried to stack the little dishes, to make the pile of dishes look like less to wash, but they kept falling off the top.

"Janie, don't stack things that don't want to stack," Mother said, "or you'll chip the edges."

"I am always very careful," I told her, quickly spreading the individual ramekins out on the counter and tearing off a little piece of a bread to put in each one. "We have just finished my pretend dolly's tea party," I said, trying to cover up what might be construed as less capable than my brother.

"I don't see any dolls around here," Bobby said. He was sarcastic because he always thought my imagining things was dumb.

"Well, that's what 'pretending' means, silly," I retorted.

"Now, children," Mother said, trying to keep us from getting into one of our tit-for-tat tangles. It wasn't big enough to keep us going, anyway, so we ended it.

The last of the evening sun came into the kitchen, making little patterns on the linoleum, and outside we could hear the birds settling down for the night with their purring *chirrup, chirrup*, a sound that always sounded like a sleepy "good-night." Daddy tipped his chair up on its back legs and leaned against the wall, the usual signal that dinner was over. Our kitchen was as warm and comforting as flannel.

Then, suddenly, we heard a man outside yelling, "FIRE! FIRE!" followed by wild hammering on the door. Dad's chair banged down on four legs and he leapt up, crying out, "Come on in!" When Daddy threw the door wide open, I could see the big bay stallion out by the garage, all covered with globs of bubbly white sweat, its reins thrown over our fence post.

"Tom, what's happened?" Dad wanted to know.

"Sorry, Ma'am," he said to Mother, taking off his hat, "I'm in a terrible hurry!"

The man was wearing coveralls over a shirt that had holes in the elbows. He was out of breath, but finally he blurted out, "Bring buckets to the Barker place! They say some kid was playing with matches. . . . They're afraid the barn'll catch!" And he was gone, galloping out our driveway on his horse, the gravel flying.

"Where is it?" Mother asked, standing up, tense.

"Over at Barker's place, Tom says." Dad said little else. Instead, he ran to the back porch, yanked open the back door and grabbed the galvanized pail Mother called her scrub bucket.

"Can I help, Merrill?" Mother asked.

"Just stay out of my way!"

Activated by such speed as we had never witnessed, we two shadowed him, caught up in the drama and the hunger for details. How did Tom find out about the fire? How many other people had he rounded up? What did he want Daddy to bring pails for? He stopped, thought a minute, and then said, "You two want to see a fire, what can happen if you monkey with matches?"

"Merrill, you can't take the kids!" Mother said.

"Why not? It'll be a good lesson for them. Besides, I'll take Frieda with us. She'll keep an eye on them."

"Yes, yes!" we said with one voice.

"Okay. Grab a sweater, it may get chilly past your bedtime. You'll have to stay out of the way. Do you hear! Have to stay inside the car."

So I pulled down my sweater that hung on the hall coat tree and followed Daddy out the door, one arm stuck in one sleeve. I was still trying to get the other arm in as we clambered into the front seat of his Model A. Daddy ducked into the garage where he dumped out another pail filled with apples, and just let them roll around on the floor. Then he nested that pail in the first one, threw them in on the back seat.

He whistled for Frieda, "Here, girl!" He slapped his palm on his leg. "C'mon, Frieda." He opened the door wide, put one foot up on the running board, and motioned her inside. She came bounding to him from wherever she'd been, her tail wagging like a metronome. "Atta girl. Scoot together tight, kids, she can sit by the window." He patted her rump and said, "Over," and she clamored over both our laps and sat down on the front seat next to him, her head looking out the windshield just like a real person. We sometimes thought he loved that dog more than he loved us, giving her the best seat and all, but we were glad she was coming along.

To Mother, standing on the sidewalk by the house, worried, he shouted, "I've got the kids, Zee. And Frieda. She'll keep 'em in line, don't you worry."

Daddy craned his head out the window and we backed out of the driveway in such a hurry the gravel sprayed out on either side. We could hear it scattering. He swung into the road, shifted gears, and drove across the bridge at breakneck speed.

"How far away is it?" I asked him.

"Bite your tongue, girl. You'll see for yourself, soon enough." So, both of us just shut up and waited, not wanting to make Daddy cross. He was driving like a maniac.

Not very far away, we could see the plume of smoke rising into the darkening sky. As we got closer and swerved off the road, we could hear the crackling of what sounded like a big bonfire. It smelled awful, sharp in our noses. We sped over bumpy ground never intended to be driven over, only to park with some other cars on the grassy edge of a field beside the river. Bobby reached over and took hold of my hand, for neither of us had ever seen our father push the gas pedal to the floor, to make the car go so fast. It was almost as scary as the fire was. We could see it blazing, not very far away.

Dad stopped abruptly, set the brake, grabbed the two pails out of the back seat and bent down to us, speaking in a terrible voice.

"Now you listen to me, you two. I'm only going to say this once, do you hear? You can watch from the car, sit on the hood if you're careful, but if I catch you anyplace else, I'll beat the tar out of you, understand? A fire is terribly dangerous, and I hope to God the wind doesn't pick up. I had no idea it'd be this big." We nodded. That tone of voice was authority itself. To Frieda, he said, "Stay, girl. Stay with the kids!" And he reached over and scratched her behind the ears, patted her on the back, and left, running. As we spread out to take up the driver's seat vacated by Dad, Frieda stretched out a bit, put her paws up on the seat, and stared at us. We began to pet her and talk to her, glad finally for her company.

The gathering together of more men than we had ever seen at one time, the panicked shouting as they formed a bucket brigade from the Raccoon River up to the house and barn, seared itself vividly in my mind. Whose farmhouse caught fire, I cannot remember. It has an echo in my ear like a double consonant, Bill Barker's, or Jake Johnson's, or something close. And the year? Maybe the dry summer of 1929 or '30.

Someone had tied a rope to a sturdy tree at the waterline, helping to steady the hand that hoisted the water up the steepest part of the bank, one pail at a time. The man at the river's edge shouted out a number as he filled each bucket. "One. Two. Three. Four." We could hear him counting, and all along the line, the buckets were passed along from one man to the next. When he had filled ten of them or so, he gave that hardest job to the next man in line, and he went to the back; otherwise they could never have endured the shoulder work of lifting those heavy loads of water like a practiced relay team, alternating the crossing arm. Nor could the man nearest the flames endure the heat much more.

We had never seen anything so scary. The fire raged, making a huge roaring and popping sound like breaking a million dry sticks over our knees all at once. Tall orange and yellow tongues licked the sky, now dark brown as chocolate pudding. The billowing smoke had erased all the stars. The flames were bigger even than the stoked fires of the brick kilns and we, small humans huddled in a car with a big dog, felt frightened and vulnerable.

Even when the burning house began to settle down, after the crackle and snap of breaking beams slowed like the last kernels of corn in the popper, the heat radiated out to where we were parked. Frieda's breath came out between her teeth, her tongue hanging out of her open mouth. She was thirsty and so were we, but we had nothing to drink.

"Open the window, Bobby."

He refused. "No. It'll only make it worse." Then, after a little argument to prove his point, he changed the subject.

"My Sunday-school teacher says Hell is a burning fire you can't put out. It must be like this. But, she never said it was so stinky."

"Where is Hell, exactly?"

"It's down underneath the ground. It's where you go if you've been bad all your life. If you've been *really* naughty, God will punish you with Hellfire and brimstone. And there isn't any water down there, either."

"Do you burn up?"

He pondered this awhile. "Maybe not all of you, but you get blisters and there isn't any Unguentine. The Devil keeps that all for himself."

We talked less and less, getting sleepy and waiting to see if the men were going to save the barn with their buckets of water splashed up over the boards and the shingles. The house was a roaring blaze that crackled and fell in on itself. The noise scared us more than the terrible leaping flames, and we could feel the heat clear across the field. Between the house and the river was the barn. The men were throwing water on only the barn now.

In fact, the house was left to burn to the ground. In my memory it was a huge house, but in reality it was relatively small. As we stared at the terrible bonfire of a house, we heard the woman who lived there yelling, "Help me! Help! Joey is still inside!"

I was terrified, imagining that small boy sizzling into a crackling if someone didn't rescue him. The men were all too busy with the bucket brigade to stop, and I turned to my big brother, desperate for the mother's fear. "Can't you help her, Bobby?"

"Dad would kill me if I left you here alone. Besides, her boy's probably run out somewhere, or is dead already."

"He'll *die* in there," I pleaded. I began to cry. Just then, we saw Joey clutching his mother's leg. She was patting his hair and hugging him, swaying from side to side to keep the baby quiet at the same time. We were enormously relieved. Bobby was right; Joey'd run to her from some hiding place.

"He's safe!" I yelled.

"I told you so." We kept hugging Frieda, just to feel safe ourselves in this horrifying scene of fire and smoke.

The woman was crying on the dry grass of her lawn among the few things that had been dragged out of the house, some chairs, some dresser drawers, a wicker baby carriage. She clutched the baby in her arms and wiped her nose on her apron—which Mother said no lady ever did. But we could see her shoulders shake and her apron go up to her nose, so we knew she was terribly sad, and we forgave her this breach of etiquette. They did manage to save the barn, or at least enough of it to allow for some future repairing. Daddy came to get us when it was very dark, both of us by then huddled together inside the car, layered on the front seat with Frieda like a litter of puppies, tired and sleepy, awed by the destruction a single match could cause, still a little bit scared, and wanting to get away from the smell of the smoke that made our eyes sting and made us cough.

Dad was smudged with mud and ashes and sweat, and he smelled awful. When we asked him about his dirty clothes, he said, needing to catch his breath, maybe, "Never mind." We were quiet as church mice driving home. So was he.

Only by eavesdropping on the conversation he had with Mother when we got back did we learn the extent of the loss.

"What a damn shame. . . . They lost practically everything they owned! No one was burned, though. That was a godsend. Even the black-walnut bedstead that was made for their wedding present went up in smoke," Daddy said.

"And her braided rugs and quilts?" Mother asked.

"Practically everything."

We faded as they gossiped about what the burned-out family would do next. Mother and the women of the town would gather at a church meeting and collect what necessities would tide the family over. Mother said something about a bolt of outing flannel she had stored away for making winter nightgowns that she could use to hem up new diapers for the baby. The family was going to be staying at the neighbor's house for now.

The men in the community would form a work party to rebuild some semblance of a place to live. From the lumberyard, they could get the siding, and there were enough capable carpenters among them to get a roof over their heads before winter.

Many times during the next few toy towns we built by the creek side, one of us would play the horseman, bringing the news, clapping one hand on alternate legs to imitate the hoof beats, *clickety-clack, clickety-clack, clickety-clack.* The other one would push a toy Model A through the streets and across a vacant space as fast as chubby hands could push it, yelling, "FIRE! FIRE!" And of course, we had "built" a hospital in our strange little crisscross of roads to which we subsequently carried innumerable burn victims, for our make-believe disasters were always larger than life. Bob was always the doctor, and I, as always, the nurse.

For years, I think, the terror of a fire raging out of control would freeze us with fear. Anything to do with burning—a struck match, the kitchen stove popping with a new piece of wood, a candle being blown out, even the stack of dry leaves raked up for burning when

Dad set it ablaze.

"You can't be a sissy forever," Bob told me. But he was only pretending to be brave. I had seen him wince and pull back whenever he got near a fire, too, for the sight and the sound of that farmhouse crackling and being totally destroyed seared itself on our consciousness.

Getting Down to Bedrock

Standing high above the wide meandering Missouri River, in the loess hills of western Iowa, where wildflowers and tall grasses dance in the wind, we saw around us the effects of wind and water on the land's face. Contrary to the popular image of a flat state, smack in the middle of a flat prairie stretch, Iowa is a land of gently rolling hills. Not only did the recession of the Wisconsin Glacier leave the huge runoff channels that became the Missouri River on the western border and the Mississippi River on the eastern side, it also left indentations on the land, drainage paths for smaller rivers and creeks, as if some god had raked long fingers through the mud. Great slabs of basalt were ledged where the waters had cut away the earth beneath them. Words like "cut bank," "gully washers," "bedrock," and "caves" peppered the speech of Iowans, inheritors of this land, this climate. From often-repeated allusions to geology, I learned the source of Dad's frequent references to bedrock. It was the bottom layer, the bare facts, the truth.

Our father had a compulsion for identifying things. From him, we learned to be curious about the names of plants and animals, about clouds and the birds that flew under them, about weather. Although it was from Mother's passion for reading that we learned about vocabulary, about new words and how to pronounce them, it was he who taught us to be specific, to name the world we lived in, to ask about the how and the why of things. We did not say, simply, "a field of hay," but, more accurately, a field of "alfalfa" or "timothy" or "wild clover."

I could not appreciate the logic of such fine distinctions, then. He was bent on teaching us to distinguish a winesap from a Jonathan apple, and we knew this. One crisp autumn day I remember, we went to a neighboring orchard to fill our burlap sacks with apples for the winter. The smell of that ripe fruit, the damp leaves underfoot, the delicious feeling of harvesting, of choosing the best apples from the windfalls on the rain-softened earth, made our mouths water with anticipation of Halloween or Mother's juicy apple pies. Then one of us would say, probably Bob, who was always seeking Dad's approval, "Those are Jonathans, aren't they?"

"You betcha," he'd say. "You're absolutely right, that's exactly what they are," and Bob beamed, smug in his perceived brilliance.

Perhaps Dad's dogged insistence on accuracy, his quick corrections of childish errors, helps to explain the burden of perfectionism we both carried. His exactitude left me striving for good grades, the right word, honest teaching, a clean house, good health. And Bob, with the same legacy, became an internist, loving a profession that identified even the invisible parts of the body, knowing how they functioned, how they were connected, how best to heal them.

Dad's nature, training, and cast of mind were scientific. He draped a moral cloak over his natural tendencies, calling it honesty, a trait he insisted we emulate. For this reason, in so many of our family conversations, he insisted on getting to the heart of any matter, to the root cause, to the " bedrock." If Bob and I told slightly different versions of the same incident, Bob insisting that the gate had been "left open," and my saying Bob had "unlocked the gate," Dad would take the two of us aside as if our future were on trial, and say, "I just want to get down to bedrock, here."

Then, the inquisition began, way out of proportion to the deed we two would agree, usually in a healing confession up in our treehouse. But he was bent on teaching us to tell the truth, for he was a fair-minded man, and he could not brook a liar. "A man's word is his bond," he said. He would always straighten up when he said that, which was why he did push-ups, we decided.

Bob would usually be the one who tried to outwit him. Of sterner stuff than I, Bob could outlast his probing with the lie still intact. We "borrowed" Mother's long-handled wooden spoon, the one that was stained purple from stirring a big batch of simmering grapes, to dig out the secret holes where we'd hide our treasure maps, down in the woods. We reasoned that she would never miss it for one day. But fate moved in and she went looking for it, maybe to reach something up high or to skim the suds from the washing machine, who knows, and, not being able to find it, she asked Dad if he'd seen it. Of course he hadn't, and he knew where to go for an answer.

"Wonder what happened to Mother's big spoon. You kids seen it?"

"No," Bob said. "I don't know what we'd do with that old thing, " he continued, making matters worse it seemed to me.

I just shook my head, mortally afraid of telling a lie to Daddy.

"Just wondered," Dad said, staring holes through both of us.

Neither of us confessed. But I knew we had broken the handle, trying to dig deeper through that packed earth, that Bob had buried the two pieces down by the riverbank. He told me nobody would ever know what happened to the spoon. And I guess he was right.

But I sympathized with Dad's wanting to know the truth, no bones about it. He wanted the facts, and I would most often give them, despite life-threatening daggers from my brother's eyes. More than once, I took the blame for something I did not do, just to get it over with, keep peace in the sibling pact. The consequences for telling on him were dire.

Wily first-born, Bob was imaginative and inventive sometimes. When he, six, and I, his four-year-old tag-along, went to a neighbor's house to see her new baby chicks, he did a terrible thing. Whole pens were filled with soft squares of yellow fuzz I could pet and purr over, like boxes of ripe dandelion heads. But Bobby picked up a little yellow ball and wrung its neck. The little eyelids closed forever. He stuffed it back among the living. He repeated this, to my horror, several times, just to see me wince and wail, begging him to stop. I finally ran to the neighbor lady. She was in the kitchen, wearing an apron made of the same printed flour-sacking Mother had made my summer nightie out of, and her socks wrinkled down around her ankles.

"What's the matter, honey?" she asked me, the tears undoubtedly making little rivulets down my dirty face.

"Can I call my mother?"

"Yes, of course." She rang the number of rings on the party line, and when Mother answered, I told her what Bob was doing.

Then, furious as could be, embarrassed at having such a naughty son, she charged down the road, a hickory switch in hand. After she had apologized about a million times, and offered to pay the woman for the chickens that would never grow up to give her eggs, she lashed the backs of Bobby's legs all the way home, repeating, "I cannot believe you would do such a thing! If you *ever* do that again, I will do the same to you, do you understand? I can't believe this. I am just mortified!" Bob yelled and yelled he was sorry, but I was glad to have Mother switching him. In retribution for my squealing on him, he made me eat a whole cup of chopped green acorns, and I, obedient to his orders, got terribly sick.

I wasn't as sweet as spring water; vacillation was my curse. I waited to see which direction the wind blew before I would decide. Once, on our cottage-cheese route in Redfield, a way Mother thought to make a little money, I swore a blood oath with my brother never to tell who threw the extra cottage cheese in the bushes. The lady whose house was on our list for the last delivery was not at home, and we were tired. So Bob tossed the pint jar into the bushes, that delicious creamy homemade cottage cheese I hated to waste, because he didn't want to carry it home again. He told Mother he had "lost the money," but I knew better. Should I be loyal to Bob and keep my promise, or should I confess to our father, who suspected the truth? It was not simple, this getting down to bedrock. Truth is a hard taskmaster.

There came a time when we learned what " bedrock" really meant. It was our father's birthday, probably in 1929 or '30. When we learned that Dad was born "in the last century," we thought maybe back then they still wrapped babies in swaddling clothes and laid them in mangers. Whatever Grandma Belton did with her new baby on May 16, 1896, it was a long time ago, and this year we were going to have a party. Mother said Daddy was "way past thirty and thought he was getting old," so we were going to do something to make him happy. We were going to take a picnic out to Hanging Rock.

Whoever heard of a hanging rock? To my child's ear, that was impossible, for all the rocks I knew lay flat on the ground. Bob and I looked at each other behind her back, thinking this must be a joke. How could we have a picnic where rocks hung, and where did they hang from, anyway, the sky? She said we'd just have to be surprised.

It was a Sunday afternoon, after church. We took a long, bumpy ride in our Model A Ford to an oasis in the middle of Iowa farmland, a shady place on the bank of the middle fork of the Raccoon River where people came for summer boating or swimming. We piled out of the car, hot and sweaty, our hair tangled because they'd kept the windows down in the front seat. We could now run free, explore the place, maybe find some shade, or wade into the water to cool our feet when nobody was watching.

A huge rock platform, flat as the river during dog days, jutted out like a natural roof over the water and the grass along the edge. It certainly did seem to just hang there. It was as big as our dining-room floor, and dirty gray, with little green holes or bumps on it, like chicken pox. Tilting ever so slightly toward the river, the angle wasn't very reassuring.

"What if it falls down?" I asked Dad.

"Never in a million years," he laughed. "God put that rock there to stay!"

Bob and I imagined that a great flood, like the story in Sunday school, had once covered this earth, maybe as long ago as the last century, and that, when the world began to dry up, the rushing out of waters had simply torn away the earth beneath the rock. Proud of our theory, we took it to Dad. We knew he would praise our clicking brains, since he usually praised clear statements. So he listened to our theory about the hanging rock with more interest in our reasoning than usual, this being a day of leisure.

He patiently explained to us the great age of the glaciers that once covered the whole continent, rolling the history deliciously over his tongue.

"Once upon a time, eons ago," he said, "the huge ice-cap of the world began to melt. The part that came down here was called the Wisconsin glacier. All that ice turned into water when the glacier melted, leaving gullies and gigantic drainage ditches. But that wasn't why this spot was called 'Hanging Rock.'"

He put his hands behind his head and drew his knees up to make a kind of rocking chair. He must have been thinking of how good it felt to relax, to enjoy a summer afternoon with his wife and little family.

He would tell us a story of his Iowa, teach us something.

"See those trees up above the rock, how they hang over it?"

"Yes."

"Well, a long time ago, the Indians who lived here used to hang their dead people up in the trees."

"If they were dead already, why did they hang them again?" Bobby wanted to know.

"Why didn't they just bury them in the graveyard?" I asked.

"They didn't have graveyards then, Janie. This rock was their place for hanging. Maybe they thought the souls of the dead would be closer to heaven up in the trees."

We could understand that. We had a treehouse in the maple behind the house, with steps we'd nailed up the trunk. We could climb up to the single board in the crotch and see a long way off. We used to spirit away stolen raisins and graham crackers to eat up there. That was what a treehouse was for, as far as we were concerned, and we felt hidden away by the leaves, halfway to the clouds.

But Dad was not through talking. After all, it was his birthday.

"That's a beautiful rock, though, isn't it? Look at it. It's made of shale, sandstone, coal, and limestone, the bedrock of this state, like a kind of skeleton under the land. In the early part of this century, they built a swinging footbridge here, made of barrel staves and rope. Ropes were strung on the sides to hold onto. It extended from that big tree on top of Hanging Rock across the river to a tree on the East, about over there." He flung his arm out in a wide arc, pointing to the likely spot.

He loved a story. He made an adventure out of the simplest explanations, and though he adhered strictly to the truth, he lent suspense to the details, perhaps imagining just a few of them.

"Did you ever walk across that footbridge, Daddy?" I asked him, lying beside him on the grass.

"No. That was before my time. Years later, old Lafe DeFord pushed to build a sturdier bridge in a different spot, down closer to where the icehouse is now. And the town bought the idea. They built it out of steel and cement, 'Hell-for-stout.' That bridge'll likely last until the last toot of Gabriel's trumpet. At least that's what they claim."

Dad loved the leisure of a slowly unwinding tale, almost as much as he loved an audience. Usually, he had something interesting to say, especially when he was relaxed. This day in May was warm and lazy, and he told us lots of things we had never heard before. He told us that the Mormon people had pulled their big-wheeled carts across the state from Iowa City to Florence, Nebraska, back before the Civil War, and that instead of horses pulling the wagons, people were the horses, harnessed in between two shafts, pulling, usually with someone behind, pushing.

"Why are they called Morons?" Bob asked. Daddy burst out laughing in that rare abandon brought on by a lazy day, which made Bobby feel even more confused. Then he explained the name.

"I think Mr. Mormon was a prophet, you know, something like a fortune teller, who wrote down what he thought was the truth on some golden tablets. And then a man named Joseph Smith found them and turned them into a book for the people to read and believe."

"Like the Bible?" I asked.

"In a way, but not exactly. They didn't believe in some of the things in the Bible, but they had their own rules. You know, like our Golden Rule? D'ya know what that is?"

"Yes," Bobby said. "Do unto others what you want them to do to you?"

"Close enough. The Mormons were religious people whose town got burned down in Nauvoo, Illinois, by some people who didn't believe in their rules. So, they decided to move out West. Their leader, a man named Brigham Young, told the people in Iowa City to build the hand carts. They used Iowa hickory and oak with very little metal, to save money. Even the big wheels and the axles were made of wood. Boy, were they heavy! No one was allowed to bring more than about seventeen pounds of personal belongings, and one lady tied a colander and a teapot to her apron strings, so they wouldn't count it in her baggage!"

"Did it bang against her when she walked?"

"I'll bet it did, honey."

"Where did they sleep at night?" I asked, always wanting to know about a warm bed.

"In their wooden carts, I guess," Daddy said. "They'd build a fire, take the pots and pans off the cart to cook with, throw a straw pallet on the wagon, maybe a blanket or two.

"The Mormon Trail went by here, by Hanging Rock," he said. "They camped just up on top. I guess it was a relief to them to find bedrock, because the whole State was a sea of mud then. That's why they eventually had to drain the land with hollow tiles. But back then, it was so knee-deep in mud everywhere when they came across they got mired down. Do you know, it took them one whole year just to come this far, it was so muddy. They'd sink in, and the wagon wheels would sink in, and they couldn't move very fast in that mess."

"Did they wash their clothes in the river?" I asked, worrying about cleanliness and Godliness.

"When they washed at all," Dad said. "Chances are they stayed pretty dirty until the next year rolled around." He was losing interest in the story, just as we were being pulled in, imagining the details of life on the trail. He got up and went over to where Mother was fussing with the picnic.

We loved his stories. We thought he was the ultimate authority on everything except chocolate cake. There, Mother was the champion.

She had spread an old bedspread out on a little rise for us to sit on. Perched there, near our parents, we felt protected, from imagined Indians, from mad bulls or unexpected rainstorms. Then Mother unfolded an ironed tablecloth on the grass and opened the basket. Out came fried chicken, corn fritters, deviled eggs, potato salad, and, of course, the birthday cake. Chocolate. It was Dad's favorite, and he made a great show of licking his chops.

We two were giddy with the smell of the river bottom, the cotton from the tall shimmering trees that stuck like white edging to every irregular clump of grass or wild rose bush. The air was fresh and sweet-smelling, the little riffles of the river sang along, and the picnic basket was full to overflowing with mouth-watering food. It was like a dream of heaven, where everyone is always happy, lounging on the clouds, eating apples.

But all through that memorable picnic, I kept scanning the trees that hung over the rocks. How could the Indians have hung their dead people up there? Wouldn't the branch break? Had they put them in an old gunnysack, or just hung 'em up naked like a pig after slaughtering?

Bob grabbed my arm, leaned over toward my ear as if to warn me. "Look, Janie! Look up at that farthest tree. D'ya see that old sack hanging in the middle of the tree? Oh my gosh, it's moving! It must be some dead Indian come to life, like Lazarus!"

"Don't!" I yelled, "Dead Indians can't get alive again!"

"Oh, well. Maybe not," he said, tickled to have spooked me even a little bit. A piece of balloon or cloth or kite that had been snagged out of the wind by the claws of that old branch was all it was.

After the picnic, after we sang "Happy Birthday" to Daddy, he blew out all the candles and we each had a big piece of chocolate cake. The twins were excited by the happy singing and they clapped their little hands when we said, "Pat-a-cake, pat-a-cake." But they were too little to eat any, and they mostly slept. We were all full to bursting, and Daddy stretched out on a little hillock of grass and rubbed his stomach, pretending to groan with satisfaction. He leaned back, put his hands behind him to cradle his head and took in deep breaths, encouraging us to do the same. We imitated his body position, one of us on each side of him. Mother picked up the picnic, folded the cloth, and put the dirty dishes back in the basket before she came over and sat down behind Daddy. He put his head in her lap. With such leisure and a captive audience, he began the kind of lazy talk the day and the celebration inspired.

"Your Uncle Dave says you kids are part Indian," he said, "and I think he's right."

Our father and Uncle Dave—actually our great-uncle Dave, because he was Grandma Chantry's brother—a history buff who owned a stereopticon and loved to read, would exchange stories whenever they got together. Uncle Dave knew Indian lore and the history of the tribes who were here before us.

"How does he know that?" I asked.

"Well, just ask your mother. There's a drop of Sioux in both of you, can't you tell? Just look in the mirror, Janie, and you'll see an Indian maiden with long braids. That's all that's left from a love affair with a squaw a long time ago I guess!" Then he laughed. He knew how resistant Mother was to any mention of ethnic mix, though the bloodline would have been through her. Daddy was the one who looked more like an Indian, and he didn't deny it.

"Must have been one of those French fur traders from the Hudson Bay came looking for a bride, don'tcha s'pose, Zee?" At the mention of the word "bride," I perked up my ears. In my paper-doll cutouts, brides wore long frilly dresses, and I couldn't imagine an Indian maiden in a bridal gown.

"What did she wear, Daddy?" I wanted to know.

"Probably next to nothing," he said, turning his head around to look at Mother, chuckling, "wouldn't you think, Mother?"

"How come I don't have braids, too?" Bobby asked, not wanting to be left out.

"We could arrange that."

And Mother said, "Oh, Merrill, stop it!!"

For weeks after the picnic, Bob and I began to play out the roles of French trapper, Indian maiden, brave, chief, or warrior, with a little more conviction than we had had before. We pretended to harvest the wild rice in our canoes, kneeling in the grass with the longest sticks we could find for paddles. We rescued each other from enemy attacks, hiding behind the huge tree trunks in our woods, or from drowning, after wading in the shallow creek that moseyed along through the lower pasture. Bob and I both perfected the knee-slapping replication of galloping horses, our palms hitting our upper thighs with the rhythm of alternate hoof beats. Frieda, our best-friend dog, always with us, was enlisted as one of our horses, but she didn't like us throwing our legs over her back, and never would cooperate.

We could imagine a charge of thousands, stampeding down off a bluff to attack our wagons. We stashed our willow-branch arrows in our homemade quivers, half a burlap sack tied to our backs with twine. We tried to make tomahawks with river stones and sticks, but we never succeeded, the stone always slipping out of its string cage before the bloody massacre. And of course, the war cry. Such ear-splitting, blood-freezing whoops! We later referred to it as our "Indian period," and kept dreaming up ways we might have improved our imagined roles. I wanted Clementine, my doll, to be a papoose, but Bobby said it wouldn't look right, she being white and all.

We never could prove any "drop of Sioux" in either of us, but we loved Uncle Dave. His beard was "grizzled," a word Mother taught us for salt-and-pepper hair. We learned a lot from him. He kept a parrot in a wire cage, and told us he got it in South America, but Mother said he always made up things. The parrot could only say "Hello, hello," "Pretty baby," and "Polly want a cracker," which got tiresome after awhile. That marvelous bird had feathers of every color you could imagine, green, yellow, red, blue, and black, but he just stared straight at us and didn't even blink. I wanted to make him talk more. I wanted a parrot of my own. But Uncle Dave said he was a messy old bird, and how would I like to change the newspapers at the bottom of his cage every day? Bobby wanted a bird, too, but one that made sweet songs, he said, not just a dumb copycat kind of bird.

At other times, usually after Sunday dinner, which we sometimes shared with Uncle Dave's family, we learned a lot of things about history. Mother and Daddy kept asking Uncle Dave about things he knew, and we, pretending to be engrossed in putting together a jigsaw puzzle, or hunkered down behind the couch, listened to every word. Or, sometimes he would take a long time tucking us in bed, and tell us things he thought we should know.

He talked about the French-Canadian explorers, Louis Joliet and Father Jacques Marquette, on a mission to learn the direction and mouth of the Mississippi River in 1673 for the fur-trapping trade. They were believed to have explored the area that later became the state of Iowa.

The land belonged to the Algonquin-speaking tribes who lived in the Midwest and who merged in 1760. The tribe most often referred to in Iowa as the "Sac," an acceptable variation of "Sauk," takes its name from their tribal word *osaki*, which means "people of the river mouth."

The first settlers who stayed to claim the soil-rich prairie land, moving westward from the Appalachian chain, were a mix of Europeans; some came from the East, some from the South, some from Germany, Ireland, England, and Scandinavia. They found in this fertile land an established Indian population whose land rights they ignored. Later, using the native pony trails between watering holes, the settlers built their roads.

The Sac and the Fox Indians, natural barterers, were friendly and helpful to the first white people to settle in Iowa. As more settlers came, bringing wagonloads of goods, the tables turned. Bands of Indians roamed up and down the rivers, begging food or whatever they wanted or needed from the settlers. In exchange, they showed the way to the nut-bearing woods where hickories and walnuts could be gathered in the autumn.

Through the Louisiana Purchase of 1803, Iowa became a part of the United States. The Indian chiefs signed over the gently rolling hills and fertile valleys in a treaty of 1842, opening up the West. But Iowa did not become a state until 1846.

Our great-uncle loved the Civil War, and kept alive, among other highlights, the story of Sherman's march from Atlanta to Savannah. In one of those double cards that slipped into the clips of his stereopticon were pictures of the armies, building little bonfires on both sides of a river. He would lean over us and explain which army was which and where they were fighting, but I never remembered the details. We looked up the United States page of our big atlas, so we learned where both Atlanta and Savannah were.

Dad picked up interest in the Civil War when he was talking to Uncle Dave. We never tired of eavesdropping, both of us able to be quiet just long enough to hear the end of a story. Referring to Colonel Redfield, Dad told him, "There's a bronze plaque in the northeast corner of Old Settlers' Park honoring Redfield's part in the War Between the States," he told Dave. "It reads: '1861–1865. In memory of Company H, 39th Iowa Volunteer Infantry, which was mustered in on this spot.' That was his regiment."

"By God, I never knew that," Uncle Dave said. "I always thought the town was named from the red clay around there. Isn't that the stuff they made the drainage tiles from? Or did they come from up north?"

"Nope. They came from right here. The Cooley yard began its operation around 1870 or so. They got the bright idea of making enough hollow tiles to drain the whole state back then, and that made a huge difference in our economy, I can tell you. Iowa was a quagmire of mud before they laid that crisscross network of tiles. The soil was pretty rich and it eventually dried out enough to plant crops. Harvest yields really took off with drainage."

"Do you mean we walk over those tiles?" Bobby asked.

"They're probably all broken up by now," I said, needing to express an opinion.

"They're pretty well out of commission by now," Daddy said, "but they're not all gone." He turned back to Uncle Dave. "They got into the fire brick business, too, some of it was so full of iron. Ever hear of the "Redfield Reds?" They were used only in Dallas County for a while. Built the towns and covered everything, streets and all, with brick! You been to Adel? Well, that's typical. Then the word got around. Des Moines is still pretty much like a brickyard, don'tcha think? They even shipped it down to Omaha, made the face brick for Father Flanagan's Boys Town. Damned good stuff, unless you want to plant something in the thick of it!"

◆

Many of the early pioneers were anti-slavery Quakers, with a sprinkling of Baptists and Methodist among them. Their faith and often their only literature came from the *Holy Bible*. Some of the Mormons, led by Brigham Young, came this way from Illinois to Salt Lake, although the main trail was south of Redfield. On foot, they were pushing or pulling their high, twelve-hundred-pound hand carts piled with all their worldly goods, probably with a baby on top. Every so often in the line would be an ox team with their supplies. The river was so high they camped near Redfield for two weeks. During their stay, three babies died and were buried in the cemetery at Wiscotta, a little town not very far from us.

Quaker Ridge to the south and east of Redfield is famous for its Underground Railroad hideouts during the Civil War. Runaway slaves hid in caves or any place possible until they could be taken by wagon to the ferry to cross the wide Missouri River to connect with the "train." The famous escape route that followed the "Drinking Gourd," as the Big Dipper was called, kept the idea of a railroad, the "train" any means taken to ride to freedom. Iowa's underground started in Tabor, Fremont County, the southwestern-most county in the state, then crossed diagonally through Stuart (then called Summit Grove) in Adair County, a few miles from Redfield. From there, one line went east down Quaker Divide and the other crossed the Raccoon River near Redfield and on to Adel, both coming together in Des Moines. From there it ran to Grinnell, dipping down to Muscatine on the Mississippi River and on up to Canada.

"Many times blacks were seen crossing the prairie from Middle River to Summit Grove on their way to freedom," Uncle Dave told us. "One mile east of Redfield on the 'Brick and Tile' road is one of the original stops for the Underground Railroad, now known as the Reason's place. Another half mile east was the Murray farm, where a door in the fireplace used to hide six to eight slaves. Few slaves stayed in Iowa, for they were eager to press further north, even into Canada where they would be positively free.

"Didn't they get dirty in the fireplace?" I asked him.

He laughed, over and over. "Honey, they were already dirty; they were just glad to have a place to hide."

The discovery of gold in California had a marked effect on the whole region. The stories that a thousand dollars could be picked up in an hour gave many the gold fever. Down the state road, the forty-niners came by the hundreds to cross the Raccoon River below Hanging Rock. In the spring of 1850, a continuous line of wagons came through here, stretching as far as the eye could see; the promise of riches overshadowed the rumors of Indians, buffaloes, impassable mountains, and dry, desolate country.

The wave of immigration west resumed after the Civil War. Iowa was said to have much to offer the enterprising settler: the sun shone three days out of five; the climate was ideal for farming; there were no rocks or stumps to move; and the soil was so rich that when you planted a garden, you dropped the seeds and ran to get out of the way of their growth. Best of all, the fabulous land could be bought for five dollars an acre or less.

These tales enticed new blood into the state as claims were spoken for. The grassland prairie sod was actually so root-bound and dense or so clay-packed that it was hard to turn, though it did supply wonderful pasture for livestock until it could be brought under cultivation.

The people who passed through left their flavor in our history. The state was destined to be a crossroads, situated as it is at the center of the country, sifted fine by the pulls of war, of climate, of faiths. From the overheard conversations, from the stories Uncle Dave and Daddy told us, we gradually took pride in the land we grew up on, the rich prairie loam, the deep clay deposits. The history, the weather, the woods of wherever we lived were ours, and the animals that lived in them became part of our world. Too, the people who preceded us, and those who surrounded us, became part of who we were. Earthiness we inherited, and the bedrock of our geography was firm, but our heads turned with the wind and the racing clouds.

The House on First Street

With two of us going to school now, our parents decided to move into town in the fall of 1930; the school bus would no longer have to stop at the bottom of our driveway. The farm was only a little way out of town, maybe a mile and over the bridge, but the change would allow us to walk to the Redfield Consolidated School, a big brick building a few blocks down from the house on First Street. Too, we could walk to Sunday school, equally close. It didn't matter which church we went to, as long as it was Christian. Perhaps it was Baptist. We could never tell the difference.

Mother was thrilled to move, and the house we rented, a big white clapboard house in the 100 block on First Street, pleased her. There were neighbors. Lessons were available, things that would civilize her two country kids, like music and dancing and art. And for her, too, a study group, a class on flower arranging or a quilting group, the WCTU or a reading club. Her hunger for some social community had reached a point of despair, shackled as she was with baking bread, peeling vegetables, canning, scrubbing floors, hanging huge loads of laundry on the line to dry, ironing, changing sheets, keeping an eagle eye on all four of us. Trying to please Daddy and coping with the demands of farm life, she was lonesome for other women, for friends.

People called the place we rented "the Patterson place," after the family who had lived there a long time, maybe since the house had first been occupied. It was up a little hill from Main Street, with a sloping lawn bordered by a rock wall at the bottom. To us, used to gravel or worn paths, city sidewalks made of bricks were a real luxury. Our front door faced the street, but nobody ever came in that way. The back door at the top of the driveway had a porch that Daddy called the "mud porch," with an old braided rug for wiping our shoes. Mother had made it out of strips of wool from old blankets, woolen pants, Grandma Chantry's faded blue coat. It was the only entrance anyone ever used.

As Bobby and I became familiar with our surroundings, our parents trusted us to go down to the Old Settlers' Park alone, a shady square in the middle of our town about five or six blocks away. We played jacks or marbles in the grandstand there, or played catch or talked to people or just wasted time. We always hoped to find an old settler, some gray and bearded guy who had been one of the first people ever to live in Redfield. There were lots of them, and we stared a lot, but were too shy to ask any questions.

One day, for Old Settlers' Day, an annual celebration, Mother gave Bobby a dime and me a nickel. We could spend them at the Arcade, a part of the hullabaloo. A big canvas tent, not as big as the circus one, but with tables inside, had wonderful surprises in it, a glass ball full of bubble gum, a box with a handle that operated a tiny crane inside to pick up, if you were lucky, charms or rings or hair barrettes. We were ecstatic to set out on this adventure on our own, money clutched in our fists, charged with the terrible decision about how best to spend it. Running down the sidewalk, my mind on our destination, I dropped my nickel on the bricks. Both of us hunted and hunted for a long time, but without any luck. It had fallen somewhere in the cracks and I never did retrieve it. I felt bereft for years, not just for having lost the nickel, but for never knowing what it might have bought.

Once convenience made it possible, Bobby began to take clarinet lessons from the music teacher at the school, and I took tap-dancing lessons. I think Grandma Belton sent us the money to pay for them, or else it was Uncle Howard. The squeaks from Bob's room were close to unbearable at first, but Mother was confident he would get better. I had new patent-leather pumps that tied with grosgrain ribbon and had metal taps on the toe and the heel, which I could make fairly rattle on the floorboards. Mother made me a plaid pleated skirt. Over and over I would practice "East side, west side, all around the town. Boys and girls together. . . ." I got so good the piano player had to hurry to keep up with my "rubber legs," as she called them. My classmate, Harold Pitzenbarger, and I did a duet dance for the Masonic Lodge party. Those men, afterwards, told us we were wonderful. They hugged and kissed me until I was convinced they were right! It made me feel like a movie star, which is what I aspired to become. Grandmother had taken us to see a movie in Des Moines, *Mrs. Wiggs of the Cabbage Patch*, after which I was sure my destiny included performing in one way or another.

In the house in town, we had next-door neighbors, the Straights. They were people of whom my mother stood in some awe. She was aware of men who wore neckties and of women who wore silk stockings and high-heeled shoes, who changed into pretty dresses in the afternoon, after the morning's chores were done. Hers, she said, were never done. Mr. Straight was a town official, a councilman I believe, and their house was made of brick with two large picture windows in the front. The front porch had four square pillars on a built-up railing with a concrete top where guests could sit, gracefully draping a dress over one knee or smoking a cigarette. The screen door had curlicues of ironwork over the screen. They entertained a lot, and we could watch them, hear them laughing.

One of the frequent refrains we heard during those years in town was Mother's longing for more leisure, more culture. Buried under children and laundry and shoes that were worn down at the heels, Mother may have felt wrongly perceived as a *hausfrau*, something she was not. She was educated, read voraciously, was generous by nature, and bore her burdens with great dignity. Good manners, she believed, were the mark of an aristocrat, and she carried herself with poise born of a natural reserve.

"I used to walk down Grand Avenue in Des Moines, past Drake University, and long to go to college there, to take music and art lessons, to read Shakespeare and write poetry," she would reminisce, always slightly sadly, because those days were gone forever.

"You can still read Shakespeare," Daddy would counter.

"But I remember walking past the rich homes of girls who always wore white and played tennis and went to concerts," she would explain, her fantasy existence based on the adolescent dreams of a city girl.

Our neighbors had a big shiny car that Mr. Straight polished, and a garage under the house to put it in. They had a grand piano in their living room and only two children, both of whom were taking music lessons. We could hear them practicing to the tick, tick, tick of the metronome, a word I loved. When I told Grandmother, our "Gango," all about it, what it did, she didn't even say, "I know." She just taught me how to spell it. Our parents were cordial neighbors, but they never shared mid-morning cups of coffee, or evening games of bridge.

Their two kids, George and Rachel Straight, were a bit doughy and spoiled—George, a pudgy Lord Fauntleroy who was always stumbling and falling, and Rachel, a whiny prima donna, the adored and only girl in the family. From somewhat more fortunate means, she wore white organdy Sunday-school dresses and black, patent-leather Mary Janes with buckles. Her hair was cut in a bouncy, shiny bob. I felt no pride whatsoever in my dark braids, despite a common adult remark about their being marvelously thick. That meant coarse to me, and I longed for the coppery sheen of Rachel's freer hair.

But Rachel was, as we had overheard Mother say, dumb. By that, our quick-witted parents simply meant naive, I like to think, for I loved her. She and I played paper dolls for hours on end. We both had books of cutout dolls, made of stiff paper, and books of their clothes, on regular paper. We were very careful to cut them out without a mistake, because it was possible to slip with scissors and cut off one of the tabs that held the dresses onto the stiffer cardboard dolls. We decided we would make our different dolls members of the same family, because we had some blondes and some brunettes and we would be the parents of both. Rachel's book had a boy doll, too, but his clothes weren't as much fun, just pants and shirts, one jacket, and a necktie that we could never get to stick. She would let my dollies wear her dollies' party dresses sometimes, and I let her choose from mine, too. She loved to prop up our paper dolls in a line and sing to them. Because she took piano lessons, she could even make up words to fit the songs, and we pretended the dolls were a church choir, especially when we played on the sidewalk, Sunday afternoons.

As for shoes, mine didn't have buckles. They were lace-up Buster Browns, with toes of tough, pock-marked leather, bought at Younker Brothers Department Store in Des Moines, and always a size too big so that I would "grow into them." School shoes were a major expense not to be squandered on style. I remember the magic machine like a giant stereopticon. The shoe salesman let me see the skeletal bones of my little-girl feet, swimming in the opaque tadpole film of the shoes' huge outline. Rachel never wore what Mother called "sensible shoes," and I didn't see why "sensible" was necessary. I thought the several pairs she had were beautiful and I was envious. Daddy said we should be grateful we had shoes at all, that a lot of kids in the world had to go barefoot all year long. Our parents were forever comparing us to orphans or the starving children of China so we'd clean our plates and say thankful prayers all the time.

In that house, too, after the leaves had fallen off the big maple trees, we raked and piled them into mountains at the bottom of the sloping lawn. It was safer to burn them on the parking strip below the big stone wall that held in the hill. But before Daddy actually torched any pile, he would stand beside the tall stack with rake in hand, the air hazy with ground mist, with that unforgettable damp-mushroom, crushed-leaf smell of fall, and marvel at the tidy lawn, the huge trees, proud of his work. Then, we would be allowed to jump into the huge piles before they were lit. We four neighbor kids buried ourselves in the leaves, hiding the way you could in a haymow, playing "king of the mountain" and "hide-and-seek" in the crisp, cheek-pinking air of an Iowa autumn dusk.

Daddy, Bobby, and I were in cahoots in our effort to persuade George and Rachel to jump with some abandon, to have them feel the freedom of racing blood and carefree laughter. We Beltons didn't like sissies, keeping prissy and clean instead of joining in the fun. I'll never forget hearing George let out a war whoop, once, with a jump that must have sprung him free. It sounded like a squeaky trombone at first, but then a blast of joy that was earsplitting. We all laughed so hard I wet my panties. But I didn't care, and I didn't tell anybody. We played later than we were usually allowed to in those dusks, just to celebrate being kids in the witching world of swirling leaves.

It was a glorious game, and Dad didn't mind raking the leaves back into mounds after we scattered them. The twins were getting to be a part of our days, too, and, even at two or three, they loved to be included. We dressed them up, made them ride in our wagon, and were proud of having two such cute little sisters. We buried them under the leaves, sometimes, and they squealed with delight.

As different as they were from our family, Rachel and George Straight were our constant playmates those days we lived in town. From the house on First Street, Bob rolled me down the sloping front yard and into the street, curled like larva inside the stiff rubber of an old tire casing.

"You'll just fit, Janie. Come on, get inside and curl up. When I roll the tire, it'll feel like a ride on the merry-go-round. I promise. Come on. Tuck your elbows inside, so they don't get skinned."

"But what if I don't like it?"

"You'll like it. We'll take turns, okay?"

As usual, I did his bidding. I got sick from the head-over-heels momentum, and when Mother discovered this, she told Daddy to give Bob a severe spanking for that idea. It was terribly dangerous, for into the street the tire rolled, out of control until it beached on the opposite curb, blocks down the hill. The "girl in the rolling tire" idea was potentially fatal. It was probably a good thing we got caught and forbidden to play with the hard tires again.

Blown-up innertubes were allowed, though. No person got inside. One of our summer evening sports was to roll those down the lawn into oncoming cars, of which there weren't many. But we would wait until we thought we could connect with one, and let it go. Whoever was the sentinel called out the optimum time with "Let 'er rip!" An innertube hit a gasoline tanker once, got to thumping around in the tire well, terrifying the driver. It caused him to jackknife the truck when he hit the airbrakes because he thought he'd hit a kid. We never told our folks that one, and they didn't hear him give us a tongue-lashing from way down the street.

Another time Bob was willing to risk my life was his brainstorm about turning me into an angel. He had fashioned wings by bending wire hangers out and gluing newspapers to them with flour and water paste. The hanger hooks, he said, were where we could attach them to my playsuit straps so God could see them, spread out and ready to fly into heaven.

"Can I fly home again?"

"If you are brave and flap your wings just right, He'll let you come back," Bobby reassured me. He told me that little people could fly better than big ones, that was why all the angels looked like babies. I believed him. He fastened the flimsy wings to my straps in back, looped some string around my small chest and we climbed up the ladder left leaning against the shed roof. He held my hand while we walked across the shingles just above the straw-covered drip line, maybe five or six feet below.

"When I say jump," he instructed, "just lift out your wings and jump into the straw. Don't be surprised if you feel the hand of God lifting you up into the sky."

"What if He doesn't?"

"We'll try again," he said. "Ready, get set, go. Jump!"

Needless to say, I landed on the ground with a terrible thud. I began to cry. Bob scurried down the ladder and came over to me.

"Are you dead? Did it hurt you, Janie? Oh, look, you broke the wings! That's probably why God didn't take you to Heaven."

The shed was not far from the back door, and Mother heard me yowling. She came outside to see what had happened, and when she realized what Bob had devised, she was furious with him. "Just you wait until I tell your father what you've done, Bobby! He'll spank some sense into you. You took a *terrible* risk, you know; you could have killed your little sister, or hurt her badly, don't you understand?" She turned to me, removed the shattered wings, and took me into her arms. "You're going to be all right, honey. Just stop doing whatever Bobby tells you to do. He didn't know it would hurt you, I'm sure. But it was a dangerous thing to try."

Miraculously, no harm was done. But a spanking was not a small matter. Dad used his razor strop, that skinny piece of leather hide that hung down near the bathroom sink, the thing he sharpened his straight-edged razor on. This terrible weapon also doubled as a serious switch. He would instruct us to lie face down on the toilet seat, and he would whack us with his leather strop until our howling satisfied him the lesson had been learned. When Bob was being punished, my standing outside the bathroom door and pounding my fists on the door yelling, "Stop it! Stop it, Daddy. Don't hurt Bobby!" was fruitless. Dad must have known the tire-rolling game was done innocently, that the angel experiment had been triggered by Sunday-school pictures, but he also knew the danger, and he let us know why such painful consequences followed.

The lack of money was the hardest burden, for Mother and Daddy never had enough. Apparently, the Straights, who owned their own much nicer brick house next door, did. But we as children didn't know about the cost of things, about disappointment or longing. We knew the adventures of every day, of being healthy kids in a trusting world. Going out to play, in the hot sun of August or the deep snows of January, was always exciting, the thrill of freedom without grown-up supervision. We had bare feet and sun-suits for playing in the sprinkler, for playing hopscotch or reading in the porch swing in the torpid days of summer. In winter, for making snow caves, we had snowsuits and knitted caps, handmade mittens threaded through our jacket sleeves on a crocheted string.

Mother was always reading in the afternoon and, at night, aloud to us from our favorite stories, *Mother West Wind and Her Merry Little Breezes*, or *The Dog of Flanders*, which always made Bobby and me cry, or *Hans Brinker and the Silver Skates*. Sometimes she or Daddy would get down a volume of *My Book House*, to read again some of our favorite stories, "The Musicians of Bremen," "The Owl and the Pussy Cat," and "Snow-White and Rose-Red."

It was when we lived on First Street, too, that one Memorial Day, I stood beside the house while Daddy cut long stems of yellow roses from a huge climber that twined up the outside of our chimney. He laid them in my arms, carefully, slowly, like cordwood to be carried to the woodbox. These, he said, we would take out to the cemetery to put on "little Jane's" grave. How strange that sounded. What I learned, then, about the loss of their first baby girl was to haunt me for much of my life.

"Was she born at home?"

"Yep. She was born on November twenty-second, as I recall, near Thanksgiving."

"Wasn't there a doctor for Mommy and the baby?"

"Yes. Dr. Henry Kleinberg was a Des Moines physician who had a practice in Redfield. We thought he was a good doctor at the time. But he couldn't save the baby." He went silent and continued to reach up for the best roses to cut. "She was a healthy little baby, but her tiny lungs filled up with fluid so she couldn't breathe."

"Did you name her before she died?" Bobby wondered.

"Yes. We named her Jane Margaret, after each of our grandmothers. Mother had all the baby clothes embroidered and folded in the dresser. Little Jane only lived for a few hours. . . ." His voice trailed off. He took a folded handkerchief out of his pocket, whipped it open, and blew his noise, loudly.

"Did you have a funeral?" I asked. Bobby and I always had elaborate funerals for our dead animals and had just buried a baby bird in a matchbox under the oak tree.

"Nope. Doc Kleinberg and I took the little coffin out to the cemetery and buried it ourselves. It didn't take long to dig such a small hole. I remember the snow was falling. . . ." We both felt so sorry for him and for Mother that we got awfully sad, too, standing there holding our armfuls of yellow climber roses, imagining the terrible digging of a hole in the ground under the cold snow for our tiny baby sister.

Bobby whispered to me, "Poor Mother. Her first little baby, dead. She must still be crying inside her heart."

"Imagine a Baby Jane with my name before I got it next. She must be in heaven by now, maybe sleeping on a cloud with angel parents. Would they trade me back if they could, do you think?"

"I hope not," Bobby said, reassuring me that we two were meant to be together.

We three took the yellow roses out to the cemetery. Mother and the twins stayed at home. On a little metal stake out in the middle of the unmowed grass, we found her name on a white card behind some isinglass. "Baby Girl Belton," it said, and the day she was born and died. She was only one of us for one day. And then, Bobby came along. And then, me, Jane again. And then, the twins. As we stood there in that whole pasture of graves where the only noise was birdsong and the gentle breeze blowing the grass heads, I wondered how she would look down there under the ground. Would she think her little coffin was like a cradle, or could she ever see anything but the lid? If she had lived, would she be like my twin sister? And what name would I have if she still had mine?

There, too, near that enormous yellow rosebush, we built our winter tunnels like a rabbit's warren in the crusty snowdrifts. Bobby liked to crawl inside and hide, and acting as the master engineer, directed me to do further scooping and digging. My wet, red hands hurt, near frostbite in soggy woolen mittens. The snow would bead up on the wool until the frozen drops would rattle. Little shreds of red wool would stick to the snow, the only color in that tunnel against the blue white of the snow.

While we lived in that house, we learned the meaning of "quarantine." In those days, the health officials would post a house by tacking up a notice to warn visitors of contagion inside. One day, across the street and up a few houses, a red cardboard sign appeared on the porch post, quarantining the family who had an outbreak of scarlet fever, or diphtheria, or whooping cough. Before antibiotics, such diseases were often fatal, and we were instructed not even to cross the street. Mother told us, in her superior way, "Those people weren't very clean, anyway, so it wasn't any wonder. They probably had rats."

Bob and I worried about the kids inside that quarantined house. They must be sick and hot and trapped, maybe throwing up. I hoped they wouldn't die, even if they weren't very clean. When they got well, we decided we would go over to their house and introduce ourselves, maybe make some new friends. But we never got the chance. One day, the quarantine sign was gone, and so were they. They moved somewhere else but we never knew where.

Rachel and George were always clean. Mother admired that. We didn't care, even if we ever noticed. They were our closest playmates while we lived on First Street. When we moved away, we all four cried, and promised each other we would always keep our secrets, no matter how old we got.

Bending the Twig

Miss Mantz always wore brown. Her hair was brown, her eyes were brown, and all her clothes, including her lace-up shoes, were brown. It was the autumn of 1930, and I, having just turned five, was terribly proud to be starting school. Miss Mantz was my first-grade teacher. I loved her, despite the monotony of her dress, for she always welcomed me with a hug and a smile. Bobby had had her for a teacher, too, and he always told me how nice she was. Mostly because of her, I think, the Redfield Consolidated School, a square brick building with a diagonal walkway from the street corner to the front door, was a place I loved. Inside, there were playmates, and sometimes a wad of chewing gum under a desk, which I could re-chew, oblivious to germs. Mostly there were books that smelled of the ink genie, the thrill of learning how to read, how to connect the letters of the alphabet to make real words.

On a special tablet that already had lines on it, we could copy the letters of the Rice Penmanship Method, the model for which ran around the top of the blackboard like wallpaper trim, learning to make a row of Os that looked like a bedspring, to make the fat belly of a capital R come just to the dotted line, to write the capital S so that it didn't look like a music clef. Miss Mantz would pause over my shoulder, lean down and look at my work, saying, "That is wonderful, Janie! You're such a good reader and a good writer, too." Her warm voice, her gentle encouragement made me feel buzzy and special. The die was cast. I would be a slave to language for the rest of my life.

To say that I basked in her praise is an understatement. I felt like Polly Flinders in the story Mother read to us at home. I too was a poor overworked child with adored twin sisters just three years younger, an older brother to whom I deferred, and parents still struggling with Depression poverty. In contrast, the whole day at school was shining.

It all had to do with some aspect of language; even the stories Miss Mantz read aloud were aglow with the magic of words. Her soft tones and easy smile were infectious, and I wanted more than anything in the world to be just like her. Even having to buy yet another pair of oversized Buster Browns was bearable because they, too, were brown.

Meanwhile, at home, Gango, a teacher too but one who taught mathematics, was listening to the annual national spelling bees on our old Atwater Kent radio. I think those contests worked like tennis tournaments, with a state's contestants seeded in elimination rounds. But how it worked was secondary to her riveted attention. She was glued to the radio, static notwithstanding, *shussshing* us not to miss a single suspenseful moment, whooping out her excitement when some young speller would master the toughest challenges. Iowans were mad about spelling. The results would be published in the papers, and great statewide pride centered on an Iowa child who made the finals.

We nestled in her arms while she listened to the national contest, respecting her awed silences, her audible cheers. She targeted me as a likely speller, mostly I think because I could guess her riddles before anyone else got them. She said if you were good at riddles, then you'd be good at spelling. "Three men are in the yard," she'd begin. "Two of them are sitting on the fence, and a third is working. One man says to the other, pointing at the working man, "Brothers and sisters have I none, but that man's father is my father's son." Who is he?" And I would puzzle it out, wanting her to be proud of me when I got it right.

"If he didn't have any other brothers or sisters, it'd have to be *his* son, wouldn't it?"

"You're right! That's a good guess, honey. That's exactly who it is!" Another one that stumped us, but that taught us a lot about listening carefully to language was, "A man had an apple tree from which he picked bushels of apples every year. One year, though, it bore fruit but not apples! What kind of tree was it?" Unaware of the sneaky plural, we gave up. "An apple tree," she'd laugh, "but the "fruit" was just *one* apple, not *apples*, plural."

Nothing would do but that she teach me how to spell a couple of tough words until I was letter-perfect and secure. Then, as a surprise at dinner, she would ask me, feigning nonchalance, "Janie, how do you spell 'Presbyterian'?"

And, to the utter amazement of my parents, I would reel it off, cool as a cucumber.

Then, after the buzz of approval subsided, she would say, "I suppose you think you can spell 'veterinarian.'" And, of course, trying to keep our collusion secret, I would not hesitate. Words were part of our family recreation, what they meant, how they were spelled.

The word got out. One day at school, Miss Mantz announced to the class that among us was a spelling wizard who would invite any challenger. "Janie," she said, "will you come to the head of the class. Now, spell 'Presbyterian,'" which I did. "And now, 'veterinarian.'" The class clapped, and innocent as I was of vanity those days, it was a day of supreme joy, of a secret commitment to the mastery of words.

◆

After school was out that spring, Miss Mantz married a Mr. Ramsbottom. We were embarrassed to say it, even! Such a name change was a terrible tragedy. I prayed for her, hoping to lighten the cross I imagined she would carry for the rest of her life. Even after Mother's teaching us Juliet's speech about "What's in a name," I thought it was unfortunate past enduring. But finally resigned, I sadly practiced writing "Mrs. Ramsbottom," over and over, planning to send her a letter from California where we were going to spend the summer with our other grandmother.

Daddy's mother, Grandma Belton, lived in Gardena, California. I imagined her town would smell like flowers. Dad and Bob and I drove all that way in our Chevrolet with friends of our parents, the Kippings, who wanted to go to California and who would help pay for the gasoline. Two in front and three of us in back felt crowded, mostly because the adults talked a lot.

"When will we get to the Grand Canyon?" Bob asked.

"Don't know if we'll have time to see it this trip," he answered.

"But, Daddy, you *told* us we'd get to see the biggest hole on earth," I pleaded, having tried to imagine what the bottom of it looked like. One of the things I wanted to write to Mrs. Ramsbottom about was seeing the Grand Canyon.

"Please," Bobby begged.

"You *promised!*" I whined. I guess that was the last straw. He blew up.

"I told you we'd see it *if there was time!*"

Dad was getting impatient to see his mother, I guess, because he fairly barked at us. Our father's loyalties were divided. The Kippings were eager to reach their destination, too. Even when we began to see road signs for the Grand Canyon, we did *not* turn to go the fifty miles out of our way to see this wonder of the world. Bobby and I were unforgiving, vowing never to be so selfish when we had kids.

All the way I thought about my beloved teacher, wanting to tell her all the things we saw on our way, a place where they sold orange juice built like a big orange and painted orange, and a tamale stand looking like a tamale. I wondered if she knew what a "tamale" was. I did write her a postcard from Gardena, one with a palm tree on it, in my best writing, and signed it "Your favorite pupil."

When we started back to school in the fall of my second year, I so looked forward to seeing her, wondering if she ever got my card all the way from California. Suddenly, there she was, in the hallway, standing with another teacher. I didn't want to interrupt their conversation, so I stood back and listened. I overheard her laughing about getting summer mail, and she was telling the other teacher about my postcard, about my signature.

"She signed it 'Your favorite pupil,' isn't that funny?"

What I meant, of course, was that she was *my* favorite teacher. But the words didn't come out right. I felt such deep shame and embarrassment I have never forgotten it. Words had betrayed me. And, even though she began to wear blouses with roses on them, I never felt the same closeness, a distance of my own making.

My resolve was to be ever more careful, wary of thoughtless speech. I moved up in the grades, still fascinated with the reading and writing of language until once, in the fourth grade, I stole a little red dictionary from my friend, Harold Pitzenbarger. Staying after school, ostensibly to help clean chalk erasers, I dug inside his hinge-topped desk where I knew he kept it, quickly stashed it in my lunch box in the cloakroom. All the way home on the bus my cheeks burned, knowing what an evil thing I had done, imagining my life given over to the Devil. I hid it under my pillow, and looked up words by flashlight in the dark of night.

Guilt-ridden, I confided in my brother. Then, because I wouldn't do his bidding once, he told my secret to our father who, he knew, would never brook such thievery. I denied it. In the bathroom, helpless, arched across the toilet, my panties hobbling my ankles, I was razor-stopped, first for stealing and then for lying. Finally, he stopped, broken by my refusal to apologize. I never was sorry I had that little book for a while, and I wasn't going to lie about that, to compound one lie with another.

Even that crime, the betrayal of my brother who told on me, and then my spanking, my having to confess, having to give the little red book back to Harold with deep chagrin, did not rob me of my love of words. If anything, it planted a seed that grew into an unswerving love of all dictionaries.

Never did it overshadow the memory of my first beloved teacher, Miss Mantz. Her smile, the warmth of the learning environment she introduced me to, and my delight in language cast me in this role I call my life. At some level, I never stopped wanting to be like her.

Secrets in the Brickyard

Below our Patterson house, on a wide expanse of flat ground, a brick-making business glowed and clanged and smoked. Flat cars ran in and out on a railroad spur that served to carry the bricks to wide-ranging destinations. The house, far enough away to escape the din, was built on a small bluff above the long-dry flood plain. That large field contained the kilns that looked like overgrown mushrooms, and pallets of bricks, different colors in different stages of cooling. In the center of the field, in among the kilns, the pasture, so green in the early days of spring was, by summertime, unkempt and thick with wild roses. Remnants of the middle fork of the Raccoon River's subterranean flow fed the roots of huge hardwood trees—maples, oaks, black walnuts, elms, or hickories—that bordered that large space like a picture frame. The Raccoon, like many of the rivers that drain ultimately into the Mississippi, is a many-forked, east-flowing waterway, imprinted on the land by the prehistoric ice melt.

The narrow path behind our house, deepened by what my father called a "gully washer," led down across the railroad tracks to the brickyard. Clay deposits there, deep and red, colored the earth and seemed to back up the name Colonel Redfield had given our town. Such fine-grained soil, sticky as gumbo in the spring thaw, was prized most of the year for its plasticity, for its hardened durability, and the Redfield Brick and Tile Company was a thriving industry. One day when the path beckoning us like a sliding chute, we conspired to explore beyond the edge of the bluff.

"Mother," we'd begin, when we saw that she was especially busy with the twins, or the laundry or the baking, "all of the bricks down in the brickyard have been taken out of the kilns. Can we go down there, now? We'll bring you a bouquet of roses."

She frowned, seeing right through our bribe. "Absolutely not! How many times do I have to tell you? That is a dangerous place for children!"

"Please...."

"NO!"

Unrelenting in our habit of playing one off against the other, we approached Daddy, probably hoeing the garden or working in the shed. "If we be careful, can we go down and watch the men working in the brickyard, Daddy?"

"Nope. You stay away from there. It's too dangerous, full of fire and hot bricks and cooling pits. And railroad cars," he added, trying to scare us with all possible calamities.

Neither parent ever gave in. The answer never varied. We were warned. No doubt it was dangerous, but that was part of its allure. We knew the consequence would be a razor stropping if we were caught.

So, we went down to the brickyard whenever we could sneak away, easier to do in a simpler time when children roamed their neighborhoods, fearlessly. We conspired with Rachel and George, the neighbor kids, to come with us. That way, the idea could have been theirs.

"Will you promise never to tell your mom or dad where we went?"

"Yes," they both answered, loving the danger of such a secret.

"And we'll never tell, either," Bobby assured them.

But just to make sure they'd keep their word, we pricked our fingers with a needle taken from Mother's sewing basket, and smeared each other's fingers with the drawn drop, swearing a blood oath to eternal secrecy.

Nothing else in the placid landscape of our Midwestern growing up held a candle to the brickyard for excitement, and though it was, in fact, risky, it also was an irresistible attraction for curious kids. It was easy for Mother to assume that we were simply playing over at the Straights'. Mrs. Straight, never as busy but not as smart, probably thought her two were over at the Beltons', playing house. We had a signal. Both pairs of us tied an old bandanna to a stick, so we could pass as hobos, or, as Daddy called them, "bindle stiffs." In case worse came to worst and we had to run away from home, we hid them under our beds.

When one pair of us wanted to go down to the brickyard, we'd parade out the door with our hobo signal, and the other two would get theirs and join us at the top of the path. We were always afraid Rachel would give away our scheme and ruin the plot, but she never did.

When the kilns were not in use and cold, when the big iron door handles had cooled off enough to leave them open, they became our igloos, arctic hideouts in the barren land of the Eskimos. Built of brick-lined hollow tile and strapped with wide iron like belts for giants, the ball-shaped kiln domes were scattered over the pasture. They looked like the toadstools of monster dormice. Between and among them, wild roses grew in prickly bushes full of flat-faced pink flowers. Sometimes holes in the ground, places we called elephant traps in our tropical jungle, were lined with straw and used for storage until enough bricks had accumulated to ship on the adjacent railroad spur.

Down on the flats, the huge, hot kilns glowed with flames from wood-fed fires that sent sparks up into the air, shimmering like the Fourth of July. When they were firing, the heat was so intense and searing if we got too close it squinted our eyes and hurt our nostrils. Natural pyromaniacs, we tried to toss dry grass into the least-hot one to see if it would catch fire, but we could never get close enough. It hurt our faces.

"Hey, there, you kids. Get back away from here, NOW! This is no place for children," one of the men shouted. He was scarier than Billy Goat Gruff, so we stopped doing that. When the kilns grew cold, and the workmen all left, we sometimes went inside them, pretending they were Eskimo igloos or Indian hogans. We never stayed very long, fearful that something might happen.

One of our competitive delights was walking on the rails of the train tracks in the brickyard. It took a sense of balance and a lot of practice. We took turns going furthest, and then, fastest. We must have looked like scarecrows escaped from some garden, our legs mincing along like sticks, our arms straight out like tightrope walkers. Sometimes we'd have to saw our arms up and down like the blades on a windmill, to keep our balance. George Straight was never able to win, because he kept putting one foot down on the ground, and Rachel was afraid of falling. Bobby and I were good, so it turned out, really, to be a game we set up for ourselves, in cahoots like "big twins" again.

We were fascinated by the brickyard work, and the workmen were our friends. They were big men in sleeveless undershirts and huge asbestos gloves, scooping the bricks from the kilns with long-handled shovels, like the baker taking loaves out of his oven. The red-hot bricks were stacked to cool on wooden pallets. Then, when they had cooled off, they'd hoist the load with gears and pulleys, pallet and all, up and over, either into the storage pits or onto the railway flatcars, a process that provided a model for our own levering of everything from spit wads to snowballs.

Once, a whole square load of bricks crashed beside the tracks, and we heard the men swear with loud sentences that none of us had ever heard.

"Jesus Christ, God Almighty! What the hell happened?"

"God-damn son of a bitch! The fucking chain broke. Christ almighty, this is a helluva mess!" They cussed so loud and so long we ran back home, afraid such anger might follow us up the path, or, at the very least, show on our guilty faces. Mother was right. It was dangerous territory.

But it was on that bleak, purgatorial landscape that we played out our fantasy of the castle we would live in someday, when our parents threw us out of the house the way Hansel and Gretel's poor family had rid themselves of too many mouths to feed. Heaps of discarded bricks, those clinkers that had fused together in the firing, or had broken in the process, shone like burnished steel with the iridescent rainbow of high-fired ceramics, satiny, hard, and glistening like meteors from another planet. To our taste, they were ideal building blocks, and we set about constructing our version of a tower. We knew from our father that "anything worth doing is worth doing well," and we held long conferences about where the bedroom should be, how and where in the castle we would cook our oatmeal, how to protect ourselves from any invaders. We debated the pros and cons of an outhouse versus an inside toilet, given the economic considerations we assumed were a part of all adult discussions.

Bob played his usual role of construction supervisor while the rest of us hauled and carried, pulling the ones that were too heavy to lift. None of us reckoned with such obdurate resistance. We endured the sharp cuts of hard-fired clay, the broken fingernails of adamant material, and the ultimate sadness of defeat. For it could not be built. The bricks were irregular and would not stay put, and we knew nothing of mortar. A sod house would have been so much simpler. Finally, we abandoned our castle, scattering the fragments of our dream among the summer grasses. And gradually, the delicious defiance of parental caution wore off, and the limited intrigue of the brickyard began to pale.

But we found another escapade there, no doubt Bobby's idea. He was always interested in bathroom talk. Taught by Mother to refer to our excrement as "B.M."—short for "bowel movement" in the fashionable nicety of her day—we whispered the plan we devised to Rachel and George. Simply to say out loud, "Let's have a shit contest," made us feel evil and filthy, living a life as shocking as the dirty hobos that came through on the freight cars. To be vulgar in our house was unforgivable. Crudity called for washing our mouth out with soap, and to say "damn" was enough to get the bitter suds burning our tongues.

How we could defecate on demand is still a mystery to me, but my memory of this is very vivid. We wiped our bottoms with corncobs or dry grass, or maybe with stolen toilet paper. In an outhouse, it is impossible to examine one's elimination, for it falls down to take its place among the accumulated excrement of the whole family for as long a time as it takes to fill up the portable structure and move it to a new pit. So, to be able to see at close range, and more important, to demonstrate to others what feats of intestinal production one was capable of, was evidently a high order of achievement. What we had eaten made a difference. Daddy was given to adding an abundant handful of flax seed to our cooked cereal sometimes, for it was a laxative that always worked for him, and he must have assumed it was good for all of us. Or, during fresh rhubarb season, the urge to go to the bathroom was frequent. Apples helped. Dried prunes were a treat rationed out to us as effective cathartics.

Once, in cherry season, having sat up in the tree and gorged on the fresh fruit we were supposed to be picking for Mother's canning, I won the brickyard contest. For about a week before, the purgative cherries had loosened my bowels, but the day before I had not had a B.M. I was ready. I created a prodigious heap of coiled and steaming manure that might well have fertilized a dozen wild roses, more by twice that of my giggling brother or our corn-fed neighbors. With my playsuit and panties down, I produced a mound of two or three perfectly formed pieces that looked like long, long sausages. Neither Bobby nor George or Rachel could believe it, and they kept marveling at such quantity coming from such a little girl. No contest won since has been quite so memorable. It was an epic performance.

George never said much. But this contest was such a highlight of experience for him that he just giggled and twirled around in pudgy circles, having left only a little rabbit poop before he stood up and pulled his pants on. Rachel didn't like the scratchy grass on her bottom skin. But the four of us were bound to each other, now, intimate and naughty and sworn to keep our secret lives away from the ears of our parents.

"You cheated," Bob accused, competitive in all things.

"How can you cheat with THAT?"

Then, realizing the absurdity of his accusation, he said, "Okay. I give up."

A delicious concession, that. Given the role assigned him—"Take care of Janie, won't you Bobby?"—he felt compelled to discipline me, teach me, show me how to do everything. I got tired of his superiority, occasionally throwing a fit. Once, when I was sure Bob had messed up our game of jackstraws because my turn was coming and the straws had fallen in my favor, I yelled, "I hate you!" I threw the whole handful of straws at him and ran into the bathroom, slamming the door so hard it nearly cracked, and locked the door.

"Janie? Jane! Jane Ann, open this door, do you hear me?" Mother to the scene of the crime, using her full-name threatening voice.

"Make Bobby stop bossing me!" I yelled. And to Bob, standing beside her or, more than likely, behind her, I added, "Remember the "S" contest, you big bully?"

I came so perilously close to spilling our sworn secret in an attempt to establish equality that I scared myself. I unlocked the door and came out, scowling.

"Bobby isn't trying to boss you, honey. He is trying to be helpful, to protect you."

"Well he doesn't help if I already know something!" I pleaded.

And I began to cry. I could evidently summon tears as well as other bodily efflux, which reinforced my resolve to become a movie actress.

The brickyard was a testing ground for both of us, an experience we laughingly alluded to often as we outgrew the thrill of disobedience. Such collusion was the proof of our blood oath to live together until we were as old as our parents. After all, they were pretty old, being already in their thirties.

The Cattails of Okoboji

Neither of us had been away from home for more than an overnight, much less for several weeks at a time. But this summer (most likely 1932), Mother accepted Auntie Bing's invitation for Bobby and me to come with them to their cottage on Lake Okoboji. The northwestern corner of the state, known as "the lake district" or "the wetlands," had big Spirit Lake and several smaller lakes, Lake Okoboji being one of the favorite retreats from the heat in Des Moines. It was cooler, and it afforded Uncle Keith his annual fishing vacation.

Auntie Bing said children always had more fun when they shared a vacation with others their age. So Mother agreed. Auntie Bing wasn't our real aunt, but she was Mother's best friend. They had been home-economics majors at Iowa State and sorority sisters. She and Uncle Keith Merrill, a man with a deep laugh and brown eyes, for which he was nicknamed "Brownie," lived in Des Moines with their four children. He owned an insurance agency there. Uncle Keith liked to fish and I guess that's why they had a cottage at the lake. Daddy and Uncle Keith had been friends in college, too, so our families were like kin.

The twins were too little to go, and besides, Auntie Bing hadn't invited them. We were terribly excited to be rescued from the little girls who followed us everywhere, to be off on an adventure of our own. I remember almost as much getting there as being there. It was our first train ride. Mother and Dad drove us the thirty miles from Redfield to Des Moines in our Model A Ford to spend the night with Gango.

The Burlington Northern train didn't leave for Spirit Lake until the next day, but we loved any excuse to spend time at Grandma's. She lived on the top floor of the three-story Denny Apartments in downtown Des Moines, a brick walk-up with a big, round light above the front door. The stairs and the many landings were fenced in with banisters, like a brown picket fence, just made for sliding down, except for the square top of the newel posts, which could hurt. We were never allowed to try it all the way down, but we sat side-saddle on pieces of the railing and slid when no one was looking, because it was so shiny and lickety-split.

Grandma Chantry taught fourth-grade arithmetic in a nearby Des Moines public school. She walked to work, even in the snow. Her galoshes lived at the base of a coat rack in the vestibule, the space you first entered when her door was opened. A mirror sat with little flowers twined in a gold frame around it on a three-legged table that fit into the corner. On that table sat a tall vase that looked like a miniature stoneware pickle crock in which she kept a dried bouquet of cattails, their long fronds brown and twisted and the dark-brown, cigar-like seedpods full of cobwebs.

"Do spiders like cattails?" I asked Gango.

She looked at the cattails. "Looks like they do," she said. "They've been there too long. If you are going up to Lake Okoboji, bring me some fresh ones. Really big ones grow up there. Tell you what. If you two'll bring me some new ones, I'll pay you a nickel apiece."

"For each of us?" Bob wanted to know.

"Yes. One nickel for every cattail." She stood with one foot in the hall and one inside the door, her apron still on from fixing dinner, and spread her hands out open, like the picture in *Ali Baba and the Forty Thieves*. Maybe she thought we'd bring a whole lot of them, and it would cost her lots of money.

"If you brought me five, Janie, and Bobby brought me six, how much would it cost me?"

I thought awhile, and made a wild guess. "Fifty cents?"

"Add five to six and then. . . ."

"Fifty-five cents," piped up my brother.

"Right," said Grandma, who always preferred to honor accuracy over sensitivity.

"I will bring you six," I told her, hurriedly, as if that would somehow rectify rather than compound the error.

Through the open window of the bedroom where we slept in her apartment, we smelled the sharp yellow dust of coal smoke, so different from the fresh country air at our house. Even after dark, we could hear voices outside on the street. The streetcars' banging sounded like pan lids dropping or like skidding to a sideways stop on roller skates. We loved the signal bell ringing when it started up again, and we lay awake a long time, listening, whispering. It was another country.

"If we ran away, Bobby, would we end up in Des Moines?" I asked. We had just finished reading *Toby Tyler, or Ten Weeks with a Circus*, and the idea of running away appealed to us both.

"No. I'll bet if we had long sticks like tramps do and enough food tied up in a dishtowel, we could get as far as Omaha."

"We'd ride the train in a boxcar. We'd be hobos."

"I don't think you could jump up that high, Janie. You have to be taller to get in a boxcar."

I was unconvinced, just thinking about a place to bed down. "What would we do when we got to Omaha?"

"I don't know. We'd just do whatever came along, sort of like a treasure hunt. Sometimes we'd even get hungry, I s'pose, but that just makes you skinny."

"Will we stay together, Bobby?"

"Yes, silly. If you don't cry or something."

"Okay. I won't. Is it hot or cold in Omaha? Should I take my red sweater?"

"It's just like here, cold in the winter and hot in the summer."

"Well," I said, sleepily, "Let's go in the summertime, okay?"

"Okay. Okay. Now go to sleep. . . ."

A nurse named Miss Hunt boarded with Grandma Chantry, which helped pay the rent, Mother told us. Miss Hunt's private bedroom was forbidden territory to us. But nevertheless, we could not resist peeking. She had lacy curtains on her window, a dressing table with a big mirror that tilted back and forth, and pink cushions on her bed. The rug was kind of worn out, and her closet only had a few dresses in it.

Grandma's bedroom was nicer. Her bed was covered with a quilt that had tiny stitches in the white part puffed up like a pile of leaves. On her vanity was a matched set of silver-backed brush, comb, and hand mirror, which I coveted. And her dresser top was covered with a beautifully embroidered and cutout white linen runner, ironed wet, I thought to myself, having learned from Mother how to iron linen napkins to make them shine.

"You have to sprinkle linen really wet, Janie, and iron it until it's totally dry. That way, you'll see the long threads begin to shine. It's made out of flax fibers that are as long as your hair! Farmers in Ireland grow a lot of flax, and that's why Irish linen is the best kind." She told me how different threads had a different feel: wool threads were springy, cotton was smooth, linen was shiny, satin was silky. I loved ironing the linen things best even though it sometimes took a long time to stop steaming. The shine of it was my reward, and Mother always saved the napkins for me to do. Gango praised my work.

When she was young, Grandma was fond of telling us, she'd taught in little country schools, wore Gibson Girl blouses and stayed with the families of her pupils. She had to iron her blouses, which had huge sleeves, and that was a lot harder to do than flat pieces.

"I was just a slip of a girl then. Once, my beau took me for a sleigh ride on a winter evening." She stopped for a while and then, in a lower voice she said, "in the gloaming," a word that meant twilight, which was romantic-sounding. Then she told us how Wilfred—that was his name—had wrapped her in a big bear rug. "Snug as bugs, we were. But, he let go the reins to kiss me. The horse got rambunctious in the snow, and we tipped over in a ditch. We had to walk miles in the dark to get help, and nearly died of the cold before we got home. But Wilfred was more scared than I was. That's why I never married him; I couldn't abide a coward!"

"Mother!" our mother said to her, as if she didn't believe it.

The next morning we boarded the train, our lunch in a shoebox tied with twine. Our mother hesitated about having her two children ride the train without an accompanying adult, but she allowed it, trusting her good friend, her old college roommate, would be waiting at the other end.

The depot was a snarl of train tracks outside the station, like a bunch of ladders laid on top of each other, but inside was like a church with hard benches. A man in a glass-fronted box, selling tickets, wore a black cap with a greasy bill. It looked old. So did he.

"He looks older than Methuselah," I whispered to Bobby, having heard about the oldest man in the Bible.

"Shhh," he said, "You must not speak loudly on the train, either, Janie. We'll sit together, and Auntie Bing and Uncle Keith will meet us at the Spirit Lake station."

To Bob, she had given the usual advice, "Take care of Janie, Bob. Don't speak to strangers, and," she added, wistfully, "give Bing my love, won't you? See you in a few weeks!"

As the train slowly began to move, my heart pounded. We waved out the window until Grandmother was a speck, waving back at us from the wide-planked wooden platform.

We looked at each other, then, conspiratorially. "We can eat our lunch now, if we want to," Bob said.

"We could get up from our seats and walk up and down the aisles, too, if we want to."

"We could even talk to strangers," Bob said, in effect daring me to do so first.

The miles between Des Moines and Spirit Lake stretched on forever, and the countryside was beautiful and vast. I imagined that the whole rest of the world would be more of the same green fields with an occasional house tucked away among the cottonwood trees, the fences all straight and the country roads laid out with square corners, and sometimes a little red-brick town. Every once in a while a long line of tall Lombardy poplars—planted for a windbreak, as the prairie is wide and winds sweeping across a cornfield can level the crop—slashed across the train window. We fell into the rhythm of the telephone poles flashing by, too, and the clickety-clack of the train wheels on the railroad tracks. I drew a picture with the pencil and paper Mother had tucked inside our suitcase, of a landscape like the one we were seeing, and in it, I put lots of telephone poles scalloped with wires between them. It looked like the curtains draped above the stage of the movie theater. It was my best drawing ever. The cows didn't even look lopsided. Bobby liked it, too.

Across the double seats from us sat a beautiful little girl about my age, with yellow curls and a ruffled dress. She was wearing patent leather shoes and long white socks. I ventured a shy "Hello. We're going to Lake Okoboji to visit my aunt."

"What's her name?" the girl asked. Maybe she knew everybody in the world.

"Auntie Bing," I said, naive about full answers.

"I am related to Shirley Temple," she said then. "She's my cousin."

"Really?" Thrilled, I said, "My name is Jane and this is my brother, Bob."

"Have you seen her in the movies?" Shirley's nameless cousin asked, ignoring my clumsy introduction.

"Our grandmother took us to see her dance with Mr. Robinson in *The Little Colonel*," I told her, glad to introduce a new subject, now that I, too, was a tap dancer. I wasn't as good as he was, but my teacher told me, "You have a natural rhythm," and she was always smiling at me. One day I *might* become famous.

I sat back in my seat, smiling at our new friend, basking in our common connections. She didn't respond to that, so Bobby and I began to talk about the movies, about another one we'd seen, *The Littlest Rebel*, about her dress and the plantation South, and why Gango was the only one who took us to see movies.

Shirley Temple's cousin didn't comment for awhile. Then, instead of telling me her name, she said, " Well, my mother says I look just like her." I couldn't see the resemblance, except that she had worked hard to make corkscrew curls. But she didn't have dimples.

We had no one famous in our family, so I changed the subject.

"Did you bring your lunch?" I asked.

"Yes, I am going to Spirit Lake, and the train won't get there until afternoon," she said, with a superior air.

"We're going there, too," Bobby said.

"We have cookies in our lunchbox. Maybe we could share some

stuff," I said.

"I don't think my mother'd want me to," she said.

Willing to allow her disinclination, I asked outright, "What's your name?"

"Dorothy," she said. I had expected "Temple," but she didn't say more.

"My name's Jane, and this is my brother, Bobby," I said again.

"You told me that, already," she said. So we decided to ignore her. She was spoiled, we could tell. I bet she had lots of frilly dresses and a bicycle and dolls with real hair.

We finally arrived. The conductor came to tell us this was where we got off. So we did and there, on the platform waiting for us, were Auntie Bing and Uncle Keith.

"Well, you made it," Auntie Bing said. "It is wonderful to see you." She nearly squeezed my breath out with her bosomy hug.

"Mother said to give you her love," I told her right away, so I wouldn't forget.

Uncle Keith talked to Bobby. "Any trouble with the train, young man?"

"No. It was kinda bumpy sometimes but we saw a lot of cows on the way." Like Daddy, Bob was always talking about cows.

"I bet you did," Uncle Keith told him, "lots of milk gets made into cheese up here. Well, let's pile in the car." First, we put our little suitcases in the trunk of the car and climbed into the back seat. From there we could see Auntie Bing's curly hair and a tiny bald spot beginning to shine on Uncle Keith's head. Very soon, we turned a corner and there, lying directly in front of us, was the blue, blue lake. Like a huge bathtub for God, it was more water than we had ever seen at once, even a little bit scary it was so big.

Vacation cottages were sprinkled around the edges of the lakes, most of them with a dock where a sailboat or a rowboat was tied up. One of these cottages, on West Okoboji, belonged to Auntie Bing and Uncle Keith. A paradise for fishermen, for game hunters, for holiday visitors who enjoy the summer coolness of the wetlands, the Lake District is a favorite place to go in summer. A Sioux Indian word meaning "wind spirit," or "windiness," Okoboji is often choppy in the late afternoons when the breeze comes up. Little whitecaps caused by the breeze that sweeps over the water look like egg whites, beaten stiff and curling over. The wind rustles the willow leaves, bends the cattails.

The Merrill family had a summer house on the sloping banks of Okoboji, to which they went every year. They weren't really related to us, but it was the custom of the day for children to call intimate adult friends by "Auntie" or "Uncle." We never thought of the four kids—Skip, Trish, Anne, and Gretchen—as our cousins, though. Uncle Keith came and went periodically from his business in Des Moines to get away from the summer heat of the capital city. Auntie Bing and the kids stayed on. It was a typically Midwestern white clapboard house with screen doors and a lattice petticoat around the bottom of the lakeside porch, where the land dropped away.

Also, there was a large, screened-in sleeping porch with rows of metal cots, sagging with old mattresses and limp pillows but heaped with quilts. Before antibiotics, sanitariums for the treatment of tuberculosis included such fresh-air porches, so that if we shivered or sneezed out on the sleeping porch, it was probably good for our young bodies. All the kids slept out there.

The six of us kids ranged in age from about six to twelve, and we could whisper and giggle, tell scary stories, put frogs in each other's beds, and throw pillows as late into the night as we wanted. No one ever interfered. That the pillows and mattresses were musty from disuse all winter didn't bother any of us, then, but the stench of old feathers in stale ticking stained with the aftermath of pulled teeth, runny noses, or sleep drool still reminds me of Okoboji.

But sleep out there we did. To wake up each morning, the world having been cleansed with dew, the birds absolutely raucous with joy, to look out on the calm lake and think about the day ahead was paradise for me. It stays in my sensory memory to this day, and often when I cannot sleep I try to remember that hallowed summer.

Mostly the nights were warm and humid. Crickets chirped and the bullfrogs belched in the lakeside edges. The little creatures of the earth were the noisiest at dusk. Sometimes a warm, summer rain would dimple the dust and smell so sweet, so intoxicating, no one could stay inside. We ran out and lifted our faces up toward the sky, stuck our tongues out to taste the heavenly rain. At nightfall, when the moisture from the vast expanse of water began to cool the day, a million fireflies would appear out over the scrubby grass, their little lanterns magic sparks that jumped like fairy circus performers. We used to catch them in a fruit jar and pretend they gave off enough light to see by. I wondered if they ever lit the way for the smaller animals or bugs who couldn't see in the dark and who had no other flashlights.

Auntie Bing had made bedside tables for our sleeping porch out of orange crates onto which she tacked squares of cotton flour-sacking for makeshift curtains. Behind one such curtain, I could hide my diary, a little locked book into which I wrote secrets, mostly about Skippy or things Bobby had done or said, adventures we had during the day. Sometimes I drew pictures, mostly of the lake, behind which I always added imaginary mountains, none of which existed in reality. But the wetlands of the lake region inspired me to try many sketches, always hairy with pencil strokes of tall, reedy plants growing along the edge. Once, I let Bobby draw a picture in my diary, but it was so much better than mine that I didn't let him do any more.

Along the wall, Uncle Keith had pounded big nails for hanging up our clothes, trying to keep a semblance of order in the natural chaos. Even though Bobby and I had been instructed to put our little cardboard suitcases under our beds, six kids, sneaking crackers or cookies under the covers, stripping their pajama tops off to keep cool, or throwing shoes across the room, do not keep order. But no one seemed to get mad those long days of summer. The adults lounged around in bathing suits or shorts, eating or drinking or reading books they left open on the chair arms or little tables, coffee cups lined up on the mantle like sparrows on a telephone wire.

During the winter, Bob and I had a trap line to catch the small animals whose pelts brought us money. Maybe it was our trapping experience in our own woods that caused our fascination with muskrats in Lake Okoboji. We spent hours looking for their burrows in the bank, houses made of cattails and other reeds. From their holes, they would peek up, with their big heads and little beady eyes, then dive into hiding again when they saw us. They were quick swimmers, their feet webbed like a duck's and their tails hairless as a rat's. Their thick, brown, shiny hair looked soft, and we thought if we could catch one, it would be a pet more cuddly than a teddy bear. Daddy had told us he once had a muskrat coat, the warmest thing he'd ever owned. How many muskrats would it take to make a coat, I wondered?

Those little brown bodies played and splashed in the water toward evening when we loved to walk along the edge of the marsh, listening to the crickets tuning up and the chorus frogs clearing their throats. The house sat close enough to the water so we could go back and forth easily. The green smell of the water, the damp land that fringed it, the little gray scallops on top as the breeze quickened or slackened, reminded me of how Pocahontas must have lived. I imagined I would have a birchbark canoe but no dock. I would just slither to the shore among the cattails and no one could ever hear me. When we heard the deep voice of the huge bullfrogs, we would speculate about the risk of catching those, asking Auntie Bing to cook us frogs' legs, of which we had only heard.

"They'll give you warts," Skip, who was the oldest of the Merrill kids, told us. He was a real smart aleck, and just because it was his cottage, he pretended to know everything.

Bob, who always liked to be right, said, "That's not true. You can't catch warts from frogs or toads. That's an old wives' tale."

"What's an 'old wives' tale'?" I asked him.

"It's just gossip and not true," he said. "That's what Mother told me."

But it was enough for me to avoid catching bullfrogs, just in case.

Those twilight hours were a magical part of the day. Animals abounded, and that hour seemed to draw them out of their daytime habitat. We hunted the discarded shells of the pond snails or mudpuppies, the salamanders. The squirrels scurried about in the Burr oaks, trees with the largest acorns of any North American tree, Uncle Keith said. We kept our eyes peeled for the otters, minks, and badgers that lived along the sedgey banks of Lake Okoboji. Too, the cricket song of that time of day marked the last of daylight's freedom to explore, for it would soon be too dark to see and Auntie Bing would come out on the porch, cup her hands around her mouth and yell out, "Suppertime!" Suddenly hungry, we would leave the quiet lake water, the gentle iridescent ripples turning into shimmering silk as the sun left the sky, lulling us into peace with the liquid *lap, lap, lap* along the shore.

———◆———

Auntie Bing's body was square as an icebox. Around her wide eyes and strong jaw, little red-brown curls framed her face like wood shavings.

She had big, soft breasts. Her shapeless apron looked more like a sandwich board than anything else. She rolled her stockings below her knees and she easily hiked them up, rolled them down again, and looped the excess into the roll. She wore glasses. Through them, I think, she noticed every little detail of the natural world. More than that, she saw the needs of others, fed the hungry, listened to our stories, braided my hair when I had made a mess of it. She was a natural-born biologist, though her education had been in music and home economics. Sometimes she would sit down at the upright piano in the cabin and play and play; even after we had gone to bed, I could hear that loving touch on the keys and vowed to take my own music lessons more seriously when I got home. But in addition to her other talents, she took us on long nature hikes, pointed out the foxes' den beneath the beech tree roots, spotted a green frog the rest of us had overlooked. She taught us to imitate the song of the yellow-headed blackbirds, to marvel at the delicacy of the dragonflies that flitted over the surface of the water.

When she and Mother first knew each other, her name was Rachel Garst and she had been an accomplished concert pianist. But after she married and had four children, she was too busy. We all loved to snuggle and be squeezed into her broad shoulders and soft arms, for she had a bubbly laugh and twinkling gray eyes the color of the water at sundown. She could make cornbread that was almost as good as Mother's, but the pies she made weren't half as pretty.

Uncle Keith was a fisherman who hung his huge wet waders out on the porch. But he was also a reader. And a storyteller. He would keep all of us spellbound with his accounts of fur trappers that used to catch animals around the lake, of Indians in their birch-bark canoes, of the Hudson's Bay traders who would pay money for the pelts they'd collected. There were two fur companies, he told us, and they were jealous of each other, so the Northwest Company and the Hudson's Bay Company would try to outsmart each other for the most animal skins. He said fewer and fewer beavers built their dams in the lake anymore because they had been trapped out, long ago.

He taught us about the headwaters of the great Mississippi River, which begins as a small, clear stream rushing out of Lake Itasca in northwest Minnesota, "north of where we are now," he would add, just to engrave a sense of geography in our curious minds. Down this river, the French-Canadian trappers had come in their canoes, and sometimes they married Indian squaws, who came along to guide them. I was glad to learn that, for they, too, had long braids and someone had fallen in love with them anyway.

He even tried to imitate the sound of a swarm of grasshoppers, a cross between a cat's purr and a fast lawnmower, when he told us the history of the devastating invasion of the Red River Valley in the early nineteenth century. The grasshoppers would swoop down to eat up every last blade of grass, he said, and it completely destroyed the grain crops, leaving the farmers destitute. He said it was called "a plague," like the ones they had in the Bible.

"Those little devils even sawed the leaves off the trees," he said. "Can you imagine what it would be like if you looked down toward the lake and couldn't see anything but the raw dirt and rocks?"

Long after we had gone to bed, I pondered the wonders of the world, after I said my prayers—"Now I lay me down to sleep, I pray the Lord my soul to keep; if I should die before I wake, I pray the Lord my soul to take. Bless Mother and Daddy and Bobby, MaryLou and Merilyn, Auntie Bing and Uncle Keith," . . . "and me," I'd always add, not wanting to die in the night. Before the dreams began to hover over my head with their transparent wings, I would lie awake in the sleeping porch, slapping at the mosquitoes that had succeeded in sneaking in and whining like miniature machines, or listening to the June bugs bump against the screen. I could not imagine how God had planned it all, the rivers and the lakes, the animals and the clouds of grasshoppers. But then, I would drift into a deep sleep until the sun rose.

The first rays that slanted into the sleeping porch those Lake Okoboji mornings always made me happy, eager to jump up to greet the day. The sound of the cockcrow in the distance has remained my favorite alarm clock all the days of my life. Dawn still calls me to leave my bed, to look out at the world with an explorer's sense of discovery.

One morning from our summer on the lake is etched in my memory. A haze lay over the water and the hint of a morning breeze moved the tops of the trees, bent the tall reeds at the edge of the water. I imagined it was God, combing the snarls out of His slept-on hair.

After breakfast of oatmeal with raisins and flax seeds (to keep us regular), milk, and oven-baked toast with all the apple butter we wanted on it, Uncle Keith pushed his chair back, got up, and strolled over by the big stone fireplace where he dropped into his stuffed reading chair, clawed raggedy by the black and white cat called "Knickers." He always heaved a big sigh once he settled into the cushions, as if he were shrugging off the last semblance of worry. His mouth, usually downturned at the corners, would relax into a straight line and he seemed softer, somehow. He picked up a book he had left sprawled open on the end table. We had been taught never to do that, because we might hurt the book. Mother said books were our best friends, and like people, they had spines and wonderful adventures and even sometimes wore jackets, so we should treat them well. Uncle Keith's book looked like it was doing the splits, and doing the splits hurt my legs, so the book must hurt, too.

"Dad? Dad?" Skip wanted his dad's attention, but, as usual, it was glued to whatever he was reading.

"Dad!" Again, louder, more intense.

His father put down his book with an impatient twist of his mouth, for one of the sacred manners we had all been taught was never to interrupt someone while he is reading. "What is it, son? What do you want?"

"Can we take the boat out this morning?"

"Who is "we"?"

"Bobby, Janie, Trish, and I."

"What do you plan to do with it?" he asked.

"The Belton kids want to gather some cattails to take home to their Grandma. She said she'd pay them a nickel apiece for every fresh one they brought her."

"How are you going to cut them?"

"Borrow Mom's flower clippers, I guess," Skip said quickly.

"Well, I guess you're old enough to be responsible," Uncle Keith said, "but be careful with that wobbly oarlock. Make the kids stay seated while you're rowing. Okay? You're in charge, Skip, understand? Are you old enough to be trusted?" He must have been about thirteen.

"Yes, I am," Skip assured him, "and we'll be back before lunch."

Auntie Bing had already put some apples and some cookies in a little paper sack for each of us, for "elevenses," she told us, a *Winnie the Pooh* word. She bustled about keeping track of everybody's plans. She had already tied a string around the handle of her garden clippers and she told Skippy to be sure to tie the other end of them to the gunwale of the boat, just in case they might drop into the water. He promised he would.

"Don't pick the too-ripe cattails or they'll burst before you get back to Des Moines. Are you going to cut them, Janie, or is Bob?"

"Both of us are going to bring her six new ones because the ones she has are dusty," I told her, and she smiled.

"Well, be careful, won't you?"

We always listened to Auntie Bing's advice.

Skip untied the rope that anchored the rowboat to the old wooden dock and got ready to shove off. There were two board seats crosswise in the boat, so two of us sat on each one. The lake was like glass, now, calm and hushed. We put on the bleached old lifejackets from the bottom of the boat, settled ourselves in the middle of the seats, being careful, since we were wearing shorts, not to get splinters. Skip tied the garden shears to the side of the boat, as he had promised, and handed them to me.

"You cut the ones you want, Janie, and hand them over to Bob. Bob, put them under the seats at the sides, in case we have to bail out any water. And Trish, you've got the can, haven't you, in case we start to leak?" Skippy was in fact, the skipper, and he let us all know it.

We rowed out into the deep water. It was wonderful to be floating on top of the world. After a while, we circled back toward the shore from the deeper water, and slowly the prow of the boat nosed its way into the thick of the cattail patch, almost impenetrable. The water was scummy in the dense growth, home of tadpoles and other water creatures. The reeds pushed against the side of the boat, and Trish hated the long leaves that kept brushing across her hair and face. But there were thousands of big cattails to choose from, all so much fresher and nicer than the dusty ones at Grandma's house. She would be amazed. They were wonderful specimens, some of them probably prizewinners at the county fair, and I was proud to be the designated cutter. Snip, snip, snip. The stalks were thick and each took several whacks with the garden clippers.

The string tied to the boat was too short and was always twisting around my wrist, and my fat life jacket kept me from leaning very far out. In frustration, I untied the life jacket strings and threw the bulky thing into the wet boat bottom. That was much better. Now I could reach some of the really good ones.

"You can't do that, Jane," Skippy said, "It's against the rules."

I pretended I didn't hear him. He kept feathering the oars to keep the boat steady, and Bobby said he'd hang onto my feet if I'd like. So, I stood up on the seat and reached for a big, dark brown cattail I knew would be Gango's favorite, stretching out a little farther, then a little farther. I could feel my feet slip on the wet seat. Then, I teetered, grabbing for a handhold in mid-air until I completely lost control and plunged into icky green water with a loud belly flop and a terrifying splash. The boat rocked back from the wake of my splash. I could hear them yelling, even when my head went underwater. I could not swim in that mesh of algae and sedge, and went down, down into the very roots of the world.

The voices in the boat screamed, "HELP! "HELP!" filtering down to my ears like a faraway call. "Don't . . . be . . . scared. Janie! We . . . will . . . save . . . Janie!" I could hear their slurry words. But I had opened my eyes under there and was shocked to see the underwater stalks as pale and wobbly as newly cooked asparagus. The light was crooked under the water, with motes of mud my falling in had stirred up from the bottom floating all around me. Little minnows darted, and wavery grasses danced around the base of the dense roots gnarled together down there. It was like an aquarium almost, even if I didn't get to look very long.

I was afraid, too, of not being able to breathe, so I flailed my arms trying to surface, holding my breath for fear I would suffocate in that green slimy mess. I kicked my feet and could feel my body heading back up.

Suddenly, a hand grabbed hold of my blouse neck and tugged and tugged, pulling the cloth up under my armpits until it hurt. But, with a dramatic surfacing, I broke out of the deep to gulp down quick little breaths of real air again. It was Bobby and he pulled me toward the rocking boat.

"Janie, are you okay? You nearly drownded! Can you breathe? Did you get hurt?" He was frantic.

His grip guided my dripping hand. I grabbed hold of the edge of the boat and held on for dear life with one hand. With the other one, I tried to push my hair out of my face and nose, so I could breathe without choking. The boat wobbled with the water churned up and Skip said, "Trish, hike out over the opposite side to tilt the boat for balance! And Bob, help her put one foot up over the side and roll into the center."

"What happened to the clippers?" Trish asked. I couldn't talk. Besides, I didn't know. Probably down at the bottom of the swamp.

"Here, honey, put one foot up over the side and I'll pull you in," Bobby said. He hardly ever called me "honey," so I knew he was glad I was rescued. We all did what Skip told us, gasping and laughing with relief. Awkwardly, because the sides of the boat were slippery, too, I hooked one leg over and let Bobby pull my sodden body in. I began to gulp the air as if I could not get enough of it, and my heart was pounding so hard I could feel it shake my ribs. We were all so relieved that I wasn't dead that we began to chatter about how it felt, what it was like down there, how terrible it could have been if there had been crocodiles in the lake. But we were all drenched, I from submergence and the others from the desperate splash of anxious oars and reaching hands. I began to shiver from shock, although the air was warm. Finally, the boat settled down and we did, too, gathering our wits to head home and give up on any more cattails.

"Did Auntie Bing's clippers get drowned?" I wanted to know, feeling responsible and embarrassed at causing such a commotion.

"No, they're here," Trish said. Auntie Bing was smart to tie the string on them.

Now that I was safely back in, Skip maneuvered the oars backwards, keeping an eye on the wobbly oarlock, and turned the boat around to head back for the dock. I kept wondering if God had punished me for taking off my lifejacket, wanting to teach me a lesson, or if he wanted me to see the underside of the lake. Bobby kept his arm around my shoulders. I felt strangely special, singled out for an experience the others would never have, given a second chance as if I were one of the chosen people who had a great future ahead, though I didn't yet know what it was.

All four of us were glad to have survived an accident, to have collected seven cattails, even to be wet, for the hot sun and the summer air soon dried us out. We laughed a bit giddily, and decided that we would never open up a cattail store, nor train to be pirates. Maybe Lake Okoboji was really most beautiful viewed from the grassy bank that sloped down from the house to the dock.

Auntie Bing washed my hair in warm water at the kitchen sink. Uncle Keith rubbed me with a towel until my skin was red. I put on clean pajamas and lolled around the living room until suppertime, reading *Little Women* and the *National Geographics* that were scattered everywhere. After we went to bed, I lay there in the cozy dark, the stars blinking at me through the screen, and thought about Bobby, how brave he was.

From his cot next to the screened-in window, Bobby whispered, "I'm glad you didn't die, Janie, really I am."

"Me, too. You were very strong. . . ." And we fell asleep trying to multiply seven by five cents and divide that by two. I promised him he could have the extra penny.

The Artist's Life

Uncle Walter was a hunchback. What had caused his deformed body no one would say. The first time he came to visit us in Redfield, I pressed my parents to know why his eyes were not much higher from the ground than mine were, why his lopsided suspenders did not match, stretched in different lengths across his spine, crooked and grotesque as a Hubbard squash. Rumored whisperings and childhood imaginings had him kicked by a horse, bewitched by the Devil, or born in a caul. Maybe his mother was a gypsy. He was the older of Daddy's two brothers. Uncle Howard was next, and Daddy was the youngest.

Whenever anyone mentioned Uncle Walter's name, either something he had done or had not done, the voice dropped or slowed or paused, as if his life were somehow shrouded in a mystery, unspeakable and strange. And whenever, as a child, I would ask blunt questions, I was hushed. For the facts of Uncle Walter's life and the consequences of his childhood misfortune in the late 1880s, in provincial Algona, Iowa, seemed to shame the Puritans he was fated to be born among. The realities of rural life revolved around good seed corn or the breeding stock from which came ribbon winners at the county fair. Cripples were often cloistered or kept away from the public eye.

But Uncle Walter had left his family home and moved to California at the age of nineteen. Not until I was privy to adult truth did I learn that he had suffered from polio when he was less than ten. It had made his life a tragedy, according to my parents, whose measure of normalcy was to be not too different from other folks. But Uncle Walter *was* different; he could draw. He had enormous talent with pen-and-ink sketching, even as a boy, and his parents enrolled him in an art school.

Uncle Walter's piercing black eyes peered out between the top of his round glasses and the bottoms of his brush-thick eyebrows, which angle had carved deep, horizontal lines into his forehead. His large nose seemed vegetable or mineral, perched as it was on top of his mouth. His lips stretched across crooked teeth that resembled a cowcatcher bent into a wedge.

He played jacks with us, standing up. In fact, it was hard to imagine how he could sit down on the floor. He whisked up the little red ball along with the jacks, like a cat swiping at a fly. His fingers bent down at the first knuckle like the scary claws of a Halloween witch, disproportionately long and stained a yellow-brown from constant smoking. So were his fingernails long and yellow. His thumbnail had been filed to a point, a terrible mark of idleness, we thought, compared to the ragged blunt ends of hard-working men's thumbs. Mother, uneasy with some of the values that made his suffering harder, explained to us that Uncle Walter was an artist, and artists had to take care of their hands. We came to regard him as a genius because no one else we knew had ever gone to art school. We plagued him to draw our faces, and we hounded him to play jacks with us at every opportunity.

"You have quick fingers, Uncle Walter," my brother said, trying to be conversational, to think of something to make him feel comfortable.

"And quick fingernails, too," I added, then burning with embarrassment, for that isn't what I meant to say. But he understood, and smiled with his twinkling eyes. He whistled through his teeth in admiration whenever one of us gathered up a lot of jacks at once.

"You kids are good," he said, "better than anyone in California. Why, out there, we can't even pick up the alligator pears as fast as they fall!"

"Alligator *pears*?" We wrinkled up our noses.

"Are you kidding us?" Bobby was skeptical.

"No. That's the truth. It's a pear-shaped fruit as green as dog days on the Raccoon River and the hide you peel off is bumpy, like an alligator skin. Or a bullfrog's," he added, watching our suspicious faces. "Some people call 'em 'avocados,' but I like 'alligator pears' better. Don't you? More mysterious. Their skin is like leather, but they taste like butter. I have two big trees of them in my back yard."

His beady eyes shone and he laughed with us, then licked his lips. We loved to think of the foreign land where he lived, with alligators in the trees. Stories spilled out of his funny body as fresh as spring water. He kept us spellbound, sometimes, making up mysteries and describing worlds we knew he just imagined. We waited for that licking of his dry lips and protuberant teeth after ending every sentence, a habit we, cruel children all, delighted in mimicking behind his back. But, in fact, we became unaware of it the more we came to love him. There was a sweetness in him that completely won me over. After dinner, he helped bring dishes into the kitchen, hobbling until we thought he might drop them. But he handed them to me, saying softly, "Nice to have a good little helper like you, Janie." I sponged up his compliment, hungry for approval as I came to feel only he could understand. When I looked at him, I thought "an artist!" as if that were a kind of god.

He was married and had two boys, and he brought his wife and children with him to visit us. His two children were noisy and rude, and we hated to call them our cousins. We asked Mother how it was possible for Uncle Walter to love them.

"Shhh," she said. "He can't help it." Uncle Walter had advertised for his wife in *Wallace's Farmer*, she told us, and he ended up with Aunt Bessie, who came out to California to marry him.

Aunt Bessie. It was obvious to us why she'd answered the ad. She was more buck-toothed and strange looking than we thought it would be possible to love. A dwarfish creature whose feet were too big for the rest of her, she was even weirder than her husband, and she couldn't even play jacks. Most unforgettable thing, though, she was dirty. Nearly blind, she wore round glasses that kept slipping down her face, the rims of which had collected so much grimy dirt from her pushing them back into place that we plotted to steal them while she slept, to ream them out with a toothpick and wash them with soap. Imagine how dazzling the world would be to her the next morning! But we never had the nerve. We had not yet learned to be tolerant of difference, and longed to see that everyone else live the way we were taught was the right way.

She had a tick. Or a snuffle, more accurately. Sucking in air after she'd say something or get amused or embarrassed by what someone else said, her tongue would slip halfway out between her seriously mismatched uppers and lowers, and she would exhale in several short snorts, sounding like a stutterer, struggling to say "cat."

"Walter doesn't *k-k-k* like *k-k-k* Cream of Wheat," she'd tell Mother, or, "It sure gets *k-k-k* hot out here in *k-k-k* Iowa!" She wore my mother to a shred of civility, but for Bob and me, she was the model of an elocutionary horror, and we only had to imitate her in a phrase or two to break into hysterics.

After a two-week stay, they returned to Gardena, California, to their brown-paneled house on Normandie Avenue, where, a few years after their trip to see us, we went to see them. Aunt Bessie invited us children to stay overnight, to play with her two boys, Ralphie and Donald, to help her pick the figs for drying. We did. To our disgust, she pulled down a bed from the cobwebbed wall, an old-fashioned In-A-Door or Hide-A-Bed, the likes of which we'd never seen, and said we could sleep there. Quite obviously, everyone else had, for the sheets were grimy and smelled of mice nests. When I tactlessly suggested we could help her change them, she demurred, saying they were the only ones that fit.

On the walls of the living room, though, hung the drawings Uncle Walter had done himself. I stared at them, at how perfectly real they looked, almost like photographs.

"Uncle Walter, did you draw all of these *yourself*?" I asked him, honestly amazed that any human being, let alone someone whose hands were scrunched up the way his were, could make anything so delicate, so beautiful.

"Yes. I did. Do you like them?"

"Oh, yes, I do. They're wonderful. The horses in the barn look just like real horses in a real barn, even the wood is just the way wood looks." The frames around each one were also beautiful, sanded to gloss and perfectly cornered, then varnished to a shine. "Did you make the frames, too?"

"Yes, I did," he said.

A finish carpenter by trade, he had a shop in the back yard near the big avocado trees, attached to the house like a lean-to. Usually open, it had two sawhorses outside with a plank across them where he worked. He took small jobs like remodeling or refinishing or making new cabinets for money. At the back, on a bench just low enough for him to be comfortable, were his tools—three different saws hanging on nails, a plane with a sharp blade at the bottom of what looked like a flat iron, a rasp, some chisels, a miter box, and lots of sandpaper. In contrast to the house, his shop was kind of tidy, the shavings from work he had done underfoot.

In their house, on the wall above the fireplace, hung two large, glass-covered, pen-and-ink drawings edged in flyspecked black wooden frames. The heads of two fine horses faced each other, their arched necks proud, their ears perky, their large eyes so real they seemed to be watching us. Drawn in lines as fine as spider webs, drawings startlingly crisp in that squalid living room, this diptych must have been a memory of his Iowa childhood. From what I had gleaned through Dad's stories, from Grandma Belton's memories, I imagined him, lonely kid with a cross too heavy to carry, leaning across the worn boards of the corral fence, watching the silent world of horses. Maybe he had a pad of newsprint and a pencil by his bed, maybe he tried his first sketch, then, and found joy in the drawing.

"Have you ever tried to draw, honey? It's something you could learn, you know."

"I could *never* do that," I said, too loud, denying a secret wish that I'd rather learn how to do that than anything I could think of.

"All of us can learn to do artistic things, if we want to, I think. People don't even try to do half the things they could, if they wanted. When I went to art school, that was the hardest thing I had to get over, that feeling that I could never do it. It takes practice, sure, but it takes confidence, too."

"Where do you get the idea of what you're going to draw?"

"Inside me. There are lots of different kinds of artists, but every one of them has to depend on some idea that comes from inside. Imagination, some people call it." He sat in his square oak rocker with the brown leather seat, squashed down in the middle from all the hours he must have sat there, and rocked back and forth, gently, leaning his arms along the wide chair arms and hunching forward, intently.

Then, in a quiet voice I didn't want anyone else to hear I told him.

"Sometimes I try to write poems about things. Is that a kind of artistic thing that lives inside me?"

"You bet it is, Janie. Will you let me see one of your poems?"

"I didn't bring them with us. But I can tell you about the song I wrote when our canary died. Bobby and I buried him in a matchbox, and I imagined, when we were asleep, he sprouted new wings down under the ground, and flew up and away the next day. It was like Jesus did to Lazarus, remember, made him get up and walk? I called my poem 'A Little Miracle.'"

"I would love to read it someday. Maybe you could copy it out and send it to me when you get home."

"I will. Oh, I will. I've never ever known a real artist before you, Uncle Walter. Do you think it could run in our family?"

"Well, you and I are the proof of the pudding, aren't we?"

And so, my idea of a possible life was irreversibly altered. Something felt secret, somehow, like more breath inside my ribs. I never forgot that conversation. He had understood and made me feel special in a different way than I'd ever felt. When I told him, he had taken my dream seriously. I began to put my ideas down on paper, calling them poems. They were the romantic yearnings of a pre-adolescent, but they cast the die for my adult life. I remember one I called "The Cold River," in which I asked God to wrap a blanket around those dripping shoulders, having seen a river-dunking preacher baptize a young woman. Death was one of my earliest themes, too, and I could make myself cry just describing it!

◆

Uncle Walter's single-story brown-shingled house had heavy timbers on the porch that made it seem low to the ground. It was like a bulldog's face, that entrance, the pillars flanking the steps like canine teeth.

Bob and I thought it mustn't have been easy for our two cousins to go back in there every day after school, to the chaos and the filthy fireplace, heaped half full of ashes that spilled onto the hearth and into which was tossed anything combustible—empty boxes, egg shells, used up toilet-paper rolls, old papers. Or to have to go to their rooms where socks and shirts and shoes were strewn about. Even the threadbare chenille bedspread, bunched up with their covers, smelled brown and musty. Their disheveled dress reflected the disorder of their lives, and even the bathroom, that sacred spring where transformation can occur, was uninviting, the ring around the tub as dark as some old throwaway tire. But return they did, all the smelly days of their growing up.

They were asocial, almost reclusive, as were their parents, and between themselves, given to fig fights or digging caves in the back lot. We thought they were probably embarrassed by the way they lived, because they had few friends. If anyone suggested, "Let's go over to your house and play Monopoly or something," they would find some excuse to say no.

"Naw. Not today. Uh—my dad's been sick and he don't like the noise."

But from anything we later learned, they both turned into nice men. The older one, Ralph, became a taxi driver, "and a damn good one," Uncle Walter would always add, licking his teeth after saying the only thing he could think of to ease the conversation along. "Ralphie," as we always thought of him, married three times, the last time to a Mexican woman with a massive pile of black hair around her pretty face.

The two of them seemed compatible, she happy to ride around town with him all day in the front seat of his cab, her bottom expanding noticeably through the years. They never had any children.

Donald, the younger child, loved baseball. His usual dress came as close to an imitation uniform as he could muster, striped knickers wrinkled from their days off under the bed. And always, the billed cap. He grew up to become a pitcher for the Baltimore Orioles, a high position of which his bent-over father was inordinately proud. Donald was a tight-jawed, disciplined personality, never very verbal, for he lisped when he spoke. All of his pent-up frustrations with life must have been hurled from the mound of whatever sandlot chance he'd ever had. Aunt Bessie said he had "the Belton determination." He never did marry.

So Uncle Walter never had grandchildren who might have inherited his artistic gift. I always hoped he passed it on to me somehow, his brother's daughter if not his own.

True Grit

A long dirt road, humped in the middle, with two parallel grooves worn down by car tires, led from the main road up to the house where Zeb lived.

"What a funny name, 'Zeb,'" I said to Mother, one day when we'd driven out to our farmhouse to get fresh milk and eggs.

"It comes from the Bible, Janie, a man named Zebediah. 'Zeb' is just his nickname. Down south, where Zeb came from, lots of people have Biblical names," Mother explained.

"Zebediah, Zebediah, pants on fiah, nose as long as a telephone wiah," we sang, loving the unfamiliarity of his name. He had a wrinkled-up little wife, whom we called "Mrs. Zeb," but we rarely saw her. Once, she came out on the porch in a faded dress cinched around the middle with a string or something. All either of us remembers was Zeb's referring to her as "the missus." When she died, Zeb lived on in the house, all by himself.

He was our hired man who took care of the "Peppard farm," a few miles outside Redfield in open country. We were renting this house and land so Dad could have enough pasture to graze his herd of purebred shorthorn cattle. We frequently drove out from town to get eggs, to check up on cattle feed, or to find a chicken for Sunday dinner, and so we knew Zeb very well. He was a whiskery character, but a lovable and dependable old man. We always loved going out to the farm, so when our parents told us we were going to move there, we were excited, imagining that Zeb would be one of the family. But he moved into the barn when he learned we were going to occupy the house, which disappointed us. He built a cozy nest for himself in the tack room where a little heater with red coils kept him warm. He washed his dish under the tap that filled the drinking trough, stored it on a wooden shelf where he also kept his comb and a small mirror with a broken corner.

He continued to stay there for a while, helping us put in a garden, feed a few hogs, milk the cows, and clean the barn. One day, he just disappeared and we never knew why or where he'd gone.

"Reckon he went back down south to be with his kinfolks," Daddy said, sounding exactly like Zeb used to.

The Peppard farm was a very different place from our house in town. The washing machine was kept on half a back porch, a lean-to built out from the kitchen. A hand pump in the corner of the kitchen, screwed into the wooden drain boards by the sink, brought water up from the cistern, the only running water in that house. There was no electricity; we relied on kerosene lamps. Our only bathroom was an outside privy, a two-holer down a packed-dirt path from the back door. Bobby and I thought this primitive life was an adventure.

All during the spring and summer of 1933, our parents talked of weather. Daily, men gathered in the yard or on the porch to exchange their deepest fears or to share their losses, and women told each other horror stories over the hand-cranked party lines, how the curtains were black with dirt, how everything they cooked was gritty from the dust. The telephone was a wooden box that hung on the wall with a crank on the right-hand side. It was our country network of news. Two little metal bells in front would ring a different code for each family on the line. For example, one long and two shorts, or two longs and three shorts, or one short and two longs signaled the family to whom the call was being made. It was sort of like Morse code. When the telephone rang, we would all go silent, just freeze while we counted the rings, then decide who was getting a message on the line. The cradle for the receiver, a miniature black megaphone one could listen to by pushing it close to one ear, hung on the left side. It was easy to pick it up and listen in on someone else's business.

Shirley, our neighbor down the road, did just that. We called her a gossip, but she was more like a town crier. She would swoop up our driveway, bearing a burden of news. Once she burst in the kitchen door to announce, "Mrs. Walen had a baby girl, poor thing, it's their fifth child and how can they afford to feed one more?" Mother forbade us to eavesdrop on someone else's conversation, so of course we did. When she was out of earshot, hanging clothes outdoors or changing the upstairs beds, we had our chance.

"You pick it up, Janie," Bob would suggest. Then he'd whisper, "Who is it?"

"Mrs. Smith. Shhh." After I'd heard something worth reporting, I would ease the receiver back in its cradle, hoping the ear on the other end would not hear our interference, and report to Bob. "She said since water was so scarce, her kids took their Saturday baths in the same water." We knew the kids. The water must have been mud after the first one.

The Peppard place was flat, parched, and desolate. Animals hovered motionless under whatever shade they could find, until the eye-burning sun went down. Certainly we, young as we were, could tell how hot it was. After a muggy hot night, our arms would stick to our sides and the sheets were damp and clammy where we had slept. The chamber pot under the bed didn't get used much because we just sweated out the water. Every morning, our bed sheets held the wet outlines of our sweaty bodies, looking just like our winter snow angels. After the first snowfall of winter, we could hardly wait to bundle up, go outside, flop down on our backs in the beautiful white world and, with windmill motions, make angel wings with our stretched-out arms. Hot summer mornings, it helped to remember how good the snow felt as we threw the sheet over the end of the bed to dry out.

Everything else was as dry as a curled-up shingle. One day, two of Daddy's best cows had broken through the fence at the end of our pasture. Resigned, he said, "They're probably still looking for water." For days and days on end, during the worst months of the drought, his prize cattle had lined up along the driveway fence and bawled and bawled, their heads low and their chins raised, mooing a most pathetic cry into the dry air. They were thirsty, their watering tank empty. We had watched Daddy sitting in a chair, looking out the window at them, the tears streaming down his cheeks. Since he never cried, we knew he was *really* sad about something. His beautiful roan-colored animals with blazes of white on their faces grew thinner and thinner by the day.

He was terribly proud of his cattle, most of them the offspring of a registered prize-winning bull, El Capitan. Mother told us he had one of the two finest herds of shorthorns in the whole state. He spent hours in his study, poring over pedigrees, recording on long sheets of paper with lines on them each cow's ancestors. On one column he wrote under "Out of" the name of the mother cow, and in the other column, under "Sire," the father's name. He gave their new calf another name, then mailed the sheet in to register the spindly-legged baby with the Iowa department of animal husbandry.

"What's a 'sire,' Daddy?" I asked him one day.

"It means 'father.'"

"And is the mother the 'out of' cow?"

"Yes. She is the 'dam.'"

"You're not s'posed to swear!"

"You're right, Janie, but it isn't swearing. It actually is related to 'dame,' only with four-legged animals, we say 'dam.' A 'dame' is usually a human, a kind of old-fashioned lady."

"Like Mother? Am I 'out of' Mother, 'sired' by you, Daddy?"

"You're getting too big for your britches, young lady, but you got it right."

We were fascinated with his recordkeeping, there at his big oak, roll-top desk under a mounted pair of steer horns. "Texas longhorns," he would say, proud of that monstrous possession. The horns spread like big wings clear across the width of the desk. It was hard to believe one animal could carry those big horns; he must have been a giant. The drawer with Dad's red-cornered ledger was always locked, which made his entries in it mysterious and somehow important. He must be a very special person, we thought, to have such very special cattle.

I would ask Zeb if Daddy was a "sire." He would tell me. He called me "Sissy gal," let me ride on top of the hay loads, skim the horse hairs out of the drinking tank, play with the barn cat's new baby kittens. He earned forty dollars a month as a hired hand and he chewed tobacco. Once, riding into town with Daddy and us kids, he spat brown juice out the window. But to his surprise, the window wasn't open and that sticky stuff splotched onto the glass like snot.

"God damn it, Zeb," Daddy blurted out, "when are you gonna give up that filthy habit!"

"Awful sorry, Doc," he said, squirming around to get a hankie out of his back overalls pocket. We got the giggles while Zeb smeared the tobacco with an equally brown handkerchief.

"Bobby," I whispered in the back seat, "Could we take his hankie home for Mother to wash?"

"You can't ask him for that; it'd hurt his feelings! Besides, it's full of old snot."

I gave up on the idea. He came from the South and maybe down there, that's the way handkerchiefs looked instead of pure white.

After lunch one day, sitting by the window, Daddy began to cry, unable to bear the low bawling of thirsty cattle. His shoulders slumped, and he blew his nose. We kept our distance, not knowing how to make him feel better. His tears made us feel sad, too. He finally said to Mother, " I'll have to go to the spring again, for water."

"You're going to have to, I think," Mother answered. "There isn't a cloud in the sky or a breath of wind. It feels like the calm before the storm, somehow; maybe before the week is out, we'll have rain."

"Will you take the sledge?" Bobby was already making plans.

"Yes. Those two hogsheads full of water are all the horses can pull at a time."

"But it doesn't last very long," I chimed in.

He looked at me, proud of my powers of observation but hating to be reminded of the terrible shortage. He knew only too well how quickly the water would be drunk. The Smiths who lived across the road had a spring about two miles away. They had allowed Dad to fill the barrels from that spring water to keep his cows alive in the desperate drought. Mr. Smith's face looked like a field plowed up by dwarves, with little rows of dirt in the wrinkles for planting peas.

Going for water was backbreaking work. Dad harnessed Doll and Pat, attached the singletree to the sledge, wheeled the two heavy hogsheads onto the rough planks of the flat bed that had a raised lip around it, and took the big, galvanized bucket from its nail by the barn door. He had made the sledge out of railroad ties for the runners and planks for the bed.

"Okay, kids, hop on. Be careful, now, to keep your feet away from the barrels. Even empty, they're heavy enough to squash your toes."

The large casks held 140 gallons of water apiece, he told us. We were very careful, loving our bare toes, dirty as they always were those days. We were excited just to be included. The big sledge reminded me of winter, when we jumped on top of each other on our red Flexible Flyer with the shiny runners in a "pig pile," making the sled go even faster down the hill.

But this was summer, and we were going to the natural spring that bubbled out of the hillside. It was cooler there, under the shady trees, like a fairy hideaway. Stuck in the ground near the spongy green circle of grass around where the spring gurgled up, a tin cup hung on the crotch of a stick, driven in beside the circle of spring water, for anyone who might want a drink. And we all did. Up close to the water, boards now slick with moss and moisture had been laid to step on, to lean down for a drink or to ladle up the clear, cool water with a bucket.

Daddy held a pailful up to each horse's mouth and they slobbered and slurped it up like we thought camels in the desert would. Then, he got the first long drink from the tin cup. Then, he handed it to me. It tasted like rusty tin, kind of like the sensitive filling in my tooth. But I loved it, so cold and fresh I splashed it over my head as well. Bobby got a turn, next, and he and I had a water fight while Daddy worked hard to fill the two barrels.

It was wonderful to play in the cold water, to get our hair and clothes soaking wet. They dried almost immediately, and the feel of hot air evaporating the moisture from our skin was delicious. We watched the water's choppy splashing in the barrels on the long trip home, and felt Daddy's relief when he scooped out the water into the cattle trough when we got back. No sooner did a pailful get dumped than the cows licked it up. He kept it up until he tipped each barrel over into the trough for the last trickle. But even with all that water, he couldn't completely slake the thirst of his parched herd.

We watched the sky for the promise of rain in times of drought, or for the end of rain in flood times. Only the wisdom of experience could be counted on. Water witches were called upon to judge the best location for digging a well, and Indians were invited to do a rain dance in hopes of alleviating severe drought. But Daddy watched the leaves on the trees for signs of wind, licked his forefinger and held it up to determine the direction or the strength of any air motion, used the size and direction of small dust devils to determine the probable drift of the wind. He was aware of how connected everything was; the drier the air, the less moisture was stored in layers down in the ground. Once the force of the wind started a field moving, soil moisture was critical. Whole acres of dry ground could be ripped away if no water anchored it.

———◆———

Months later, when he discovered his big bull was missing from the pasture, he was doubly concerned, partly for his valuable stud, and partly for what he believed was evidence of a broken fence. The faucet in the trough was still dry as a bone, so maybe the cows were just looking for adventure, I thought to myself. Dad decided that he would take his fence stretcher out, in case El Capitan had broken through the wire. It was a heavy metal tool like a big crowbar that he linked into the wire squares and snubbed the fence back up to the post. Then, with a hammer, he'd drive big fence staples into the wood, securing the wire against another break.

He told us we could all go down into the woods together when he was through, to look for our bull and drive him back through the gate. That sounded inviting. We might even see places in the cutbank where we could set our traps, once winter came. All summer long, the traps, those black hinged jaws that we would set ever so carefully with a piece of cheese or bacon to tempt the animals, hung on the side of the chicken house. Bobby and I made Christmas money by trapping animals—moles, skunks, groundhogs, squirrels, muskrats, rarely a fox—skinning them, stretching their hides on shingles we hung on the side of the chicken house to dry, then mailing them off to the Shenandoah Fur Company in Shenandoah, Iowa, way down in the corner of the state by the Missouri River.

As Dad was gathering up his tools after mending that one piece of sagging fence, we were by his side. "Can we come with you?" we pleaded. Anything to stay far away from the house and out in the world.

"Don't see why not . . . but put on your jackets, it's chilly and kind of windy out in the pasture."

Something about the flat land we had to cross to get to the pasture, furrowed in the relentless pattern of the plow, empty of any sheltering tree or an anchoring rock, threw the two of us closer together. We had not yet seen the ocean, but we felt the safety of sticking close, as if each of us were a kind of life raft for the other. The world was big and empty. The sky had no lid to it. We knew God and Jesus lived up there above the clouds, but when there weren't any clouds, they must be sleeping in *their* upstairs, very high up, or higher. Only the distant horizon stretched away, every way we looked, like a giant rubber band holding us in.

So we played in that soft dirt, digging tunnels and shaping the earth into castles and moats, oblivious of time, while Dad found the larger fence break he had predicted. Sure enough, it was down, and he set about to fix it. Pretty soon, we could go hunting for the bull who had broken through, probably hiding down by the creek.

All of a sudden, the land came to life. A few little wind whips took the dirt off the ridges of the furrows like a broom, sweeping, the fine dust blowing in our eyes. The sky grew dark so suddenly, we looked up.

"Just like Chicken-Licken, Bobby," I reminded him.

"No," he said, "this is bigger'n that, I think."

The tumbleweeds were dancing, as if they were alive, playing hopscotch and tag. It was like magic. What could be happening? Over toward the road, the sky was dark brown and yellowish, a most strange color to come on so fast. We could see a little spiral in the middle of it, and the wind picked up with such a force my bangs blew back off my forehead. Then we heard Daddy, yelling, his voice loud above the howl of the wind.

"Come on, kids, we're heading home! Quick. Get a move on!" His voice was urgent.

"What's happening, Daddy?" He didn't answer.

The light in the sky had gone out, like a burned-out wick in the lantern. Before I could move, I felt Daddy's hand grab mine and yank me to my feet. He'd already got hold of Bobby's hand, having left his fence stretcher, hammer, and little sack of staples back by the fence.

"You've gotta hurry up, now. It looks like a dust blow-up, and it's coming fast. Janie, run as fast as your legs can carry you!" We began to fly. He was breathless.

"You're hurting my arm!" Bob cried out.

"Don't talk. Run! I mean it. RUN FOR YOUR LIFE!"

I stumbled once or twice and he lifted me right off the ground until I could get my feet going again. The three of us were going into the wind, then with it, and my hair whipped around and around in a circle. We bent over, hunching our shoulders close to the ground, concentrating all of our energy trying to get back to Mother and the twins, to the house.

"Could be a twister!" Daddy yelled, his voice tight. "Hurry up, now. HURRY UP!" It frightened us. Wind lashed the grit, the pieces of cornstalk, and the whistle grass against our bodies, stinging my ankles. A deep sound like a low rumble ran beside us, spooky as a Halloween ghost. Dad was pulling us faster than we could run, and I began crying. Daddy had changed. He was hurting my armpit. His wild, dark eyes looked scared. He kept looking behind and ahead and up at the sky, like his head was on a swivel.

We doubled our efforts, got to the edge of the plowed ground, up over that fence, through the barnyard, past the barn that loomed up suddenly like a witch's castle out of nowhere, up past the cistern by our back door, then up the steps at top speed and, barely able to open the door, stumbled into the kitchen. The screen door flapped back like a crowing rooster's wing and nearly blew off into the yard before Daddy grabbed it and pulled it back in, shut it tight. But the dust had arrived before us.

"Merrill! Merrill," Mother said, "I was worried sick!" Her apron was crooked and she kept waving her arms out from her sides like a pull toy. She gave each of us a quick hug, but it didn't feel very loving. "I'm so glad you're back home, you two." Her voice was tense with terror.

Wind puffed and sucked at the glass, at the wooden edges of the windows, threatening to blow them out. Fine gritty dust blew in through all the cracks around the panes. She was rolling up every dishtowel and rag in the house, pushing them around the frames and windowsills, but tiny particles were leaking in. It was as fine as face powder, scratching our noses, our teeth, and our eyes. It blew through any tiny crack it could find, all over the floor and the counters and the dining room table like fog, only sneezing dry.

The twins had hunkered down in the corner by the stove, where Mother had told them to sit and be patient. They were hugging their dollies tight, mystified. When Daddy put his arms around Mother's waist and told her not to worry, he was there, now, and the worst of it was probably over, she settled down a bit. The little girls turned their attention to us.

Suddenly, a terrible whoosh and thud seemed to move the house. "Merrill!" Mother screamed. "How can we keep the glass from breaking out?"

"Where are the leaves to the dining room table?"

"In the wash shed."

In one load, Daddy brought four oak table leaves into the kitchen, near the windows that were bending in and out. He put two of them up against one window and told Mother to lean against them as hard as she could. The other two, he managed to wrestle into place against the glass of the other window and held them there. Bob and I were comforting MaryLou and Merilyn, feeling safer with the boarded-up windows. Both of our parents suddenly realized how their fear had translated to us.

"Anyone want to bet on how long this dirty wind is gonna keep blowing?" Dad asked.

"One hour?" Bobby guessed.

"I'll bet it's gonna stop before that," I said, though I had no inkling of how to predict anything. Wild guesses sometimes were right.

We got out the soda crackers and gave some to the twins. I wanted an apple, and so did Bobby. Mother and Daddy, of course, had no hands free for anything but the boards at the windows. I thought of the story Mother had read us from *My Book House*, of the little boy in Holland who plugged up a hole in the dike with his hand, to keep the sea from flooding the land. We thought our parents were very brave, protecting us.

They leaned into the boards against the windows and kept talking between themselves.

"Did you see that picture in the *Tribune*, Zee, those huge cracks in the earth?"

"You mean in Oklahoma?"

"Texas, too, and Kansas I believe. Nebraska, no doubt. Feels like the earth is drying up. God-awful loss of livestock, too."

"How long has it been since we've had a drop of rain?"

"Years, really. A real rain. I didn't think a drought could keep getting drier and drier. . . . This wind is fierce. From the plowed land, the open prairie, nothing can grow. . . . The topsoil just blows."

"I don't know how much longer I can stand the heat, Merrill. It's been over a hundred every day this week, and with all the windows down now, it is suffocating in here! It can't be good for the kids, either. My throat is so dry. And my face and hands are shriveled up like parchment."

"It's got to break before long," he said, wanting to believe it. Then, after a pause, " You should have seen that dust wall loom up over the horizon out there! It just seemed to climb up the hot sky toward the sun, yellow at first and then kinda orange-ish and brown. . . . I looked over my shoulder as we were high-tailing it for home and the whole sky was black, clouding out the sun. It was the damnedest thing, Zee; I confess, by God, I was terrified."

"You wouldn't think a dust roller could travel that fast, from so far away, would you?"

"Air currents are like the ocean. They affect the whole world. Look at the fallout from volcanic eruptions that drift over whole continents." He paused, shifted his weight from the right shoulder to the left. "Did you hear about that farm, in Kansas I believe it was, where the dirt buried a shed so deep you could walk right over it and never know anything was underneath!"

Mother shifted her body weight too, tired and only slightly interested in the facts and figures Daddy was quoting. "I think this one has deposited several tons in our house, already! The days have been so hot I'm just done in by noon. But today takes the cake!"

"I know it," he said, sympathetic.

Interrupting their nervous talk, a loud slam of flying earth would lash against the house, dump on the roof, then go still. Out across the barn yard we could hear the flapping of what we guessed was the chicken house tarpaper tearing off. Worse yet, maybe it was the barn roof. The filthy air must have been swirling around like a giant eggbeater in the sky, whipping the world.

"Do you think we'll get the chinch bugs back? Or grasshoppers?" Mother worried about all kinds of vermin, but the chinch bugs ate up the cornstalks, and the grasshopper plague chewed everything in sight, all the grain, all the cornstalks, the leaves off the trees, and even the paint and wood off houses.

Bobby turned to the three of us and grinned. "Grasshoppers even eat the hair off little girls."

MaryLou, whose head of hair Dad had shaved off to keep her from pulling it out to suck her thumb, knew what it would be like to want a piece of hair and not to have any. But Merilyn began to cry. She was easy to scare, because she believed everything Bobby said. I knew him well enough to realize he was kidding, but I didn't want to be bald any more than Merilyn did, so I got mad.

"Shut up, Bobby. You're a LIAR!" I yelled.

"Listen, children, calm down. There is enough anger in the wind out here to do us all. Bobby, cut it out now, do you hear me?"

After a long, long time, the howl of the wind softened. Bobby and I cuddled together with the twins, all four of us getting sleepy.

"By God," Daddy said, "Listen. I think it's letting up. We can't see the sun, yet, there's so much dust in the air, but I think the wind is dying down."

"Has it blown itself out?" Mother wondered. Her arms must have been aching from holding up those heavy table leaves for so long.

"Be patient. We'll have to wait and see. It's a devil. Could start up again, who knows."

But it didn't. Time passed. And so did the dust storm. When the wind finally died down to an intermittent whoosh, our parents took the boards down from the glass, which had not broken out after all. We looked around us at the dirt in the house. Gritty. Everywhere fine dust you could write your name in had settled. Mother began to cry, from relief and from despair. She took a jug of cold water out of the icebox and poured each one of us a glass of thirst-quenching water when the ordeal was over. Water, a godsend in this dry land. It would be weeks before we rid the house of dirt.

The next day began the clean-up. All of us were given chores. My job was to shake outside the rags used for dusting, rinse them in a pail of water, wring them out, replace the pole that propped up the clothesline, and pin the rags on the line. They dried almost as fast as I could pin them up. Bobby worked with Daddy outside, trying to right things that had blown askew.

Even a flat, plowed-up piece of land can be a playground. Across the field near our house we watched the tumbleweeds playing tag, giant balls of prickly spines like rough straw the wind loved to drive into the fences. And big old El Capitan came wandering up from the ravine to stand beside the barn as if nothing had happened.

The rain held off for a long, long time. We found ways to amuse ourselves. We were allowed to chase the tumbleweeds, and it became a contest, as most things we did together did, just to see who could catch the biggest one, or the most. It was a dangerous game, too, because, although they look as friendly as huge balloons, tumbleweeds are dead, dry branches full of brittle thorns. In the autumn, the wind will blow the round weeds off their stems, and set them dancing across the world. If we tripped in a furrow or lunged to grab one, greedy to win, we could get badly scratched.

We devised a way of corralling our catches. From the tack room in the barn, we borrowed the lariats that hung on big nails, and we wove them through the lowest branches of the tumbleweeds, keeping away from the prickly centers. Bobby got the longer lariat on the assumption that he would be the more successful. But I knew he wasn't as quick as I was, and I planned to win, anyway. Unless the entire hobbled catch rolled together, they would stay more or less captured, bound together by the long ropes.

"No fair!" Bob would shout, always the arbiter of rules. "You can't lasso more than one at a time."

"Why not?"

"Well, it's against the rules."

"Who says?"

"I do. If you want to play this game, you have to obey the rules."

"So do you, then."

"I haven't tried to grab more than one at a time."

"No, but you get the biggest ones."

"Who said there was a rule against big ones?"

"No one."

"Well then, shut up, Janie." So I did, running to catch a little bouncy weed ball that was quicker than I was, and it got away.

To keep track of which were whose, we began to name our tumbleweeds the way Daddy named his animals. Our horses, Doll and Pat, were real workhorses with feathers on their feet. Daddy said that was because they were part Percheron, big draft horses that could pull the plow or the wagon or the harrow, and that the long hairs on their feet protected their hooves. So it made sense to name our tumbleweeds. I named the littlest one in my corral "Baby." Bobby named his biggest one "El Capitan," after Daddy's shorthorn bull.

Another pastime in the fallow fields was chasing dust devils. Made of wind, they always got away from us, but we really did dance with them. We couldn't predict when they would start to twirl; it only happened once in a while. But if either of us saw one begin to circle, even a long way from where we were, we ran toward it. If they started up in our big vegetable garden, they weren't worth chasing because there wasn't enough space to try to dodge them.

A dust devil is a tiny tornado, a little whirlwind made of dust from the field the wind travels across. Its inverted cone extends up from the ground like a funnel, sometimes hundreds of feet into the air. At its base, like the lead in a pencil, it writes across the landscape like when you scribble from trying to write too fast. The trails of a tiny wind funnel look like the slimy trails of earthworms, only they are dry as sand. The ones we tried to twirl with were the tiny ones, because they picked up speed the faster they ran, and we knew our limits.

The little ones are as wiggly as a loose-jointed tap dancer, and we loved to imitate their shimmy and shake. I laughed at Bobby's dance interpretation, and did my own. Our hips gyrated, our arms waved upward and our toes pointed down like ballet dancers. Of course, we could never catch them, whirling along the ground at dizzying speed, but we never gave up pretending. Often, we'd fall to the ground in our great dancing frenzy, only to roll over and watch the little devil disappear in a gritty cloud of dust.

"Where on earth have you been?" Mother would ask when we came in, because our clothes would be streaked with dirt. "Dancing with dust devils, did you say? Well, now you've each turned into one! Strip down on the back porch and shake that dust out of your clothes. The state they're in, if I put 'em in the wash, the water'd turn to mud!"

———◆———

Our farm endured not only drought and wind erosion, but also the devastating curses of hailstorms, blizzards, plagues of rabbits, grasshoppers, locusts, and spiders. Several times we were warned about black widows because children had been known to die from their poisonous bites. It is as if the terror of those times rolled down and out like marbles in a slot machine, bringing with them every trial imaginable. In the very center of Redfield, once, Daddy showed us a car with its roof dented in like chicken-pox marks, the aftermath of hail as big as cue balls beating down on it.

Adults of our acquaintance talked of little else but weather, of seeds blown out of the ground, soil from plowed fields drifting widely, corn on the brink of tasseling withering and breaking from lack of water, chinch bugs. or searing winds. The telephone conversations were reports of dire events, of animals dying, of a family deserting their farm, of deep gashes of wind erosion. Suicides were common.

Dust from Texas, Oklahoma, Nebraska, and Kansas blew brown film over everything where we lived. Huge shoulders of wind shifted tons of restless dirt, ranging from a gray haze to billowing clouds of suspended pulverized earth, denuding some places, burying others. The area of the "Dust Bowl" reached into Iowa, but the residue of dirt reached across the nation.

Mother's friend Hilda was flabbergasted by what she called the "ruination" of our lives. She called on the telephone with every new bit of information to support her prediction of doom. Even though we could not visualize the power of the wind or the amount of dirt it carried along, or imagine the places everyone talked about, we were

Mother's "little ears." She turned to us after she hung up the telephone from talking with Hilda, incredulous herself.

"Do you know what Hilda told me?"

"What?"

"That the dust storms that start right here turn the snow in New England, thousands of miles back east, brown. Can you believe it?"

"No," we answered in unison, not knowing how we were supposed to know.

Mother told Daddy that night at suppertime, "Merrill, Hilda told me the papers reported that the biggest storm discolored snow in New England! Twenty-five tons of dust per square mile were deposited. Is that possible? She said there have been several deaths from dust pneumonia."

"I can believe it," he said, "The *Des Moines Register-Tribune*, even *Wallace's Farmer* are gathering up pretty scary statistics. Damned tough on everybody, isn't it?"

All Bob and I knew was that our teeth were always gritty. If you ground your molars, it would feel like sandpaper. We practiced spitting a lot, cutting off the spit with our front teeth. Even though Mother said spitting was crude, I got pretty good at it, but Bobby could always spit further than I could. He was the one who taught me to saw the spit between my top front teeth and my tongue like a bread knife. That, he said, would cut it off for a clean spit. And he was right. It did.

Bullet Holes and Bloody Rags

I cannot swear that the gunshots we heard in the distance that afternoon were actually from rifles. But the posse that eventually captured Bonnie and Clyde was riding that day, and the final hideout of the Barrows gang was Dexfield Park, an old amusement park halfway between Dexter and Redfield. It was no more than a mile from the pasture where our father was digging postholes in July 1933.

My brother and I heard the sharp retorts of what we thought at first were hunters. But it wasn't hunting season. Our father stood up abruptly from hunching over his clamshell digger, turned his head this way and that and said, "I'll bet they've got 'em cornered, now!" What he referred to, or why the sound of bullets in that summer heat, we had no way of knowing.

Like a mirage in the desert, that episode looms large and wavery on our early horizon. Before television, everyday events, overheard stories, or favorite books fed the springs of our thirst for drama. Horror stories shivered us to goose bumps. Safe on the couch with a book, not far from protective parents, we knew such terrible things could not happen to us. But the impact of the Barrows tragedy on our young minds—Bob was nine, I was seven—was profound.

Innocents find such violence delicious, a sort of primitive release, narrow escapes, an unconscious "there but for the grace of God go I."

We reveled in Hansel and Gretel stuffing the old witch in the oven to singe and scorch and scream. Although we sided with the Gingerbread Man being chased by a farmer with a pitchfork, we secretly hoped he could not run fast enough to escape a stab in the back. When the Wicked Queen gave Snow White a poisoned apple, we devised sadistic ways to get even with her. In our garage cave, we concocted a deadly recipe of quicklime and lemon juice on ground-up acorns which she would mistake for nutty candy and die, writhing.

So, as the events that followed those overheard gunshots unfolded, we built extravagant theories, based not on facts but on the lack of them. As we learned fragments of the truth from our vigilant eavesdropping, we exchanged, sometimes incorporated, diabolical plots of intrigue, of sinful sexual adventures, walking around naked for everyone to see you without any clothes on, or with silk pajamas and filmy nightgowns on blood-saturated mattresses, of concealed weapons and the depraved dividing of wads of green bills at gunpoint. There were always shadows, and trees to hide behind. Evil beyond the dreams of God-fearing humans was stalking the very land we lived on, the Devil on the loose. We perfected a duet of the posse's hoofbeats, too, clapping our hands together and then on our thighs, over and over, faster and faster, riding, riding to the "Pow! Pow!" of guns.

Real or embellished, the saga of Bonnie and Clyde brought us the most delicious horror we had ever dreamed of, spookier than the Gustav Doré illustrations in Victor Hugo's *Toilers of the Sea*, where a man being strangled by a hideous octopus in an undersea cave struggled for release, and more shivery than the episodes of *The Shadow* that we listened to once a week, sitting on the floor in front of our old Atwater Kent radio, our ears glued to the speaker, breathless with suspense to hear what it was the Shadow knew that we didn't. Mother reassured us, always, that it was "just made up."

The drama of Clyde Barrow and Bonnie Parker, however, was not made up. Their trail of cold murder and petty robbery that blazed across backroads America came to an end almost in our back yard, a coincidence which brightened the drab dailiness of life in Redfield. The individual characters of Bonnie and Clyde, the rest of their ragtag gang, the bullet holes that frayed the bark of trees in Dexfield Park, the blood-soaked residue of their campsite, the captured car, these were in our real lives, raw and wicked and tainted with evil.

Small towns in the rural Midwest, then, were little more than brick and wooden villages fairly close to one another. News traveled by word of mouth through Van Meter, Redfield, Adel, and Dexter, where the candy factory flourished. All of these small prairie towns fell within a radius of about thirty miles from Des Moines, smack in the middle of the state, and from Des Moines it was a straight shot along Highway 80 into Chicago, capital of gansterdom in the decades between the two world wars.

The day we heard the shots, Mother had convinced Dad to take us with him because Mrs. Vath was coming out to help her with the washing and we would just get underfoot. But we were torn. We loved being with Mrs. Vath and her funny accent.

She was a Norwegian immigrant chore woman, as it was called then, a colorful character in our drab landscape. Her accent was foreign and funny to our ears. We chattered away at her, and she would answer. In the privacy of our bedroom up in the quilt-covered attic with splintery floors and unfinished rafters, after she'd been in our house, we would imitate her accent, making up stories about having our boat sinking in the icy water of the fjords in which huge icebergs floated.

"Ahoy zere, Matey!" the captain would shout over the wind. "Keep baling ze vasser or ve go oonder."

"It ees comink in faster zan goink out!" I would respond, flailing my arms in an imitation of desperate baling. I'd finally collapse on the bed in laughter, tired from the usual role of Bob's subordinate. Never was there a question about who played captain. We sometimes imagined being blinded by a swirling snowstorm, or freezing to death in a snowdrift twice as deep as we were tall, all to the best we could, mimicking a Norwegian accent. To us, Norway was solid ice and snow. Our best performances entailed the rescue, where one of us would throw a blanket from our bed over the other one, twitching in the throes of death, and breathe into the drowning victim's mouth. It always ended in our laughing ourselves sick with exaggeration.

Mrs. Vath had a son, Isador, about whom she spoke all the time, calling him "Eesadoor," and she got her V's and W's all mixed up—"Vee alvays try very hard." We imagined Isador hanging onto the doorjamb as his mother tugged at him to bring him to America, and we'd argue vociferously about which of us got to play Isador. Mrs. Vath primed our imaginations. We knew little of geography, but she helped us find Norwegian stamps in the packets Mother brought us to sort through, saying "Ja, ja!" and nodding her head. Thick gray braids hung down her back, tied together at the ends like a swing, and her dresses came clear down to the tops of little black boots. We hated to miss her and we hated to miss watching her do laundry.

Our laundry process was a complicated mixture of soaking white things in a lye bath on the back of our wood stove the night before washday. A gas-powered tub jounced the clothes around and then, through the hand wringer attached, they fell into a tub of rinse water. Mrs. Vath, whose arms were as big as legs, would yank a sheet up out of that water and wring it around her arms like a snake. Bob and I thought it would make a terrific circus act, maybe with a real python.

But we went with Daddy. While he dug postholes, we could spend the summer day however we wanted, as long as we didn't get in his way.

"Can we go to the park since we'll be close?" Bob asked. Once a thriving amusement park, Dexfield Park had had a swimming pool, a pavilion, and a merry-go-round, a setting we imagined full of bathing beauties and handsome cars, men with moustaches and happy kids eating cotton candy or winning big toys in the shooting galleries. It had been closed for some time. Still, it drew us.

"Don't think we'll have time today."

"Please. If we be good until you get that hole dug, can't we go?"

"Not today. Not enough time between now and dark."

"How long will you be digging, Daddy?"

"I said NOT TODAY." He was all sweaty and tired. Then he softened, a kind of kid himself much of the time, and added, "But we'll go by the next time we're this close, I promise."

As fate would have it, the timing was perfect, for between the rifle shots we heard shortly after that exchange and our next visit to Dexfield Park, empty cartridges had fallen among the leaves, bullet holes pock-marked trees they had used for target practice, and rags, saturated with blood, were thrown across a downed log.

◆

The Feller farm in the small town of Van Meter played a sinister role in the escapades of Bonnie and Clyde, too, a fact that our mother and father dwelt on. Our parents knew the Fellers, and Daddy had taken a detour on one of our Sunday drives to show us the barn against which little Bobby Feller, as he was locally referred to, practiced pitching. The typical gray-board barn, peaked above the haymow door but windowless on the opposite end, rose at the edge of the cornfield. We walked back through the plowed furrows about as far as a pitcher usually stands from the plate, "just to get the feel of it," as Daddy said. There, on the barn, was a huge circle with a bull's eye in the middle. And that was the training ground for a farm boy who rose to pitch for the Cleveland Indians, rivaling the fame of Satchel Paige by putting out one batter after another. We imagined ourselves in his shoes, imitating what we thought a pitcher would do, winding up and heaving clods at that circle.

Because we had been there, we could picture what we overheard of the dramatic escape, imagining exactly where the gangsters had crouched around the edge of the barn, tousled and limping. The shots we heard that infamous afternoon had rousted them from Dexfield Park, but two of the gang escaped. Clyde with a bullet through his cheekbone which bled profusely, and Bonnie in her ankle-length nightgown drenched with dew and stained with her lover's blood, made their way under the cover of darkness to Van Meter. Early in the morning, they crawled out of a cornfield on the Feller farm and stole the family automobile at gunpoint. In it, they made their getaway. The car was later found wrecked in Polk City, Iowa, and Bonnie and Clyde died in a heavy volley of bullets a few months later. He was twenty-four; she was twenty-three.

Where they died, or where they were buried, if they were buried, we never learned, but we imagined and then dramatized them croaking out their last words to each other as life leaked from their wicked bodies. We even enacted the final hours of their lives. With vivid recall, we recited all the banks we had robbed with a death-defying "Stick 'em up!" and all the people we had killed. This one clutched his belly and pitched forward, dead as a doornail, we tied that one to the car bumper and dragged him over stones, or that one who threw out his arms, staggered into a river, riddled with bullets, and drowned. No limits of violence were beyond our reach.

About Dexfield Park, Dad kept his word. After the posse had ambushed the five-member Barrow gang, capturing all but two, sightseers poured into the area around there to dig bullets out of the trees, to collect other souvenirs from the scene. We were among them. We scuffled through the leaves at the fringes of the abandoned amusement park, and I found one fired bullet casing, to my immense delight. Bob, however, found the most wonderful piece of evidence, a torn bit of rag brownish on the edge obviously with dried blood. We speculated about what garment the rag had been torn from, how long it had been a poultice for that bullet-ravaged face. Having considered a torn-off shirt tail, a petticoat, or an old dishtowel, we finally agreed it was probably a piece of Bonnie's underwear. I have no idea, now, whatever happened to these, our best souvenirs, but for years they shared space in a cigar box full of treasures, along with petrified rocks and the docked tail of our pet black lamb.

The memory of that violent escapade remains vividly etched. Bonnie and Clyde were our heroes for years. We could be like them. But we would be smarter and not get caught.

Bursting in Air

Our ancestors had few choices. They were up against it, virtually alone in the world. Those bleak years focused on survival. Forced to make do, they were doers—quilters, rug-makers, sock-darners, bakers, gardeners, canners, and cooks. Wagon-building, wood-cutting, horse-breaking, cattle-milking, tail-docking, sheep-shearing, posthole-digging, fence-building, earth-turning doers. It was survival on the vast flat pan of Midwestern prairie life, until mechanization began to ease their load. No wonder they made virtue of necessity. How else could it have been borne? Now, in an easier time, such dogged labor is often reviled as the Puritan work ethic. And, by God, it was a work ethic, a necessity for survival in the years of drought, dust storms, and Depression.

Mother's solo feats of endurance, alone except for Mrs. Vath, who came out from town to help her with the weekly washing, unassisted by running water or electricity, were heroic. Buckets of water, hefted from the well and heated in copper boilers on the stove, were dipped into to boil potatoes, wash our hair, soak laundry for washday. Bobby and I were her "little helpers," as she called us, and we worked alongside her, especially with raising the twins. "Take the little girls for a walk with their dollies," she would suggest, or, "Will you read the twins a story, now?" She was a home economist, squeezed mercilessly beyond her college training, which never included the exigencies of poverty, water shortages, searing winds and dust, or bank foreclosures.

Pushed to the limits of enforced frugality, proud and resourceful, she devised ways to augment the meager cash flow with her culinary skill. With Bobby and me as her delivery team, she started a weekly cottage-cheese route for neighbors or townspeople who would pay for the delicious quality product from Xela's kitchen.

"Will you kids take the cottage cheese up to the door and collect the money?"

"Yes, yes."

"You carry the cottage cheese, and I'll collect the money," Bobby volunteered.

"Maybe we could take turns."

"You must always be polite when you talk to them, you know. They are paying us for something we make and you must be honest," Mother admonished. She, herself, could never dream of doing the delivery, for she was slightly embarrassed by our need. Shy by nature, she preferred to remain invisible. We, on the other hand, relished the prospect of another adventure.

Production began. The whole milk was left to sour in enamel basins on the porch. When it was curdled, it was ready for transformation. Then, from muslin dishtowels made of old flour sacks, tied up at the four corners and hung from the cupboard handles over a catch basin, the curds dripped whey until they were dry. As the liquid drained, the makeshift cloth sack would sag like an old cow's udder, the curd inside ready to be made into cottage cheese. Mother would pat and gently squeeze the bottom for any last moisture left, then she'd take down the heavy towel, open one corner and turn the gelatinous mass into a large bowl. Breaking up the curds into edible crumbles was my job. I could use my hands if they were clean. That squishy sensation was the Play-Doh of Iowa farm life, circa 1934. I was almost nine and felt indispensable to the process.

Into the broken-up curds, then, Mother poured rich cream and a little bit of sugar, stirring it up for ladling into cartons she bought from the butcher, waxed cardboard containers she lined up on a sheet-cake pan for transporting, eight at a time. They fit onto the front seat of the car Dad drove into town. From Mother's list, we told Daddy where to go, and we took one carton to each lady's front door, collected the money and put it in the envelope Mother had marked "Collections." She charged twenty-five cents apiece, and sometimes we were given pennies and nickels, which we re-counted with great care back in the car. We felt proud to be a part of the business.

With a taste of entrepreneurial success, Mother enlarged her clientele to include bread customers. The dough, covered with a damp dishtowel, would rise in large crockery bowls set on top of the warming oven. Punched down and patted like little footballs to fit into each of the eight bread pans, the yeast would rise again. After the second rising, the mouth-watering smell of baking bread would fill the house. Bobby had to make sure there was always wood in the wood box to keep the stove hot enough. Once baked, the mounds of golden crusts cooled on wooden planks Daddy made for that purpose. Usually, on bread delivery days, she made a second batch of eight, and that row of sixteen finished loaves was a work of art. We made her promise to save some for our peanut butter sandwiches. She always did.

When they were barely cool, we would go on our "bread run," collecting twenty-five cents a loaf. Maybe more, maybe less. They were never wrapped. Once, Mrs. Diddy gave each of us an extra dollar, which we gave to Mother for her hard work, only because Daddy said he thought that was fair. But her sense of fairness gave each of us a nickel of our own. Mother entered orders and deliveries on her customer cards, with a column for the date and another one for the amount of money. Poring over her primitive bookkeeping records with a sense of accomplishment, she would report the total to all of us, dealing only with the gross income, ignoring the cost of ingredients or gas or labor.

"Merrill, we made three dollars on the cottage cheese this week, and four dollars on bread, isn't that wonderful?"

"You put the Little Red Hen to shame, Zee! Good work. Did the children keep it straight?"

"Oh, yes. They are born little bankers and do a wonderful job," for which praise we glowed with pride.

In the bleakest days of winter, she peddled whole chickens, cleaned and frozen solid from hanging by their feet in an upstairs bedroom window. In our spare room, she would close the door and leave the carcasses to freeze through below-zero weather. For each of these, she collected seventy-five cents, but the demand exceeded the supply and the drive into town was treacherous on the icy hill. So, that enterprise soon ended.

Beyond the contribution to her stringent budget, there was pleasure in her work, too. She loved the praise from every one of her customers, loved Daddy's pride in her augmenting the family coffers, and felt proudly maternal in teaching us to "do business" honestly and accurately. Her resourcefulness was much lauded at our annual Fourth of July picnic at the Kellehers' with its groaning feast and kid roundup. We had four children, Auntie Bing had four, and the Kellehers had six or eight, and we waited for this reunion all year long.

◆

Helen Kelleher was the third of a triumvirate of sorority sisters who had shared their years at Iowa State. When they were all together, at one point they would sing out an old Pi Phi toast, "Ring ching-ching, ring ching-ching, Pi Beta Phi," and begin a litany of mutual memories. All three had majored in home economics, so the July Fourth picnic was something like a bake-off, each one contributing one of her specialties. As they married and had children, they were like the three legs of a milking stool for each other, the life-saving support women need to survive. No women's groups or hotlines existed, so they used the telephone as a lifeline among them, never losing the closeness of their college friendship. They shared stories of the children's antics, exchanged recipes, divulged plans, and confessed intimacies to which another ear could lend perspective. The gathering at the Kellehers' large farmhouse in Winterset this mid-summer holiday became a tradition.

On the spacious cement front porch, the men took turns with the last and hardest cranking of the handle that turned the ice cream. In the huge wooden keg, packed with chipped ice and rock salt, the shiny steel cylinder held wooden paddles that connected to a gear on top. The crank had a wooden handle on the outside that was turned by hand, but the curved metal on top, the apparatus that ran the gear, was solid. Sometimes little droplets of cold formed there. The trick was not to stop, to turn until the pure cream, ripe fruit, and liquid sugar was smooth, frozen solid. The lid had to fit tightly for fear that, as the surrounding salted ice began to melt, salt might seep in. When the mixture began to congeal, the gears on top would stiffen, requiring more and more muscle power. When the men began to spell each other off at the crank, the ice cream was nearly ready.

"It's your turn, Doc. You'll probably gobble down most of this if we don't keep an eye on you!" Uncle Keith would tease.

"Damn clever way to be sure you get your share, Brownie," he'd retort.

"The way I'm sweating, I'll need it. How hot is it, anyway?"

"Pushing a hundred, I'd guess," Mr. Kelleher would volunteer.

They kept the paddles turning until they could no longer budge the cylinder. The water-stained oaken bucket, into which the full cylinder was inserted, lived in the basement of our house most of the year. But the Fourth of July brought it out, for the ritual of homemade ice cream was as predictable as the talk of temperature in Iowa's high summer. Through the oaken slats banded by strong wires seeped the melt of the ice as the rich mixture inside blended and solidified. Pure ambrosia, this delicious concoction, made the more heavenly I think for the amount of work it took to produce it, never mind the hidden labor of raising the cows, milking them, separating the cream, tending the orchard or the vines, picking the choicest fruit, peeling, slicing—peach or raspberry, our usual favorites—then cooking it with sugar until it was ready to blend into the unforgettable treat of summer.

"I scream, you scream, we all scream for ice cream!" we sang, all the kids trying to out-shout one another, running around in the Kellehers' apple orchard after supper. We had been told to go outside and play, to run off our dinner so there would be room for ice cream. And there always was. It was a time when we were free to let off steam, to be wild and silly without the interference of adults. They were too busy enjoying each other to notice.

Served in glass bowls, the ice cream dishes reserved for this occasion, the heavenly dessert was accompanied by a slice of the big layer cake either Auntie Bing or Aunt Helen or Mother had baked —black walnut, applesauce, or chocolate, if my mouth has an accurate memory. After chicken, mashed potatoes and gravy, fresh and cooked vegetables of several varieties, homemade rolls with butter and jam, tomato aspic and dishes of olives and pickles, a Jell-O salad with little marshmallows in it, that we could eat such a lavish dessert is phenomenal.

Ice cream was not the only thing we waited for. It had to get dark before the fireworks could begin. So, the Kelleher kids enlisted our service in a hideous chore. Aunt Helen and her husband had a huge and productive farm with cattle and grain and a big chicken house, one end of which was for storing sacks of grain. A sea of rats lived there, too, and we'd turn the beam of a flashlight on them to see them scurry away. One of the older boys had a shovel, and he would hit one to kill it, if he could. I hated it. I kept jumping up and down to avoid the rats, and pretty soon, all the girls left the boys to reduce the rat population. We went inside, ostensibly to help our mothers clean up the mountain of dishes. More than likely, we just got in the way and eavesdropped on their conversation.

We were all rationed a few innocuous sparklers at twilight, but not until the first star appeared could we come sit on the porch steps that led down onto the sloping lawn, like ringside seats at the Colosseum I'd seen in Uncle Dave's stereopticon. At the bottom of the cement steps, the men, gleeful as boys and as important to the show as gladiators had ever been, readied the launching structure for the skyrockets. Those were the big explosives we all waited for "as soon as it got dark enough." I remember squatting with Bobby in delicious anticipation on a top front step, our backs against a stone porch pillar, looking out across the vast expanse of their sloping front yard to the even vaster sky, darkening enough to see the first stars twinkling.

Red cardboard tubes were arranged in order of presentation on the bottom step. The matches in their oblong box were stashed on top of the stone baluster, for safety's sake. A launching pad, looking like a miniature of the steps leading up to the human cannonball in the circus, had been constructed. We all waited, hushed. And then, the "ooh" and "aah" of the first Roman candle sent into space! The sparkle in the sky was like a gigantic flower bursting its petals! The other big explosives had names they would call out, fondly, comparing the performance of each skyrocket to the year before, or relating where a new one had been found. This was, after all, a once-a-year production, as close as these former soldiers ever came to firearms in the peaceful years between the wars. They would hop about, buckets of sand propped up on bricks below the bottom step, and boxes of matches ready, lay the long explosive rockets in the V of the wooden trough, and talk in clipped tones, "Stand back, now, when the fuse catches," or, "Did you attach the garden hose, Doc?"

Savoring what remained of our bowls of ice cream, the soggy crumbs of the cake mixed with the melting creamy soup, we were silent with excitement. Such danger. Such daring. Such bombs bursting in air, just like the national anthem said. Everyone was assembled, murmuring. The sky opened its wide arms to welcome the burst of man-made stars, all too wondrous to believe. We were dizzy with patriotism if not from overeating, proud of our brave fathers, tired from running in the orchard and prancing about writing our names in air with sparklers.

"There's a comet!" Skippy Merrill yelled, pointing. From among the bed of stars, one had fallen, a "shooting star" we thought meant good luck. We all craned our necks to see it, but it was too fast for us. More stars began to pop out as the last of the birds' night songs could be heard and the apricot light of a summer dusk faded in the sky beyond the river. The tasseling corn turned tawny and the mice in the haymow slept. Only the barn owl stayed awake, his flat eyes watching. We were hard-pressed to stay awake ourselves until it ended. Stuffed with dinner and ice cream and cake, happy as children in the company of other children can be, we piled into our makeshift beds in the big attic and fell asleep. No one even said prayers out loud. We were too tired or too embarrassed or too full, happy in the belief of eternal Fourth of July reunions.

Help With the Harvest

We were thrilled when we had been sprung free into the world of adult chores, especially to be thought responsible enough for the prestigious job of carrying water to the harvesters. Every task, from shaking the rugs, feeding the dog, or scrubbing the bathroom, to making the school lunches or sweeping the porch, was reassigned every Friday night. The schedules were works of art, stuck up on the kitchen door that led to the back porch next to the dog's dish and to the washtubs where our scrub bucket could be filled. The porch was a place that needed sweeping way oftener than either of us could believe. But these jobs were the province of children. We were outgrowing them. Or, more precisely, we could get them done in half the time it used to take, especially with the promise of a better opportunity. Mother's rule for us was that we could go outside to play, or could read on the screen-porch swing, if and only if our chores were done. That seemed fair.

Our parents believed in teaching us individual responsibility. In a family of two, then four, and ultimately six children, this rotation of jobs was an attempt at fairness, a lesson in taking turns, sharing the workload. Dad, who had served a stint in the cavalry during World War I, talked a lot about military discipline and teamwork. Unlike the military stereotype, though, he was given to praise for good work of any kind. He harped about finishing anything we started, and set an example himself. He was a meticulous fixer—of broken wagons, of splinters, of animals' broken legs, of loose teeth.

Mother made up our complex chore grids and stuck the Dennison gold stars on when we'd passed inspection. She hoped to establish some equity among us by seeing that each of us in turn was allowed to experience the delight or the drudgery of a necessary job. She certainly needed the help. Our willingness to do our tasks was partly our knowing how hard she worked, especially cooking for the harvest crew. Way into the night, she lined four pie tins with pie dough she rolled out with her big wooden rolling pin, cut the fruit into it, wove thin strips of dough across the top in a pattern like our paper placemats, and baked it in the wood stove for eating the next day, taking advantage of the cooler evening hours.

If our record of performance had been consistently exemplary, we might be given a reward—the extra piece of bacon for breakfast, a chance to stay up later, or a trip to the IGA store with Dad to buy groceries. However, after seeing a gigantic, gruesome-looking black tarantula on a hand of bananas displayed in their store window, the thrill of going into the grocery store was slightly diminished. Dad had taken us to see it; he said it was a rare opportunity to see something we might never see again. It was hairy and hideous and huge. I backed away from the store window, terrified that he might somehow get out and get on me. Bobby reassured me that would be impossible, and he leaned his nose up close to get a closer look and to prove he wasn't afraid. Dad said such creatures did not live in Iowa, that this one was in a shipment of bananas that had come "all the way from South America." We were somewhat mollified, but loath to go shopping in the IGA store after that. A "hand" of bananas was a new concept for me, though, and I always thought of bananas after that as the fingers of giants. And the scary tarantula was a giant spider that a yellow giant had scooped out of a tree.

Prize beyond hoping for, if we had been especially helpful, or gone beyond what was expected of us, was an overnight in Des Moines with Grandmother Chantry. She would take us with her to the big-city school where she taught mathematics to fifth graders, a world of wonder for country-school kids where eight grades were lumped under one roof. She was inordinately proud of my capacity to spell, and arranged a spelling bee for her class that day. They lined up in two contesting rows along the walls, each captain choosing a student in his turn. Grandma had introduced me to the class, telling them that although I was younger than they, I would be a good competitor. So, when the captain of one side chose me for that team, I was flushed with resolve to do my Gango proud. Well, the inevitable happened. She gave me a word I could not spell, and much to the chagrin of both of us, I sat down.

As Bob and I grew older, we were bored and resisted doing the wimpy chores we'd begun to suspect were mostly make-work to keep us busy. We felt the twins should be trained "to the traces," as Dad said of his pair of workhorses. Mother appealed to Dad to find ways for us to help *him*, instead. And so, in the summer before Bob turned nine and I seven, we were assigned the job of water-boys. Water-boys had the supreme obligation of keeping the harvest crew from dying of thirst as they labored under the weight of August heat and dust, using the lumbering farm machinery of the 1920s and '30s to cut the oats or bag the wheat, from whichever field was ripe and ready.

Dad had spliced a rope around the narrow necks of two one-gallon glass jugs. They were then wrapped, both for protection and insulation, in several layers of burlap sacking affixed to the bottles with wire, making them fat as ripe watermelons. Huge hooks hung from the lip of the cistern and, attached to each hook, Bobby hung a jug, which dropped into the water and filled. The removed corks were put on top of the wooden cistern cover, and one of the terrors of the job lay in the possibility of dropping a cork into the deep well. The jugs stayed immersed, cooling until they were drawn up and carried to wherever the cloud of dust told us the big McCormack-Deering harvester was operating. Twice a day, once in mid-morning and once in mid-afternoon, we pulled the water jugs up, slung them across the neck of our horse, climbed onto its back from the back doorstep and rode off on our mission of mercy.

We kept the job of water-boy for days on end, because the men around the dining room table said we were so good at it. They were effusive with praise as they ate the chicken and homemade noodles Mother served, the pies dripping with cinnamon syrup or hand-cranked ice cream. She knew how to win the hearts of hungry men. They, in turn, knew how praise would up the ante for the next day's harvest meal. We had ten chairs and used all the table leaves for the mid-day dinner. Bobby and Daddy ate with the men while Mother and I ate in the kitchen. Those ravenous men, all eight of them could "lick the platters clean," Dad said, and that was a lot of food Mother had spent the whole morning getting ready. One skinny man on the harvest crew who had blue eyes that looked like colored glass and a reddish moustache told Mother they should all "kiss the cook." I think she would have refused. Once, Mother asked me to check the table to see that everything was set, and I observed that the salt and pepper shakers had not been set out. When I told that to Mother, she was delighted with my powers of observation, and told the assembled harvest crew that "Janie set the table today," to which they heaped on compliments about my prowess as a water-boy, too.

The horse, patient about having two jugs of water slung over his mane, took us down the side pasture, across the creek, and through the gate to the upper field where the dust cloud would tell us in which direction to point the reins. To slide down off the horse onto the stickery brown stubble that smelled of oven toast, to heft the cool jugs from the horse's neck for the thirsty men, was deeply rewarding. Never have I felt so welcomed in all the years since.

I would arrive, smelling the gasoline of the engine, the hot conveyor belt, the thick air full of dust, and the sweaty men, the armpits of their shirts wet with labor. They shut off the noisy motor, climbed down onto the swath of just-cut grain, stretched, shouted as they beat the dust from their coveralls with thick, gloved hands. Then they'd pull off their gloves and slap them on the metal, leave them there and grasp the jug of water like it was the Holy Grail. Rescued for a few minutes from their grueling tasks, they lined up for their turn. They stomped their feet, untied the sweat-soaked bandanas around their necks, and swabbed their sticky, leathery necks. Then, each would tip the big bottle up and let the cool water flow down his parched throat. Sometimes it dribbled all down the front of his sweaty shirt, and he would jerk it down, afraid to drink more than his share of the water. Bobby and I traded off the morning and afternoon trips in the same spirit of fairness we had been taught through the years of the rotating weekly schedule. But Bob, as seduced as I was with praise for this deliverance, with the jollity of the men, bribed me with the promise of his next dessert to let him do double duty. If I promised not to tell.

"D'ya want to or not?" Bobby seriously wanted to come morning *and* afternoon.

"Depends on the dessert."

"It's always good, Janie, you know that."

"Okay. You can have my turns. But just for a while."

When Daddy, seeing him bring the water twice in succession, asked where I was, Bob lied, saying I had hurt my foot.

"How?" Daddy asked.

"She fell down the back steps and sprained her ankle."

"Well, I'll take a look at it when I get in tonight. Tell her to lie down and keep her leg propped up on a pillow, will you?"

"Okay."

The lie compounded the offence, and when it was discovered, Bobby was not allowed to be the water-boy for the rest of the week. It was my glorious triumph to be heralded by those burly men for three more days, morning and evening, as a second Florence Nightingale. I loved the way they said my name, the attention they lavished on me.

"Janie's here!" someone would yell.

"Bless your sweet bones, honey."

"You've saved my life, girl."

"Thank God you got here. My throat's so dry I can't even spit!"

When the grain was all harvested and sacked and the big combine put back in the garage, we missed that daily ritual. But it was getting close to the end of summer and school would be starting soon. The harvest in, at least that part of it, we all felt cleaner and began to turn our minds to the next set of chores we might be assigned. With our eyes peeled to the new schedule, we hoped to be allowed to do even more things for Daddy, he always appreciated our help so much. Maybe he would let us help him castrate the lambs, or curry comb the horses, or replace the big white squares of salt where the cattle had licked them down to the ground. They were heavy, but both of us knew, if he'd let us do it, we would rise to the task. We knew he would think of something. He always did.

Give Us This Day

Our "daily bread" meant everything we ate from when we got up in the morning until time for prayers, Mother explained to us. Even if on Sunday nights we only had crackers and milk or popcorn and apples, God thought it was "bread." He spoke the language of our Sunday school, she said. Before we could take even one single bite at suppertime, Daddy would say grace and we were supposed to bow our heads in thanksgiving, even though we thought that was only when we went to Gango's for turkey.

"Bless this food to the use of our bodies, and us to thy service, amen," he said most often, and it didn't take him very long to say it because he was always hungry. If he wanted to feel like all of us were talking to God, he'd ask us to hold hands around the table, like a Maypole. Sometimes Mother would say the grace, although when she said it, she always started "Our Heavenly Father." Bobby and I thought it must make her sad, because she never had a daddy, so she'd adopted God.

Rituals of faith or the habits of religion, such as they were, were an essential part of our growing up. Salt of the earth and hard-working, Midwestern farm families were essentially Protestant, formed by the traditional Puritan values of the Golden Rule and the Lord's Prayer. Pawns of the seasons, of the scorching sun or the howling blizzards, tillers of the soil, keepers of their own flocks, they were instruments of God's love on earth. But they needed reassurance. Much of the time it didn't feel like love. They went to hear a sermon or to take the children to Sunday school hungrily, for once a week everyone was clean and presentable, and they would get a spiritual lift, a bit of singing, exhortation to cleave unto the Lord for one more week, no matter what the temptations or the trials.

We went to whatever church was handy, provided it wasn't Catholic. For now it was the Christian Church in Redfield. It once had a tall, graceful steeple with a bell inside you could ring by pulling on the rope, but it blew off in a wild winter blizzard, so the white clapboard church ended up with a square top. Our drawings of towns always had a church in them, but every church we imagined had a steeple, on top of which we drew a "rugged cross," innocent of any distinction between denominations. Bobby said it was necessary because it meant reaching up to Heaven, closer to Jesus who lived up there with God.

Our Grandmother Belton who lived in California was a Baptist; our Des Moines grandmother was a Presbyterian; and all the rest of us were just "good Christians," we were told. Our Sunday-school teacher said it didn't really matter what we were called, that we were all God's children and He had a lot of different houses. We imagined that some of them were full of sheep, since the Bible told us the Lord watched over his flock.

Since we were headed for Sunday school the next morning, on Saturday night we had a bath. Our scruffy old shoes were cleaned up and sometimes polished with a brown liquid from a bottle that had a little wire dauber with a felt puff attached to the lid. When that painted over the front part, they looked new. At Eastertime, Daddy used his shoe polish and rubbed and rubbed them until they were shiny. Mother said to be clean and dress up a little showed our respect for God.

As well as the weekly Sunday morning trip to church, we sometimes went for special programs. Once it was for a baptism, at which several members of the church were to be dunked in the tub of water up by the cross. Bobby and I sat with the adults instead of going to our Sunday school to color pictures of Jesus in his nightgown patting several different colors of kids on the head. I loved to color the burst of sunlight that was always behind Jesus' head. He never ever got a haircut, so we colored his long curls with our brown Crayola. But now, we had to sit still and be quiet.

"Why does he keep a lid on that . . . swimming pool?" I whispered to Bobby.

"It's *not* a swimming pool!" he said in his I-know-everything voice.

"What is it then?"

"It's a dunking tank for sinners. Now, *shhhh*! You're not s'posed to talk in church."

I was quiet for a while, thinking. With our neighbor, Cole Mashur, Dad had taken us with him to watch the annual sheep dip. The poor, scared animals were herded into a chute that led them into a narrow concrete tank full of awful-smelling stuff. Their feet and woolly coats were saturated by the time they scurried up the other side.

"Like Daddy's sheep-dipping tank?" I whispered.

"Kinda. But the people aren't infected or anything. . . . *Shhhh*. Watch up there. . . . The preacher is gonna take the lid off."

And he did, propping the oblong wooden top that looked like a giant shoebox lid up against the back wall. The minister had taken off his black jacket and rolled the sleeves of his white shirt up over his elbows. He turned to face us, spreading his arms out like the welcoming God, and introduced the sinner waiting in the wings. She was a girl in our town who had "seen the error of her ways," he said, "and wanted to give her soul to Jesus who loved us enough to forgive all our sins."

And there the sinner stood, a white sheet with a hole for her head draped over her like a Halloween ghost. Then she walked out to the dunk tank and took the preacher's hand. He guided her down the steps into the water. She leaned back into his arms and he pushed her head under water. We were too fascinated with the action to remember what he said, but after a while, he lifted her up and she walked out onto the floor again, looking like a drowned rabbit. Her hair was pasted flat around her wet face, but she tried to smile.

It was embarrassing. When she came up out of that water, the sheet stuck to her breasts so tight you could see her nipples. She might as well have been naked. The preacher just held her in his arms. We thought it wasn't the right thing for him to do. Maybe he was trying to hide her immodesty. I wanted him to kiss her, but he didn't. That would just be one more sin, Bobby said.

When they drained the big oblong tub below the altar, lined with tin, more like the horses' drinking trough than a bathtub, I thought all the sins of the baptized got drained away, too.

One of the saddest extra times in church was a funeral for our little friend, Tommy. He had been our schoolmate and awfully good at marbles. We didn't know why he died, a ruptured appendix, someone told us, but the church was full of people and we sat for a long time in the hard pew, looking at the coffin up at the front of the room. Mother told us he was inside, sleeping eternally.

The night before we went in for the funeral, I just cried instead of praying. I wanted him back out of the box so bad. I hoped the Lord had already held out his arms and wrapped them around Tommy, his soul to keep. He was my friend, my playmate at school who gave me his marbles and taught me how to shoot them with my thumb doubled back like a pig's knuckle and tucked along my finger. Then, let it spring open onto the shooter, aiming at the aggie in the middle. We used to play jacks, too, and even if he was skinny and wore his dirty overalls to school, he was full of jokes that made all of us laugh. Bobby didn't like him as much as I did, maybe because he was better at marbles and jacks than Bob was.

And now he was dead. Dead was sad. Our canary had died and we lined a matchbox with cornsilk and dug a hole underneath the sunflowers and carried a Bible and sang "Jesus loves me, this I know" because it was what Daddy said the canary would like. The house seemed kind of empty when they put the birdcage in the garage and no little yellow chirp filled the mornings. But friends were different; people who were just like you weren't supposed to die until they got old, or awfully sick. What did it feel like, I wondered, being dead? Did a moonbeam shine down like a ladder in the night so Tommy could climb up to Heaven? Or did he float up like Jesus did at Easter?

Everyone at the funeral was crying and singing "God Will Take Care of You," and we cried, too. I hoped He would make Tommy a soft bed of clouds up in Heaven, with a new warm comforter and at least a few of the angels who could play marbles.

The wood along the top of the pew ahead of us reminded me of the river, swirly and brown, where we watched the preacher once wade into the water with his shoes on to baptize a fat man. He probably wouldn't have fitted into the dunk tank inside the church, and our Sunday-school teacher told us Jesus, Himself, had been baptized in the Jordan River, so maybe the man was even closer to God than you could tell by looking.

It was the custom of our days, then, to walk up the aisle between the pews once a year to put our birthday offering in a big glass jar the preacher held in his hands. Everyone in the congregation could tell how old we were by counting the pennies we dropped into the jar through a slot cut in the lid. On the Sunday closest to our birthdays, we would tie the number of pennies we were years old into the corner of a handkerchief until the time came to untie them for the ceremony.

"Does anyone in the congregation have a birthday today?" the preacher would ask. Bobby said he already knew or he wouldn't have come down the steps out of his pulpit carrying the birthday jar. But maybe he didn't know exactly who. I raised my hand. This was my first time, and Bobby pushed me to the aisle side of our seats and pinched my bottom.

"I do. . . ." I said, barely audible. To Bobby I said in a loud whisper, "Stop it!"

The people who were sitting nearest us heard me and began to chuckle. All eyes turned toward me, so I had to do it.

"Bless the little children to come unto me, saith the Lord," the preacher said, lifting his one free arm up like he was going to take off his shirt. That was my cue. In my new dress Mother just finished hemming the day before and with my shoes as shiny as they could get (but still not patent leather, like Rachel's), I stood up and walked down the aisle toward the altar, embarrassed and shy, praying I could untie the knot in my hankie without spilling my seven pennies on the floor.

"And how old are you, Janie?" the minister asked while I was plinking my pennies into the jar, one at a time. I guess he forgot to keep track.

"Seven," I told him.

"Seven?" he repeated, as if in disbelief. "My, my, aren't you growing up fast!"

One of my pennies lodged for a while, stuck in the rough slot in the jar lid, as if his knife couldn't cut it smooth, and I was terrified.

"Here, dear," he said, pushing the coin down into the jar, "Jesus blesses you for this gift." I felt good when I finally got back to my seat and slid in beside Daddy. He patted me on the knee and I felt almost an adult, now.

For Sunday dinner the day of my birthday we had chicken with dumplings, my favorite sweet potatoes, Waldorf salad, and a cake for me to make a wish on, then blow out the seven candles all in one breath. I never failed to blow them all out, and then got to lick the frosting end of the candles as I took them out to put on the cake plate.

Eating is a such a sensual pleasure for a child, starting with the very first suck of breast milk to the sight and smell of fresh bread loaves just out of the oven, looking like haystacks of wheat and yeast, cooling on wooden racks on the counter tops. Long-cut egg noodles dried on a dishtowel thrown across the back of the stove, across the roll-top warming oven, promising the soul-satisfying boiled chicken, the noodles saturated with rich broth. Or the steam rising from a dish of glazed carrots or brown-sugared parsnips Daddy just pulled from his garden, or homemade sausages on a bed of home-cured sauerkraut on a snowy winter evening, not to mention the desserts Mother loved to create—elderberry pie spiced with rhubarb because Daddy had brought home a sack full of berries from the edge of the hayfield, or cinnamon rolls with currants in them, slathered with butter freshly churned that morning. It is no wonder we lingered long at the supper table, full as ticks, talking, savoring the effort that was put before us.

"Zee, I swear to God you are the world's best cook," Daddy would tell her, and we would chime in our own versions of appreciation.

Our whole family loved to eat, and all of us had a sweet tooth.

Fudge. Fresh strawberries and thick cream. More butter than bread in a good sandwich, peanut butter and jam, of course. Mother's wooden recipe box was stuffed with terrific ideas, bulging with white eight-by-five cards filled with recipes and menus compiled from experience, from the *Fanny Farmer Cookbook*, or from recipes exchanged with friends. For Thanksgiving dinners, there was turkey with wild hazelnut or oyster dressing, creamed little white onions, pickled peaches, candied yams, mashed potatoes, and giblet gravy. On other special days, green piccalilli (a relish made of blended pickles and sweet red peppers) to go on a pork roast, leg of lamb with mint sauce, or gooseberry pie.

Mother was a wizard in the kitchen. One of our favorite treats was "scrapple," flexible slices of pork scraps in solidified cornmeal, slathered with maple syrup. We were allowed to pick it up, drag it in the syrup, and eat it with our fingers. Another recipe Grandmother Belton taught Mother how to make was thickened milk, a warm kind of bland pudding we saturated with butter and brown sugar.

"Mother, can I learn to make a pie like you?" I asked one day.

"Sure you can, honey. Do you want to help me make the crust, first?"

"Yes!"

"Well, you'll need a big bowl, big enough to hold the flour, the lard, and the salt, like this. Then, you have to mix the two with your fingers. See. Rub them between your fingers until they begin to feel like cracked corn. Can you feel that?"

She helped me of course. When the two ingredients were combined, she poured in some cold water, "just enough to make it easy to roll out on the board with a rolling pin." The flour on the board, the rolling pin pushing it all over the kitchen made her laugh. "You'll get better at this the more you practice, honey. We'll clean it up later."

The final touch, after the piecrusts were settled into the pie tin, was fluting the edges.

"Look, Janie. You can do this. Squeeze some of the crust between your left-hand thumb and forefinger. Now, push the crust in between them with your right forefinger. See? Doesn't that make it look pretty? When you go all the way around the pie tin, I'll have the custard ready to pour in. Then we can put it in the oven, okay?"

It was a triumph, and it tasted like the best pie in the world. To this day, I never make a pie crust without following that exact pattern. Her specialty was pie. With any filling, fruit or custard or cream or raisins, the flaky, lard-made crust was mouth-watering.

Genetically tall and thin, we all enjoyed the best of health, partly, I think, because we lived in a time before the earth was poisoned. I think of those tasty three meals a day as I eat a cooked bran breakfast, or nibble on an oat wafer to stave off hunger until a suppertime salad. Perhaps because everyone worked hard enough to burn up the calories, those early years in Iowa seem full to overflowing with delicious food. Playing outdoors in the fresh air gave us a healthy appetite, too, so everything tasted wonderful. We grew our own vegetables, slaughtered our own meat, canned the seasonal fruit, made bread and biscuits and piecrust from scratch. Prepared foods, frozen or boxed, were unknown.

In the cold cellar, an underground cave with steps leading down into that smelly darkness, cabbages, carrots, and parsnips grew limp, the fruit jars dwindled, and the potatoes began to sprout before spring rolled around. Our daily meals began to change. Without refrigeration, we relied on the icebox into which the ice man slid his big squares of ice. He dragged it off the truck with huge tongs that looked like giants' scissors and carried it into the house, resting the freezing cold square on a folded gunnysack thrown over his shoulder. As the ice melted, little pieces of stick or leaves would collect in the gutters on either side of the metal lining of the ice compartment. Once, a dead fly. Those big squares came from the icehouse beside the Raccoon River, and had been cut from the frozen winter river and stored in sawdust to keep them from melting.

Food production and preservation were still preoccupations of the rural Iowan long into the twentieth century. In our Redfield days, putting in the garden was a family affair. After Dad had plowed and smoothed the huge plot of ground and spring had warmed the earth, Mother would gather up the seeds she had ordered from the Burpee's seed catalog, and we would all join together in the task. Long strings of twine were tied to sticks and unraveled across the dirt to mark the straight rows, and Dad, "who had the best eye," Mother said, would dig the furrows, Mother would drop the seeds, Bob and I would take turns filling the row in gently with dirt, the other tamping it down. Peas, radishes, lettuce, spinach, beans, cucumbers, tomatoes, sweet corn, squash, watermelons, turnips, carrots, potatoes. Stories were told back and forth across the readied earth, too, to break the monotony of planting, or as an excuse to straighten up a tired back and catch a breath.

"Old Mr. Young put in a single row of corn last year," Dad would tell Mother, "Can you believe it? Of course it never amounted to anything. Nothing to pollinate it. Never did form ears."

"His wife doesn't have a green thumb, either. She planted squash and pumpkins together in solid rows of seeds. They grew so thick all the energy went into the leaves, a real tangle, you can imagine. She bought her pie pumpkin from a farmer she knew because the two little pumpkins she raised were the size of apples!"

"Well, they moved out here from the city, thinking they'd retire, but they never learned anything about planting a garden." Then, our parents would bend back to the job at hand.

And, gradually, an eye kept on the need for watering or thinning, came the harvest, the heavenly meals along the way, the autumn ritual of canning. Cucumbers for pickles would soak in brine or vinegar in big stoneware crocks covered with wooden lids, the dill weed and garlic filling the basement with spiciness. And the stories would center on the county fair, or the state fair, how the prize for the best canned string beans was divided this year, who baked the prize-winning chocolate cake, or the biggest Hubbard squash coming from a farmer in Adel, a small town not far from where we lived.

It was not only vegetables that were preserved for the winter. Fruits were more fun to can. The way the peach halves could overlay one another was beautiful. Peaches, pears, applesauce, pickled peaches for Thanksgiving, all were lined up on the shelves in our root cellar, where sacks of onions, turnips, carrots, cabbages, and apples were also stored. It was a source of tremendous security to see the fruits of our labor waiting there for a winter dinner. Not to mention the beauty of it, for Mother liked to copy the canning style of the state-fair winners, and she did a little bit extra to make necessity a work of art. As the jars on the shelves began to thin and the stored food began to dwindle, we knew the robins would be coming back soon and Mother would get out her seed catalogs. And then, the garden again.

Bobby was fondest of the butchering and curing of meat, wild game or farm animals raised for slaughter, part of the self-sufficiency of those years. With some hired man or farm neighbor, our father would kill the pig or the cow or the lamb behind the barn where it would be skinned, drawn and quartered, then left to hang there to drip blood, to "cure" for awhile. This they usually did after the first frost had killed the flies, for they could drive you mad, buzzing in big black clouds, hungry for blood. Sometimes the carcasses were covered with gunnysacks, just in case. I was not allowed to witness this ritual. But Bob was, and perhaps he got his first fascination for surgery, watching the sharp knife cut through flesh and bone. Dad, wanting to train him to cope with a skill the future might demand of him, would hand the knife to Bobby to cut off a piece of meat to be discarded. Bob was given to exaggeration, and when he told me the knife made a sound different from the sound of a bread knife, that it was more "gritty," he would imitate it dramatically, saying he cut off the whole leg, or "sliced the whole carcass in two."

"The blood spurted out like the neck of a chicken without its head all over me," he told me, "and it tasted like salt and stuck to my hair."

"Did you eat it?"

"No!"

"How do you know it tasted salty, then?"

"It spurted on my face and all over my mouth, but I spit it out."

A gruesome business, it seemed, and I never really wanted any part of it after that.

After a communal butchering, where two or three farmers brought their animals to where a big chopping block and black iron pulleys and ropes were waiting, each family sorted out its portion. The big hams were taken to be cured or smoked in a cooperative smokehouse in Adel, first. Then, our share would hang from our attic rafters to tide us over the winter.

Mother put up boiled beef in jars for winter dinners. Mincemeat and butchering always went together. Into the same tub that heated water on the stove for our weekly baths went the ingredients for holiday pies, chopped up meat, raisins and currants, suet, lots of finely cut apples, and sugar. We had a huge wooden paddle with a long handle to stir it with, and Daddy pretended he was a French-Canadian trapper, paddling his canoe down to New Orleans as he dug through the tasty mix. It smelled like cinnamon at first, but by the time it was ready to can, it had sharpened to smell more like vinegar.

Pure butter, lots of sugar, bacon drippings, and salt made everything taste delicious. The delicacies Mother served from that big iron stove were legion. With unadulterated ingredients, she roasted a leg of lamb, baked fresh pecan rolls, seasoned pot roasts, created popcorn balls, breaded parsnips, baked apples, made rhubarb pie, cinnamon cake, penuche, fudge. We had corn fritters, sweetened tomatoes with chunks of bread softened in them, tapioca or custard or chocolate pudding, crunchy fresh apples with cheese. Stories about recipes, good cooks, creative conservation made up the conversations women shared whenever they congregated. Mother's reputation was undisputed.

One of her proudest efforts was the annual batch of "sunshine preserves." These were freshly picked, deep red strawberries, lightly mashed and mixed with an equal amount of sugar. Then, they were put in shallow pans or platters and set out in the hot sun under glass to cook in that natural heat. Daddy was always very willing to set up the sawhorses and planks on which this delicacy would bubble and thicken, his mouth watering in advance.

One year, a freak storm moved in rapidly, with hailstones as big as golf balls. The wind blew and the trees gyrated and the hail kept coming down, thicker and ever bigger. At the first click, click of the ice balls on the roof, on the window, Mother ran to the kitchen door, screaming, "Merrill! Merrill! Come quick! My jam will be ruined!"

He was already on his way, probably from haying. His first thought was for safety, for himself, his family, his animals: such an ice storm can kill a man. But his second thought had been for those bubbling pans of winter preserves, the taste of them on toast or ice cream keen in his mouth. They met across the sawhorses and planks on which the shallow pans of sunshine preserves had been placed under glass, as near to the catastrophe as hail would allow. They stood helpless as those brutal ice balls pounded the glass panes, breaking them into fine splinters that the storm ground down into the strawberry jam.

The syrup, like blood and gore leaking out, splattered onto the ground.

Mother burst into tears, repeating over and over, "All that work. All those beautiful strawberries. . . ."

Dad had run through the hailstorm hunched against the danger, his hands over his head, desperate to do anything possible. He stood beside Mother under the back-porch roof, trying to comfort her, sick himself, for he had picked those berries, had helped Mother hull the whole batch. Now, they had lost the reward. Mother cried as she threw it all away, and who could blame her?

That same summer, a shaft of lightning struck a big elm tree in our front yard and split it down the middle. It came crashing apart like a Fourth of July explosion and cracked down the whole length of its beautiful straight trunk. We, too young to worry about the danger of electrical storms, watched from the windows as if we were at a carnival. After a long time, Dad and some neighbors cut it down and sawed it into firewood chunks, their crosscut saw moving back and forth across the saw guide, a big X made out of two-by-fours crossed like a cradle. It was seasoned and turned into firewood.

Iowa storms—hail, wind, snow, dust—were a force to be reckoned with. Mother coped by planning compensatory meals, and Dad picked up a bit of money doing odd jobs for local folks, like rescuing a cow whose newborn calf was stuck halfway out of her, the little leg wedged inside. We did our chores—one of mine was trimming the kerosene lamp wicks, and Bobby fed the chickens. But ease was not a part of that time, and we talked a lot about God, his wrath, his beneficence, his eternal watchfulness and care for all of us, the dead and the living. Our "daily bread" became a sacred ritual, overshadowed by the talk of foreclosure of the farm. There was not enough money to keep paying the rent.

"Where will we go?" we asked our parents.

"Don't you worry your little heads," Dad said. "I'm thinking we could move to the farm up the road. D'ya know the one with 'Highland Stock Farm' written on the barn's hay door? That's the one." So we began to pack up our things again, excited by the prospect of a new bedroom.

Waste Not, Want Not

We did manage to move up the road to the Highland Stock Farm. With fewer acres, the rent was less. Daddy could still move the cattle and the farm equipment over. The people who had rented it before were filthy dirty, Mother said, scraping the kitchen linoleum with a spade before she scrubbed it. She and Daddy cleaned and cleaned the place before we moved our beds and clothes, dishes and furniture over.

A man with a flatbed truck helped tie things onto the back and drove the little distance from the Peppard place. For days, the trips in the car and in the cab of the truck were like sporting events for us: our chief chore was to stay out of the way. I loved to drive into the driveway of our new house and see, in big white letters on the tall red barn, "Highland Stock Farm." It felt important, somehow, like we were somebody now.

Bobby and I were happy to find a fireplace in the living room and a front porch where we could see the cars going by on the road just past the end of the lawn. On the opposite side of the road, a huge cornfield marched away to the horizon like a forest. We did a great exploration of the barn and the outhouse, the machine shed and the chicken house. It would be an adventure to live in a new house. But one bad thing was we were moving into a different school district and would go to a little country school, within walking distance if we cut diagonally across the pasture. School was a long time away, though.

It was still summer. When people came to visit, it was really to swap stories.

The house was hospitable, a big wood frame with four bedrooms and an attic, a kitchen large enough for a table, a wood stove, and an ice-box, counters that sloped down to the sink so water would drain off the wood, and that were long enough for friends to lean against and talk while Mother snapped green beans. Everyone was so friendly, welcoming us to our new place.

The days turned into August. Harvesters told the best stories. In from the dusty job of cutting hay or bagging grain, they sat relaxing around the big noonday meal Mother had prepared, jovial as workmen always are during lunch break. For all the splashing of water from the galvanized washbasin out on the back porch where a gunnysack towel hung on a nail, they still had oat hulls under their sweaty hats or alfalfa green on their nostril hairs. They would tell the human stories that rivaled any radio adventure, of a man who fell through the ice and drowned, of breeding an old mare with Gus's stallion and getting twin colts, of water dowsers who found water along the west pasture fence.

Once, all the men around the table began to laugh and get loud, or whisper to each other, because someone began to gossip about a neighbor who had a gypsy woman in town "who damn near wore old Henry out."

"Did Henry's clothes get holes in them?" I asked Mother.

"No, honey. They are just making a joke."

"Why are they all laughing? What's funny?"

"I forgot to put the milk on the table, Janie. Hurry up, and take it to the men, will you?" And with that, while she was busy cutting the pies into six pieces, I was honored to carry, full of milk, the antique pitcher, as squat-bottomed as a fat lady bending over in the garden. It had painted iris on it and gold all around the lip, a treasure that had belonged to Grandma Belton. I would die, simply die if I should drop it. She trusted me, and I rose to the occasion.

One of the men told us his story about running into a nest of baby rabbits in the alfalfa with his mower, how he had felt so bad about it but left them there, hoping their mother would gather them up again. We already knew about that, for Daddy had done the same, mowing in our hay field, and had brought two little ones home for us. We emptied the contents of the soda cracker box in order to provide a bed for our new pets, and lined it with straw. The poor little creatures were shivering with fright, which we assumed meant they were cold. So, we opened the oven door on our Majestic wood range and put them in there to warm up. Then, Bobby and I both forgot them, and when we discovered those cremated babies, we cried as much from remorse over our neglect as from losing our soft little animals. We had one of our best funerals ever, with flowers and songs and real tears.

When Grandma Chantry was visiting during the summer, she told us something about our kinfolk. When Mother was being courted by Daddy, Gango had "looked into the Belton family." She wanted the best for Mother, and she needed to learn what kind of people Merrill Belton came from. Dad's father had a terrible temper, so the story went. Atlas Leet Belton, a chicken farmer who delivered sacks of chicken feathers to a mattress maker in Algona, Iowa, once came across a hay wagon in a country road. The narrow way required one of the teams to swerve into the ditch to let the other pass. The oncoming farmer, evidently a neighbor with a reputation for being pig-headed, refused to budge. His attitude so angered Atlas that, after the impasse failed to move either wagon, he got down from his wagon, having wrapped the reins across the front, jumped up onto the other wagon and slugged the stubborn farmer in the jaw. Such arrogance on the Belton side, she feared, might have flowed down into our father's veins. Bob and I loved that story, for we thought it high drama on the highway, and would play it out on our imagined hay wagons, out-shouting each other and threatening to punch each other in the jaw. And whenever I would march into my room and slam the door as hard as I could, mad at Bobby or at someone or something, Mother would say, "She's got her father's temper!" *He*, the mildest of men.

The conversations of adults became the stuff of our play-acting. When we overheard the story of how Aunt Lizzie had died when she was only two from drinking lye she'd found under the sink, we went into our hospital drama. Mother had converted empty oatmeal boxes to toy cradles by cutting them in half lengthwise and putting the lid back on the end. We had several of them, stuffed with rag mattresses, and they became the beds in our hospital ward. Clothespin dollies, those wonderful inventions made by painting faces on the wooden-pronged clothespins and draping them with rectangular scrap "clothes," were the patients. The ghost of little Lizzie was created by dressing her in a long white piece of a pillowcase we'd found in the ragbag; the hand-crocheted hem up around her arms was her bed jacket. Bob, of course, was the doctor, and I, the nurse.

Not surprisingly, many of the stories had to do with birthing, long before birth control or abortion were available to women, long before hospital proximity was common. The blizzards of winter or the distances from a town often prevented the needed help from arriving in time for a baby's delivery. Granny midwives and concerned neighbors brought many of our ancestors into the world with, of course, hot water boiling on the wood stove.

Once, Mother and a neighbor lady named Mabel were having a cup of coffee at the kitchen table, and I was washing my dolly clothes on the back porch. They were talking about men in a whispery voice.

"She told him she had in a pessary, but she evidently didn't, because she got pregnant right after their boarder went back to Kansas City," Mabel confided.

After a pause, she asked, "Do you use a pessary, Xela?"

"No. Merrill uses a rubber, now. He found some new fishskins he likes," Mother answered.

When I asked Bob what a "pessary" was, he said it was a kind of wild pig. That didn't make sense to me. How could a wild pig keep from making a baby? So I looked it up in the dictionary, and learned a new word—*contraceptive*. Even then, I was in the dark, for my innocence could not imagine the mechanics of the whole affair.

Bobby told me he had once heard those two talking about Mother's grandpa. Our own grandmother, Gango—Ella Clementine Cowden—was born in 1870, and she lived for ninety-six years. Her mother before her, Margaret Amanda Summerville, was born in 1834 and lived for ninety-eight years. With her husband, Watson Pentland Cowden, Margaret had nine children, all of them born at home. Rumor had it that she caught him in bed with a servant girl who had come to help them, and she locked her bedroom door after that. Those were our mother's grandparents.

On July 15, 1898, our mother, Xela Margaret Chantry, was born. Her father wanted her to have a unique name, so she was christened "Xela." We thought it should be spelled with a "Z," because that's the way it sounded. She was the first child to live, for the premature twins who had preceded her did not survive.

In our family there is an unusual incidence of twinship. Orren Chantry was a twin. Grandmother bore twins. Our mother had twins, so it didn't skip a generation, as the old wives' tale has it. The big question for pregnant women in our family is, "Will this be a pair of twins?" Another twist in the generational story is that our mother, like her mother before her, lost her first baby, a little girl they had named Jane. When I was born, I got her name, second-hand. Coincidentally, Mother too, after her children were nearly raised, became a county superintendent of schools as her father had been, albeit in Oregon. And so history braids us in these looped and shining circles.

Stories about medicine, about this abscessed tooth or that mastoid operation, the loss of fingers in sawing accidents, a baby born dead or deformed, the gangrene that set in after a leg injury that prompted amputation—these were the challenges of our make-believe hospital. We loved playing doctor. We called our red wagon the "ambulance," and it made several trips to and from the hospital, set up in the corner of the garage.

Mrs. Smith lived across the road in the house with a huge windmill and a well house. She often walked over to our new place, just to talk with Mother when the day's chores were done. She loved to regale us with stories of her pioneer grandparents, Scandinavian folks who settled in North Dakota and built a sod house for a first home. She called it their "soddy." The way she gestured as she described the icy blizzards that blew across the treeless prairie, over the low roof of that primitive dwelling, or the way she squinted to illustrate the darkness inside a windowless sod house, intrigued us.

"Was there a door?" I wanted to know.

"There had to be, honey," she said, interrupting her delicious retelling of hardships, "but it was placed away from the wind, made of a big flap of buffalo hide."

She and Mother began to talk about living on dried meat and potatoes, about how far it was to the nearest neighbor, about delivering babies and carrying water, about the difficulties all pioneers had to face.

"Daddy," Bob asked that night over supper, "could we build a sod house in the pasture?"

He stopped eating, looked at both of us, wondering where on earth *that* idea had come from. Then, smiling he said, "Well, I don't see why not. It's a big job. I'd back it into that little hillock down by the creek, though, if I were you. The soil'd be easier to cut."

"Will you help us?" I wanted to know, having no idea how we'd lay the foundation, or how we could cut through the thick grass.

He hesitated, caught Mother's eye across the table, and said, "Sure. Why not? We'll need the spade, the shovel, probably the hoe, too. Maybe Mother would let us have that old butcher knife I could never put an edge on. Would you add that to our tool kit, Zee?"

"If you promise to bring it back, I will. I still use it for cutting fudge." Clever Mother. She knew the mere mention of fudge would ensure its return, for Daddy was always chocolate hungry.

The next morning, as soon as the early sun came streaming in our window, we were up and dressed before we heard the breakfast preparations. Always a man of his word, Dad had gathered the tools by the back porch. We would set off as soon as we had eaten. I think Daddy was as excited as we were. He was like a kid sometimes, like the time he had tied our sled to the back bumper of his car and drove us around the country roads in the snow, giving us a thrill ride with no hesitation about safety.

"Ready to go?" he asked us, after we'd finished our oatmeal.

"Yes!" We'd put on our oldest clothes.

And so, together, we three trudged down to the little rise above the creek. On the way, he explained the wisdom of backing into the hill, "to save yourselves a lot of work, and to protect the little house from the weather.

"But you kids will have to be careful. Don't make it too big, or you'll never have enough sod to finish the job. Cattle come down to the creek to drink, and you won't want them tromping around inside. Use the spade and shovel handles for a gate when you finish every day; that'll keep 'em out."

And so, in an exaggerated imitation of Mrs. Smith's story about her pioneering grandparents, we began. Dad cut the first pieces of sod, about two feet long and maybe a foot wide, not so big we couldn't carry them, but big enough to satisfy our sense of progress. He had shoveled out a little cutbank for the back wall, and laid the first pieces in a rectangle in front.

"D'ya get the idea?" he asked, after the first layer was in place, a place left open for the door.

"Can I dig one by myself, just to practice?" Bob said.

"You bet. I'm not going to spend the whole day here. You kids'll be at this project for several weeks, I'll bet, so you might as well get started."

My job was to use the dull old butcher knife to slide underneath the rectangle of grass and cut the roots. Then we took turns prying up the square, carrying them to our "house," actually no more than about six feet square, and laying them one on top of another, each just off center of the one beneath it, "like brick layers," Daddy said.

About four layers up, and weeks into the sod house, we got tired. It was hard work. The dream of finding an old burlap sack we could make into a rug, the chatter about where we would hang such indispensable kitchen utensils as an egg-beater, a potato masher, or a butter churn was enough interior design for our flagging enthusiasm. Then, although we built it up no higher, it served as our "soddy," and we took our toy cars down to it, pretending it was our garage, or apples and a peanut butter sandwich for our lunch picnic.

We moved our orange crate "store" down to our hideaway, too, the shelves filled with the samples we got from ordering them out of magazines. Even a miniature bowl was set on top of the crate to use for mixing such ingredients as soda from the tiny Arm and Hammer sample and flour from General Mills, to be washed later with the little box of soap flakes. We poured vinegar into a teaspoon of soda and called the bubbly stuff batter. We never actually baked anything, but we pretended to sell our products to eager buyers.

Those dreamy summer days set a pattern of planning things together, of feeling that the future would never part us. We planned to live together until we were as old as Mother and Daddy, and could have a real house with chairs and beds and an indoor toilet. We would invite our parents to come and visit us, maybe for Thanksgiving. We spent long afternoons lying on our backs inside our pretend house without a roof, gazing at the sky or the overarching trees, planning our next meal or estimating the cost of buying ourselves a milk-giving cow to stake outside where she could eat down the grass.

Summer went by quickly. Already the leaves were beginning to turn color and fall. Our new baby, Daniel Thomas Belton, who had been born in February, was old enough now to take with us outdoors. In the house he could walk, but we mostly took him in our wagon outside to please him. When he smiled at us, he had little dimples in his cheeks, and we could make him laugh. Mostly Mother took care of him. We had to wait for him to grow up as the twins had. They were more fun than they used to be in diapers, so there was hope for Danny. I got to sit out on the porch to keep an eye on things while he took a nap in his buggy. He was so cute, so delighted with things like the leaves falling on his face, we enjoyed him. Both Bobby and I were old enough to be a real help to Mother with the twins and now Danny.

Blustery winds would swirl the dry leaves in little eddies across our gravel driveway, and Danny would squeal with delight, thinking them alive, maybe. Our favorite haunt this time of year was down in the woods, the Iowa hardwoods in autumn smelling like roasting pumpkin seeds or the char of bonfires.

Soon, the leaves were deep enough to make our yearly nutting trip as exciting as an Easter egg hunt. The whole family loved the air, so pungent, so tangy, so sharp with oak and hickory and elm at the turn of seasons that we all laughed a lot, playing with the freedom of being outdoors most of the day, of squirreling away our delicious winter store of various nuts. Going nutting meant promises of fudge and penuche, Christmas cookies and candies, the crusts of an apple crisp, not to forget the buttons for gingerbread men or eyes for our snowmen. These all depended on our filling sacks with black walnuts, hickory nuts, and butternuts. We had found some new trees to hunt under during the summer, ones we didn't know about in our last house. And we discovered the hazelnut shrubs, filling a little sack with those oily and tasty balls, each one clothed in a funny elfin hat fringed like a drawstring purse.

Frieda, our big German shepherd, loved the woods as much as we did. She'd leap around under a nut tree as if to show us where the best finds were, imitating our pawing down under the blanket of leaves, barking with her contagious spirit. When she wasn't chasing squirrels, that is, for they, too were nut-gathering and stashing away their winter acorns from the huge oaks. We liked the black walnuts better. They were bigger, but they stained our fingers yellow. Their outer husk, Mother said, was used for dye sometimes.

We dried the nuts on old window screens, hung on a pulley above the ceiling of the shed, some out in the tack room of the barn. Mother or Daddy would let them down every once in a while to turn the nuts over until the husks or hulls were dry enough. Then, in some warm after-dinner time when everything seemed close and slow, Daddy got out his hammer and a piece of board to crack them, giving the shiny nut picks to us to work out the precious black-walnut meats curled inside that hard-ridged shell. Mother made a batch of black-walnut fudge to celebrate the occasion. She had to ration it out or it would have disappeared in one ravenous craving.

After nutting, it was time to get ready for school. The air had a different smell, a smell of apples in gunnysacks or the nostril-widening spice of crisp leaves when we stepped on them and cracked their edges. For both Bobby and me, it was a wonderful end-of-summer feeling, as if school arrived just in the nick of time when all our summer games and projects began to bore us. Learning was like opening the lid of a big treasure chest full of surprises, and both of us loved school. But we still had a little time to wait until opening day. Why must we always wait? Our parents' favorite word was "wait."

"When will the pumpkins be ripe enough for pies?"

"We'll just have to wait."

" When will school start?"

"Not long now. We'll just have to wait."

"Will we go to Des Moines for Thanksgiving?"

"Not for a couple of months. We'll just have to wait."

What we'd always done before was go shopping, every August or September, at Younkers in Des Moines. Mother loved these sprees. She was hungry to buy new things and in a place she knew well, felt at home. So, we used to put on our best clothes—if it was hot, summer seersucker, and if cold, woolen sweaters. The drive into the city was a break from the sameness of her daily chores, and for us, an adventure full of suspense and wonder.

We learned what window-shopping meant: you could look at everything without spending any money. Mother would stop by a store full of shoes, and tell us the ones she thought were the prettiest. And the store signs, the street signs, all the color and movement was like a carnival to us. For our day of school shopping, we all loved the hubbub of city life. We went into the department store to look at jackets or sweaters or jumpers for each of us, and always came home with at least one or two new things for school, usually new underwear.

Mother bought a little sack of chocolate candy for us each trip. Too, Mother relished the fresh dill pickles they speared out of a crock for her. The man at the counter sometimes would give Mother one just to taste on the spot, she was so pretty. When she got them home, she would open the waxy box and smell the pickles and close her eyes and say, "Ambrosia!"

"What is ambrosia?" I asked her.

"It means food for the gods. It tastes heavenly," she said.

"I didn't know the gods ate real food."

"Well, if they did it would have to be as good as dill pickles," she laughed. She was always happy when she got home from downtown Des Moines. She grew up there and all things urbane and civilized had an aura of glamour for her.

Once in a while, usually after supper before the dishes, she sat down at the piano and played a song called "Narcissus," staring into empty space as if she could see the innards of the piano strings. The house quieted down when she did this, and Bobby and I felt sorry that she couldn't get dill pickles from the IGA store in Redfield, or that we couldn't move to Des Moines where she would be happy all the time.

But there would be no shopping spree this year. Money was scarcer than hen's teeth. When Daddy went to the bank to take out their savings, the big door with the brass handles was locked up tight. He kicked the door so hard he had a black toenail for a long time. When he came home that terrible day, he was angry and swearing. "Those

God-damn dishonest sons-a-bitches! They'll squeeze blood out of a turnip, ride around in their God-damn new cars while our savings disappear like sand down a rat hole!"

After he'd paced around, "letting off steam," Mother said, he began to remember the rest of us. He put his arms around Mother as she cried and cried, telling her things *had* to get better, they'd damn well figure out some way to live like decent human beings. There were tears in his eyes, too, and he had to keep blowing his nose. By now, all available resources had dwindled. Our move to the Highland Stock Farm was a sad, raggedy comedown for our family, now with five children.

So, we dreamed together over the Montgomery Ward catalog with Mother, ordering school clothes. It was the newest catalog, last year's having been folded into a doorstop for the outhouse. She had spread the big book open on the dining room table. Bobby and I leaned on our elbows on either side, asking to turn the pages back or forward, or to look up the picture of something listed on the back page. Then we could compare the various kinds and prices, learn about the color choices, of winter jackets for instance, and, tell her which was our favorite and why. It was a book full of everything in the world anyone would ever need or want. Planning for the order was almost as much fun as going into Des Moines, into that big store with the shiny glass cases and the very high ceilings.

First, possibly to break in our writing skills before we started a new grade, or maybe to turn necessity into a lark, Mother made us make lists of what we needed. Then she showed us how to make two columns, headed "need" and "want."

"Write down first the things you need the most, in the 'need' column. Like some long underwear, new woolen socks, a pair of corduroy coveralls. Maybe a sweater. And new Dr. Dentons, since both of you have worn out the feet on your old pajamas.

"Next put down the things you want, some things you could do without, but would *like* to have in the 'want' column. When we add it all up, there may be room for one or two extras. I'll make a list, too, because the twins need some things, and I do, too. Baby Danny is growing so fast, he needs some new clothes. And Daddy has some things he needs. When we all get our wishes down on paper, then we can begin to whittle it down." Of course, we hoped the whittling down would not eliminate *our* favorite things.

Mother did the same, showing us how. On her "need" side, she wrote, "Four three-pound cotton batts for making comforters. Two new bath towels, all cotton. Four new cotton washcloths. Four 500-yard spools Coats mercerized thread, size #60, two black and two white. One roll of brown darning cotton. One 25-yard bolt of outing flannel @ 13 cents a yard. One carpet beater."

Under her "want" column, she wrote, "One Bissell carpet sweeper. One new eggbeater. One new woolen petticoat with trim. One hot water bottle. Pair of pigskin fur-lined gloves." She made a line across the middle of her page, and made two columns under it, lumping the twins in one, Danny and Daddy in the other.

In his "need" side, she wrote, "Two horse blankets. One long-legged underwear pants and one long-armed underwear shirt. Two pairs knee-high wool socks. One $1.90 horsehide razor strop. Four long leather bootlaces. One cholera-serum syringe for $4.85." On his "want" side, she wrote, "One pair heavy leather work gloves. One thick flannel work shirt, blue plaid, neck size 15, arm length 34."

The little kids needed thick corduroy overalls, too, and she knew the sizes. She put down two books for the little girls, a *Child's Garden of Verses* and *Billy Whiskers*, a story about a goat. She listed "Johnny jumpers" that would look just like the bigger ones for Bobby and me, and two little jackets with sheepskin inside. For baby Danny, she listed a woolen snowsuit with a fur-lined hood that would make him look like a little Eskimo doll.

Our lists weren't very long. With the constant talk of money these days, we didn't want to seem extravagant. I *needed* a new pantywaist with garters attached to hold up my long stockings. Like slipping a harness over the horse's head, my pantywaist, made of white thick woven tape, would slip over my shoulders and around my waist. The garters on my old one were stretched so much they didn't keep my stockings up, and I hated bulgy socks. And I *wanted* a new pillow. The feathers in mine were so squashed down, I had to double it up even to feel it. Bobby put in his "need" list a new jacket with a belt sewed into it already, with double buttons and a sheepskin collar, and in his "want" side, a new chinchilla cap with earflaps because his ears stuck out and he didn't have long hair like I did.

I wanted a new book, too. The catalog had *Little Women* for $1.37, and *Black Beauty* for $1.15. For only forty-six cents each, we could get *The Little Lame Prince*, *Grimm's Fairy Tales*, *Uncle Tom's Cabin* or *The Dog of Flanders*. Mother said we could choose two apiece, so Bobby ordered *Tom Swift and the City of Gold*, and *The Rover Boys Out West* and I ordered my two most expensive ones. That night, Dad and Mother sat down together, drawing the kerosene lamp closer toward them, and added up the numbers, several times. Finally, they decided what to ask for, and Dad said he would pick up a money order at the post office the next day. Neither Bobby nor I got our books, because, Daddy said, we hadn't read all the stories in *My Book House* yet. He didn't understand that we wanted books of our very own to keep in our very own rooms. But we were good sports, something they had drilled into us.

And when Mother finally tore the order form out of the catalog and wrote down all the things we'd decided on, and put it in the mailbox, we began to wait for the mail truck to deliver it to our door. It was better than those letters we used to write to the North Pole, because Santa was not as reliable as Monkey Wards. Like Christmas ahead of time, the bulging box with all our new clothes was supposed to arrive any day from Chicago. And we could hardly wait. But, of course, we had to.

"Will it come today?" we kept asking, always getting the same answer.

"We'll just have to wait and see."

From the big brick Consolidated School in Redfield, we were going to go to a little white wood-framed building, a one-room country school nearly two miles from where we lived. We would have to walk there and back every day, climbing over or through the fences as we cut across the pastures. We needed some warmer clothes, certainly, for winter got so cold sometimes we could not see out the windows for the patterns Jack Frost left on the glass, big feathers like ostriches or peacocks, and the fronds of giant ferns.

Our mail order for school clothes included long-legged winter underwear with a drop seat in back, with one button in the middle of the flap, which you sometimes had to undo in a hurry, and some maroon corduroy "Johnny jumpers," as we called them, thick velvety overalls with metal buttons on the straps to wear over our sweaters. And new galoshes. We had sent in papers with the outlines of our feet traced on them, so the people in Chicago would know what size to send us.

For school, Mother had knitted us long scarves and hats that pulled down over our ears. Grandma came out from Des Moines to help her with school sewing. The machine Mother'd used in town, the little hump-backed Singer with a black knee lever like a giant question mark, wouldn't work out here, for there was no electricity and nowhere to plug it in. So, Mother borrowed Mrs. Smith's treadle sewing machine because the power was in your feet, like organ pedals, except there was only one. The pedal on the black iron base of the borrowed machine just rocked away, Grandmother quite speedy with her toes and heels, making it go lickety-split. She said she was good at it because it was the way she first learned.

As Gango cut out, ripped and sewed, finished hemming with her needle, she told me about the tailors who had a contest to see who could sew a coat fastest. One, greedy for success, threaded a very long thread into his needle, thinking he would save time by not having to rethread. The other tailor used a piece just long enough to sew evenly, and he won.

"Why did he win?" I asked her.

"Can you guess?" she asked us.

Bobby who sat cross-legged with his book in the corner of the room, piped up, "Because it took longer to get the big thread off the spool."

"Nope." When neither of us could imagine, we gave up.

She sat there, waiting until our curiosity seasoned, sticking the needle into the bosom of her apron where she already had a whole porcupine of pins stuck, and then told us, "The greedy tailor got his long thread tangled up and knotted, and he spent so much time untangling it that he lost the contest." It was a way of teaching us several things at once, for she was a born teacher. And she loved riddles.

Our Grandma Chantry sang hymns, too, and recited whole poems by heart. And sometimes, she would tell us what it was like when she was a young girl. Born just after the Civil War, she had come from a world that to us, then, seemed very far away. She told us about our great-uncle Ben when he was a boy. "One of our best cows didn't show up at milking time, and Grandpa sent Ben to look for her. Probably she'd broken through the fence in the corner of the pasture, he thought. So Ben took a rope to lead her back to the barn if he found her. As he was walking along the fence line, he thought he heard a hissing sound, but it was dusk and he couldn't see anything. Then, he turned around just as it turned dark, and heard a swishing. He ran all the way back home, thinking he was being chased by a snake. You know what it was?"

We waited. She snapped a thread in her mouth and said, "It was the rope dragging on the ground!" We whispered to each other that maybe there had been an idiot in our family.

Of course, we thought Grandma was a real antique. We goaded her to tell us about *her* childhood. Mostly we waited for her strange words, like "beau" and "courting" and "spooning," which made us giggle. Sometimes, though, she'd make our mouths water when she talked about sunshine preserves, and gooseberry pie, and the piccalilli she made every summer.

She'd ask us to go down into the "root cellar" for things she wanted to cook for supper. She didn't like to lift up the trapdoor, we thought, because she hated spiders. So we would go. It was another chance to sneak one or two pieces of our favorite delicacy, "cracklins," the crisp brown rind of roasted pig, forbidden food we thought so yummy and crunchy. They were rich. Too many of them could make you sick, we were warned. We always stole a few and ate them together before we went back up the stairs.

"They look like dead spiders," Bobby would say.

"More like baby field mice, toasted," I thought.

"Even more like bits of horse turd picked up from the road." Whoever could think up the grossest thing was raised in the other's esteem, especially when we were sure nobody else would hear us.

This "cave," as we called the root cellar, was as dark as night unless we left the door open. We had a flashlight so we could see the corners. It was like a cold cupboard, or an icebox. It had an earthen floor, and above the wooden framework the roof had a very slight moist smell of earth. Along the edges, Daddy had built shelves for Mother's canning, and the rows of jars full of cherries, peaches, applesauce, green beans, corn cut off the cob, even beef for winter stew, made us hungry. Too, there was a whole section of delicacies for special occasions, apple butter, pickled peaches, spiced pears, cinnamon crab apples with the stems on, and raspberry jam. A few jars of quince jelly Mother saved for when she and Daddy had friends over for dinner.

The cracklins were stored down there, waiting for the day when Daddy and our neighbor Cole Mashur would make a batch of soap. The recipe for soap needed the natural fats provided by pork rinds as well as lye, stirred and boiled with water until it began to solidify. It was heavy work, soap making. Cole Mashur was a big-muscled man, taller than Daddy and strong. The soap making was done in a large iron kettle hung on a tripod over a fire. When the long-handled wooden paddles got sluggish, the batch stirred to the right consistency, the hot fluid would be poured into a big shallow wooden mold to cool before being cut into rectangular bars. It looked good enough to eat, oily like the pork cracklins and brown as sugar, but the smell was strong, like the Fels-Naptha soap we used for laundry, dishes, sometimes even our baths.

Cole Mashur owned a mule, which turned the sorghum grinder in a dumb monotonous circle, wearing a deep ditch track in the sawdust. The sticky molasses for pancakes dripped into a big kettle, swarming with flies. It was in the center of that circle that the fire was built to boil the soap. The same big iron kettle served for both purposes.

Getting ready for winter, Mother and Grandma sewed together salvaged squares from old woolen pants and coats to make covers for the batting sandwiched in between them. They spread these covers out on the floor, the two sides facing each other, wrong side to wrong side, with the soft batts inside. Then, Mother tied them together. They were a lot like the quilts we had, but the pieces were much bigger, and they were never quilted as finely. She threaded a big-eyed needle with a piece of yarn up through the three layers to make a double knot on the top side. She made sure there were enough ties to keep the batting in place, tied tightly enough to keep it from coming apart with use. She would get down on her knees and carefully fold the big piece back to reach the middle, like trying to make a double bed that is closed on three sides.

"You sit on the corner, Janie, so the pieces don't slip, will you?"

"Yes."

"And Bobby, can you cut the yarn pieces all the same length as this one?" She tossed him one she had cut and was about to thread into her needle. He took up the scissors and began to measure lengths of yarn for her, worrying because the wool would stretch. "Don't worry, honey. It doesn't matter that much, because I'll trim them anyway, when we're all done."

When the pieces were tied together, she basted a long bias binding around the edges and Grandma would sew it down. Those comforters were so warm and cozy on our cold winter beds upstairs. If it was freezing cold outside, we were allowed to undress by the kitchen stove and run fast into bed. Lots of times, Daddy had put a two-quart Mason jar full of hot water, wrapped in a towel, at the foot of our bed. Oh, it was delicious to find it down there with our cold toes and feet!

It was wonderful for the whole family whenever a box came in the mail. It was like winning a prize at the county fair, or getting Uncle Walter's box of "alligator pears" all the way from California, or even the thrill of a package of hand-me-downs from Auntie Oreen, Mother's sister, who lived in Washington, D.C. In the long, low light of autumn, when the shadow of the elm tree in our yard reached all the way across the lawn, when the air was tingly and crisp and the pumpkins in the cornfield were almost ripe enough to pick, our boxes from Montgomery Wards finally did arrive.

We all gathered in the kitchen where Daddy got out his knife to slit through the string and tape. Opened, the boxes made us hold our breath, for inside the wrapping paper, we could glimpse our treasures. All our new things were there, pretty colors and textures and the promise of warmth even when the lashing wind would sweep across the ground, biting into our legs with its icy teeth. Now we could walk to school and not freeze to death, like the poor little match girl, shivering in her rags.

Then, Daddy carried the boxes into the dining room to spread everything out in piles on the table, one for each of us as they were taken out of the box. We could hardly stand still, wiggling with delight to find brand-new things that fit. All except my galoshes. They were too big.

"Maybe they sent me mine from Bobby's foot picture."

"Mine are bigger, though, so that couldn't be the reason." Bobby said.

"Let me see."

He held his new galoshes against the soles of mine. They smelled like erasers. They were bigger. But not by much.

"How much bigger are yours than your shoes, Janie?" Dad wanted to know.

"About a inch."

"Well, that's not so bad. By the time winter rolls around, you'll probably have grown enough to fit them. If not, you can stick a sock in the toe!" We laughed. The mood in the house was loving and forgiving, and the galoshes not as important as my new warm pajamas, or my wonderful maroon corduroy jumpers, just like my brother's. How I loved them! They fit. And I could snap the buttons on the front into the little metal eye by myself, easily.

"Now Jane and I can be twins, too," Bobby said to MaryLou and Merilyn. They each had a pair just like ours, too, so that made four of us. Mother rolled her eyes at Daddy and said, "You didn't know we had quadruplets, did you, Merrill?"

"God forbid!" Daddy said.

Baby Danny was adorable in his snowsuit. We put it on him and took him out on the front porch, in case any cars came down the road. The world could see our little Eskimo brother, and marvel at his cute face, even though he didn't have puffy slit eyes. The twins whooped and hollered and danced about with the excitement of it all. All of us felt prepared now—for school, for winter, for survival. I, personally, thought I might just be asked to dress up and pose for a picture in the *Saturday Evening Post* or something, I felt so elegant in my brand spanky new clothes. I didn't want to take them off, but Mother said I had to save them for our first day of school.

Mother and Daddy had been invited to a "hard times" party that night. Isador Vath brought his mother, Mrs. Vath, out to spend the night with us because tomorrow was washday, and she always came to help Mother with the big things. She was going to be our "nanny" for overnight, just like they had in England. We felt very privileged.

I can't ever remember our parents being so happy as they dressed up in rags, put on crumpled hats, and tied ropes around their middles instead of belts. Dad had cut out the toes of an old pair of rubber boots, and put on holey socks that showed through. Mother had made herself a kind of dress out of an old gunnysack and blackened one of her front teeth. They laughed and laughed as they got ready to go, and they explained to us that they were *supposed* to look like that! This night, having managed to provide school clothes for all their healthy kids, having a party to go to, Mother and Daddy were as silly as kids, and all of us were giddy with joy to see them happy for a change.

Our One-Room Country School

Our grandfather, Orren Chantry, had been the county school superintendent in Adair County in the post-Civil-War days. And Grandmother, in her day, dressed in shirtwaists with leg-of-mutton sleeves and a long skirt like the girls sketched by Gibson in the gay nineties. She taught in a one-room school, where, she told us, the big boys were taller than she was. Our own mother at nineteen, before she married Daddy, boarded with a farm family and walked across a stubbly field to a country school to teach. People called these positions "teacherages," and to be assigned to a teacherage by the school board was an honor. Our family always regarded teaching as a noble profession, probably because it ran in the family.

Country schools in the early decades of the century were small, sometimes with as few as ten or as many as forty children from ages six to seventeen in the first eight grades. This size allowed for individual attention either from the teacher or from an older student. Students could advance at their own pace. The children felt carefree and secure since they all knew each other.

The rural school system had been mandated under Thomas Jefferson, who believed in an educated citizenry. So did our parents. Iowa was increasingly proud of her rural schools: one square wooden box of a school existed for every thirty-six square miles. In Iowa they had reduced illiteracy to the lowest level in the nation by the turn of the century, a position the state held for years to come. Mother and Daddy were quick to give us a sense of pride in our new school by telling us all of these things.

Our first day of school finally arrived. Daddy walked with us the first time to show us the shortest way, cutting through the fields and over the fences "as the crow flies," he said. When we asked him how far the crow had to fly, he told us not quite two miles. It was exciting and scary at the same time. We saw the schoolhouse from a long way away. It had windows all along the side that let in lots of light, and a front porch with a covered entrance where we could wipe our shoes.

"D'ya think you can find your way home, now?" Daddy asked us.

"Yes," I said, confident because I'd paid attention to landmarks on the way.

"I think so," my brother told him, sounding less positive than usual.

"Are you scared, Bobby?" I asked him.

"Yes, a little. Maybe not scared, but conspicuous."

I knew that big word. It was what I was most scared of, too, because we didn't know anybody there, and they would all look at us. We had on our new clothes, though, so that made it easier to face.

When Daddy knocked on the door and introduced himself and us to the teacher, she was so nice, so pretty, and so kind. She said she was expecting us, since Mother had called to enroll us, and she put her hands on each of our shoulders, thanked Daddy, and turned us toward the kids in that room.

"These are the Belton children, Jane and Bob, one third-grader and one fifth." Then, she showed us where our seats were. We turned our heads toward Daddy, who was lingering by the door, and he waved his fingers at us and left.

After that, dressed for whatever weather, we went alone. Lots of times, I took hold of Bobby's hand, because he was bigger and wasn't as afraid of storms. The walk wasn't hard, except when the cold, heavy rain would drench us. The sky would just open up, and we knew what Chicken Little meant when she said, "The sky is falling." In the coldest days of winter, when we shivered the whole way to school despite our warm wraps, we would take turns walking backwards into the wind, the other walking frontwards acting as the guide. Sometimes you could get dizzy, watching the snow swirl across the land as fluid as water or sand, and we were afraid we would lose our way.

But we had some landmarks, like our neighbor's big board gate, and we depended on each other to keep a lookout, to keep going. The snow drifted over the fences completely, and when the ice formed on the top, we walked right up and over them. Daddy said that if the freezing weather held, a coating of ice on snow could support a horse. We asked if we could ice-skate to school, but Mother said no. On softer days, in the late days of autumn or the early days of spring, we dawdled, for the earth was full of strange bugs, little moles, flowers we didn't know the names of. If the earth was warm where it had been plowed, we would take off our shoes and socks, tie their laces around our necks to carry them, and walk through that chocolate dirt all the way across the field. We wiped our feet off on the grass before we put our socks on again, and stuck our imprisoned feet into the jail of our shoes before we heard the teacher's bell ringing.

We had a weekend trap line, hoping to earn some money selling skins of groundhogs, foxes, muskrats, and skunks. Walking our trap line once, on a Sunday, Bobby got sprayed by a skunk, and I couldn't get far enough away from him, even walking two miles in the fresh air.

He had his head shaved, his clothes boiled in vinegar, and still he smelled strongly like a skunk. For over a month, he had to sit at the back of the room in school, because all the kids complained. That big skunk must have turned and lifted his tail right in Bobby's face, it was so awful. He felt sad, too, because there wasn't anything he could do about it, he told me, and it felt like a punishment. I would always sit with him for lunch, because I got used to the smell, and it's lonely to eat lunch alone.

Coming in sight of the schoolhouse was a kind of daily victory. We had walked the two miles and nothing had happened to us, we had withstood the weather and arrived on time. My heart always did a little dance when we got to school, for I loved the teacher and the schoolroom was a haven of safety with playmates and new things to learn. It was a place where I could prove my mettle, for I was a "hungry learner," my Grandma said, loving to imagine things, to remember clearly everything I read, to please the teacher, to be chosen by the captain of the spelling-bee team or, better yet, to be the captain, to reign over my peers. I wanted to be recognized by the older boys, the big farm boys from the eighth grade, some of whom inevitably would be sitting on the fence until the bell rang. I hung around them wherever they were, wanting to be asked to play their games. I could bat a ball farther than any of the other girls. But all they ever did was pull my pigtails until it really hurt and I begged them to stop.

A board fence marked the square schoolyard. Just outside the fence, a pony shed with a roof and a manger full of hay sheltered the horses ridden bareback to school by some of the kids who came the longest distance. A gate with a huge hook kept the animals inside until school was dismissed. Generally, the big boys were the ones who came on horseback, and they would take their places on the top board of the fence like birds on a telephone wire. Just inside the fence, in the back corner of the schoolyard across from the pony shed, the privies stood, two wooden buildings, one for the girls and the other for the boys. They were single-holers, and the doors locked from inside with a big hook and eye; pages from an out-of-date mail-order catalog served as toilet paper. Nobody stayed in there any longer than necessary because it was too stinky, too hot, or too cold.

Between the outhouses and the schoolhouse, close enough if you stared out the windows to see the leaves dancing, was a big tree with a tire swing. The ground beneath it was bare, indented and worn thin from shoes that had dragged across it to stop its dizzying wobble. A trick we all tried, once at least—it could make you dizzy and light-headed—was winding the tire round and around on its rope to give it an additional spin. Then, a hard push would send the tire and its child gyrating in all directions until it came to a hang-still. That and a teeter-totter mounted on a bent piece of steel pipe on the other side of the porch, a marbles circle for the boys, a hopscotch grid painted on the front walk for the girls, made up our playground equipment. Mostly we played games like "keep-away" or "jump rope" or "Annie-Annie over" during recess. The well pump where we got our drinking water and water to fill the enamel basin where we all washed our hands, stood beside the concrete front walk near the front steps. Inside, we hung our coats, hats, and mittens on hooks, putting our metal lunch boxes on the floor below them. The low shelf where the washbasin and the soap lived had a roller towel on the other end, and we always tried to pull it down to find the driest, cleanest part to dry our hands and face. If it was muddy outside, we had to leave our galoshes in the entry-way.

Inside, the one large room wrapped its warmth around us with wooden seats, shiny from years of use, each with a sloping desk that had a hole for an inkbottle and a little gully for keeping our pencils from rolling off. A big black stove toward the front, when the fire was hot, gave off heat waves that wiggled like a nest of snakes. Its flue was like a tall tree trunk, rising up through the room to a hole in the roof. It had a metal damper on the side that the teacher could turn and make it warmer or cooler. It could get hot, and we would watch her jump back, then pick up a hot pad that she kept near the woodbox before she would touch it again. She'd open the door, with its little isinglass peephole window, to throw in more wood or hunks of coal. Then we saw the flames dance up through the little window. In the winter, a big pot of soup would be simmering on the back of the flat top, smelling like beans and tomatoes and chicken, or maybe ham hocks and split peas. Each child, in addition to a sandwich or some cold biscuits brought from home, had a warm lunch that way, ladled into our individual cups, our names pasted on them with adhesive tape. Some days, some kids didn't have a sandwich, so they got an extra ladle full. Our soup cups were all lined up on a shelf above the bookcase behind the teacher's desk. We washed them out in a new basin of water after lunch, and let the cups drip dry on the grooved wooden drain board.

Up in front, on either side of a map case with maps that rolled up and down like window shades—maps of the whole United States or Africa or Europe—hung two big pictures of our dead presidents, Abraham Lincoln and George Washington. I thought George was better looking for a long time until someone told me he had wooden teeth. Ever after that, I couldn't imagine how dry that would taste. No wonder he kept his mouth shut and didn't smile.

An upright piano stood against one wall, and a movable blackboard was stored behind it. Sometimes, the teacher pulled her hair back with a rubber band. It tightened the skin on her face and made her look tired when she sat down to play some music for us at lunchtime. She wheeled the blackboard out when we took turns doing our arithmetic problems on it.

Her desk had a row of books in front, between bookends that looked like books, too. It stood like a castle wall between her face and the rest of us, a place she could almost hide behind to correct our spelling papers. On one corner was the big brass bell with the wooden handle, resting there upside down. Stepping out the front door, she would ring that bell for the beginning of school and for the beginning and end of recess. On the other corner of her desk was a globe where you could spin around the whole world and still see the North and South Poles. It was colder in those places than we ever were, she told us, when a blizzard howled against the rattling windows in winter.

Since every morning began with the Pledge of Allegiance, our flag stood beside the piano on a broomstick with golden feet. We all stared at it when we put our hands over our hearts. It was our way of saying what patriotic young Americans we all were, though I never knew exactly what a patriotic American was supposed to be. It was like saying "Our Father who art in Heaven" in Sunday school, the words to the Lord's Prayer printed on our hearts. How God sorted out who was praying and who wasn't puzzled me. Too, some people said forgive us our "debts" and some others said "trespasses," which I didn't like, because if God, even Jesus, wanted to trespass on our property, I would be glad to give him to eat and to drink.

Our country school had eight grades, but some years there weren't any pupils for some grades. Bobby's fifth grade only had two in it, and my third grade had three. The eighth grade had four big boys, and when their class was called up to the front bench for recitation, their voices were loud enough to make it hard to pay attention to our lessons or to reading *The History of the Thirteen Colonies*. We listened to their spelling words, and some of the ones they missed, both of us could spell. We would look at each other across our desks and smile.

On our walk home in the afternoon, we'd make fun of them for missing such easy words.

Those big boys knew a lot of things that made me scared of them in a way, and they called Bobby a "sissy" because he used bigger words when he talked, and he had newer boots.

"Hey! Lord Fauntleroy, where'd ya get them new slippers?"

"They're boots!"

"Oh, really. We never coulda guessed it. Ya forgot yer velvet dress!" they taunted.

"Bullies are just cowards," Bobby told them, "so you don't threaten me!"

"Threaten? Threaten? Did ya hear what he said? We don't 'threaten' him! He means he ain't scared of us."

"Oh, yeah? Whad'ya think, Mr. Dictionary, does threaten mean scared or not? In this school, we don't talk sissy, so the sooner you learn that, the better off you'll be."

Their teasing hurt Bobby, but he didn't want to show it. So he and I went back into the schoolhouse to get away from those mean big boys.

Once, while the three or four of them were out sitting on the fence, one of them asked me if I knew what "fuck" meant. I didn't. So they told me Andrew "fucked" his cow. Andrew got furious and pushed the boy who said it off the fence. They said lots of swear words and took the Lord's name in vain a lot. That started a fight the teacher had to stop.

"Bobby, what does fucking a cow do?" I asked him on the way home.

"Where did you hear that?" He turned his face toward me and his eyes bugged out. He was almost mad at me. Then he shrugged his shoulders, said he couldn't explain it, which I took to mean he didn't know either. I didn't believe him. He knew and wouldn't tell me, and I hated secrets unless they were mine. The way the boys had laughed, though, made me think it was naughty, and one of my friends finally told me more or less what it meant. I'd seen a lot of that with the animals, I just hadn't heard the word, and I didn't think people did it. I steered clear of the big boys after that.

We were allowed to leave our desks without permission for two reasons: to sharpen a pencil if the lead broke, or to go outside to the toilet. If my lesson in penmanship or arithmetic was done, just to break the boredom of long sitting, I would get up to go to the wonderful pencil sharpener with the handle that turned and turned, making the wood of my pencil into sawdust, which smelled as good as Mother's cedar chest. I put my nose up to one of the little holes and sniffed and sniffed the fresh scent. Too, it was an excuse to look out the window at the sky, to see the clouds rolling by or to catch a glimpse of the black and white cows munching in the pasture next door.

Closer to Christmas, we began rehearsing our school pageant. All the farm families for miles around, in addition to our own, would come to see us, and we wanted it to be a great surprise. One of the boys was a whiz juggling balls in the air. Bobby was going to be Joseph, and the parts of the three wise men were given to the boys who weren't very good actors. I was to do my combination tap-dance and jump-rope act while another girl played "East Side, West Side," on the piano.

The little audience made a big sound with lots of clapping, because we didn't miss a step or a note. In addition, I recited a long poem called "The House by the Side of the Road." It said what I wanted to do most of all, to "be a friend to man." When I came out on the stage, a platform in front of the room made by one of the fathers, there were Mother and Daddy, MaryLou and Merilyn. Baby Danny was sitting on top of a desk. When he saw me, he called out in his baby voice, waving his pudgy arms up and down with excitement, "Janie! Janie! Janie!" Mother tried to shush him, but the whole audience was amused.

I was so embarrassed I nearly forgot the lines. My cheeks were hot and I prayed that I could finish the poem and then just drop over, dead. Then he'd be sorry for interrupting our play. Mother and Daddy would put green leaves with red holly berries on my snowy grave, and people would forget what happened, they'd be so sad. But I managed to stumble through, which won praise from the teacher, later. My chagrin was so intense that I was impatient with Danny when he wanted me to tell him a bedtime story. "No," I told him, "You weren't supposed to yell out my name in the schoolroom!" Of course, he didn't understand and began to cry, sensing my cold-heartedness.

Mother said, "Janie, he is too little to know the difference. What he was really saying was 'I love you.'" And, underneath it all, I think I knew that was true.

We went to that school for two years. When the second spring came and the wonderful days burst the woods into bloom, Daddy and Mother told us they were planning to move to Oregon where Uncle Howard had a farm he wanted Daddy to manage. Mother knew we would miss our friends, so she made a party for Valentines Day, cupcakes for every one of our schoolmates and one for the teacher. We had lemonade from a big enamel pitcher that sweated on the sides. Mother wanted the students to remember us as "very talented children," and she held up a picture I had drawn of an island and a sailboat. Bob, she told them, could make model airplanes that could almost fly.

We were both excited about such an adventure as a move clear out to the Pacific Ocean, but sorry to leave our friends. Even though we were glad to have a little farewell party, we were kind of sad. Oregon was a long ways away, and we had come to love our one-room schoolhouse, standing so proudly out in the middle of the prairie.

Now, almost half a century later, my own memory of two years in our much-loved schoolhouse is vivid. The smell of sweeping compound sprinkled on the floor before the teacher swept it up when school was out, the chalk dust, the sound of the teacher's brass bell, raising the flag against the bright blue sky, the warmth of the wood stove, the cedar-perfumed *whirr* of the hand-cranked pencil sharpener, the excitement of opening up our wooden desk lids to find our books and clean paper, our class being called up front for lessons, the drowsy flies inside the smelly outhouse as the days grew warm—all of these sensuous details remain.

My Darling Clementine

Financial circumstances for farmers in those bleak years made it all but impossible to stick it out. As if the economic depression and the wave of foreclosures were not enough, the grasshopper plague was the last straw for thousands.

The skies would suddenly go dark, blackened with clouds of grasshoppers, ugly, greedy, greenish-brown creatures that stripped all the leaves and the bark off the trees, killing them. They had big heads and little teeth, wiggly antennae that stuck up by their ear holes, and legs that were bent at the knees. Some were really big, two or three inches long, and some of them, probably their babies, were smaller, but hungriest of all. They ruined the crops, chewing the new wheat shoots and the tender corn off at ground level. We could hear them zinging before we saw them coming, and everyone who was outside ran into the house. The high whine of hordes of hungry grasshoppers was noisier than a dozen buzz saws. There was no more escape from them than from the hot sun in the open desert.

"Dad, will they come inside?" Bobby had picked up the tension everyone felt.

"I don't think so, son, but I heard that in the Dakotas, the bastards even ate the paint off the houses. They've had it worse than we're seeing. We've shut everything up tight, though, so they can't come in. But it's a sorry sight. It's another year of loss for us, I'm afraid. . . ." He paced around the dining room table, a kind of mad stare in his eyes.

By next morning, they had disappeared, but on our lawn, carcasses of many of them were scattered everywhere. They were different from crickets, different from frogs, kind of brittle and mean, with veiny wings and a little mouth like a devil's grin. We had heard about plagues in the Bible, and we wondered if God was mad at us. We started to gather them up to put in a pail, but Mother opened the door and yelled out at us.

"Don't touch those dirty things, they might be carrying disease for all we know." So we just let them stay there until Daddy raked them up in ugly piles. They stayed there for a long time, drying out and curling up. At the end of the summer, Daddy burned them with gasoline, and their nasty bodies crackled like cornflakes.

It was deep into autumn, 1935. Our woods smelled like leaves burning, but without a fire. The low sun had burnished the hardwoods to leaf fall, the black walnuts, the oaks, elms, and hickories gorgeous in their September colors. The air was turning crisp, the kind of fall weather that made our nostrils open wide, that made us want to breathe like winded horses. We had cut and tied together the corn stalks to put with our Halloween jack-o-lanterns on the porch. Their dry leaves rustled like stiff butcher paper. The pumpkin pie Mother had baked for supper was cooling on top of the warming oven, but even that did not make Daddy smile, as it usually did. They were silent a lot.

Bobby and I were excited, though, for we would be moving again after New Year's. This time, we would be moving out toward the Pacific Ocean; we would be moving to Oregon. We had overheard a lot of conversation between our parents about the planning of it, tense arguments that we went outside to get away from, for their voices sounded more and more brittle.

"Merrill, if I have to choose one thing *only* to ship out to Oregon, it'll be my corner cupboard. I just can't part with it. It belonged to my grandmother. That and a dozen or more books? We can do that much, can't we?" Her voice was wheedling, for he had become rock hard in his resolution to spend very little on freight.

"What do you mean, one thing? One thing only? All right, Xela, we'll ship the damned thing, but don't bring it up again. I can't perform miracles!"

Mother was forever blowing her nose as if she'd caught a cold. But we knew better. She was sad. It didn't diminish our dream of adventure, however, for we were going to travel to a new land.

Daddy listened to the news on our Atwater Kent. One night he told us to come and listen. "Maybe it'll help you understand our moving west," he told us. The man on the radio was explaining why lots of people had made the same decision.

"With the dust storms and the terrible drought years of 1934–35, not only homes were buried in dirt, but also, the last shreds of hope were buried with it. Throughout the Plains states, two and a half million people have left for other parts. 460,000 people will leave Iowa for the Pacific Northwest."

We were dumbfounded. "Two and a half million, did he say?" I asked.

"You heard right, Janie. And we're gonna be among them."

Dad's brother, our uncle Howard, who lived in the rich Willamette Valley in Oregon, urged him to file for an "auction of his chattels," post the handbills, sell out, and come join him. Mother and Daddy reached a decision, a hard one. They would ship a few things by rail, sell everything else they had, and with the money they earned, drive to Oregon in February 1936, and stay with Uncle Howard and Auntie Mae until they could relocate. Dad would either set up a new veterinary practice near Canby, or he would manage a farm that Uncle Howard owned until we could get on our feet. With five children and a pregnant wife, it was easier said than done. The excitement we felt about their plans was different from our parents' mood, heavy as contagion in the air. After all, we would be enrolling in yet another school, and both of us, by this time, had come to look on these changes in classrooms as chances to make new friends, to learn more things.

Those were hard years in the Midwest. Hundreds of Iowa farmers were unable to pay off their mortgages. Insurance companies, farm equipment contractors, and banks were foreclosing on property because the owner could not meet payments on their loans. The spirit of camaraderie among neighbors was strong and supportive, bound together in adversity.

We knew about auctions. My best friend from school, Annie, told us at her birthday party how her family had had a "ten-cent sale" last year. We didn't know what she meant, so she tried to explain it, but none of us really understood what banks did, or why farmers gave their farms back to the bank. Although we couldn't grasp the fine points of a depressed economy, we could feel the tension everywhere.

"They call it a 'ten-cent sale' because everything went for less money than it was really worth, my mom said."

"You mean you can buy anything for ten cents?" Bobby asked her.

"No, silly," Annie answered, "It just means cheap."

"How much did things sell for?" Bobby wanted to know, because he'd just had to sell his 4-H grand-prize calf for beef, and Daddy said the meat was worth a lot more. The buyer from the packinghouse cheated him, he thought. He was money conscious, anyway. He'd cut a slot in a jar lid with Mother's kitchen knife, big enough to put pennies through. The bottom of the jar was already covered with pennies. He swore he would not take them out, even to put in the birthday collection at church.

"Lots of stuff got sold for practically nothing," Annie said, "like fifteen cents for a butter churn, twelve dollars for our plow, I think about thirty cents an acre for our pasture. Really cheap. Mom said the auctioneer was great, because he would close the bidding when it was low, because he was sympathetic to us."

Annie was older than we were, and smarter, but she wanted to talk about how her auntie who lived in Virginia had sent her some new clothes, so we didn't talk about their auction for long, but we told all the other kids that we were going to have an auction, too. They didn't seem to care.

Annie's mom had made a freezer full of peach ice cream, so that's what we were waiting for. We had a good time that day, mostly because Annie's mother had the birthday party, but partly, we thought, to celebrate their not having to move.

Daddy put the white notices up in Diddy's Drugstore, the post office, the IGA store, and the library, too. On it, it told about our auction, where it was, the Highland Stock Farm on Highway 6 north of town, and when it was to start, October 1, 1935, at eight o'clock in the morning. He'd tacked the papers on both posts flanking our front gate. The auctioneer had been hired.

"Do you remember that man we passed in his hay wagon the other day on the road, the one who was practicing his auctioneer's call on his team of horses?" Dad asked me. I did. "Well, that's the fellow who'll be working for us," he said, and both of us older kids were sure we could learn how to do it, just by listening to him for a while.

At night we practiced from our beds, giggling. "Now, here we have a fine John Deere harrow, do I hear a bid, a bid, let's have a bid. Do I hear one dollar, one dollar, one dollar fifty cents, do I hear one dollar seventy-five cents. Do I hear two dollars, two dollars? Going, going, gone to the man in the red shirt for one dollar and seventy-five cents." Bobby's voice rose and fell like a barker in a circus. I thought I did a better job than my brother, but he felt, since he had a man's voice, that he won.

"Clemmy, who's going to be the best auctioneer?" I asked my doll. Then, because I thought Bobby was a really good imitator, I made her head nod in his direction, holding her arm up as if she were pointing to him. "I guess you win, Bobby," I said, feeling unselfish and proud of Clementine. Maybe that's what he'd grow up to be.

Already October, the day of our big auction finally arrived. The hubbub was like the county fair, only there weren't any balloons. People from the town and farmers from counties all around us drove into the farmyard in their Model T's, Model A's, or old Chevy pickups, even parking up on the edge of our grass. People we'd never seen before were swarming around in the barn and in the shed beside the house. That's where our household things and personal belongings were displayed on planks laid over wooden sawhorses. That's where the auctioneer would stand on two apple boxes turned up on end and steadied with chunks of wood, so he could see over the heads of the crowd.

The auctioneer stalked into the house and spread the inventory sheets out on the kitchen table. Mother hardly looked at him. We, on the other hand, stared. He was skinny as a pitchfork, had sandy hair that needed a wash or a better brushing than he'd given it, and his faded work shirt smelled like sweat. But he had the lips for the job, big lips that could blow bubbles, I thought, if he'd wanted to.

"Smells awful good in here," he said.

She ignored him.

"Smells like a punkin pie." She didn't take the hint, although usually she was generous. He was out of luck on this day, however, since he was planning to take away some of the things she cherished, and the only way to survive the company when the auction was under way, was her aloof silence.

Later in the morning, Mother stood at the kitchen window, crying. She had on her favorite apron, the one Daddy said looked like a sandwich board. It was the same both in front and back, and could be turned around when one side got spilled on. Instead of ties, it had tabs with a button on one end and a buttonhole on the other, to attach one side to the other. Grandma had made it for her, edging every inch of it with bias tape. When the apron was new, it was bright with flowers, but it was faded now from many washings. Mrs. Vath, the lady who sometimes helped Mother wash, told us the sun was greedy and would pick the flowers right off the clothes on the line. Now, stuck into the side tab of her apron hung one of the big handkerchiefs I had given Daddy for Christmas last year, and every once in a while, Mother would pull it out and blow her nose.

She watched a man who had bought her needlepoint footstool carry it out the driveway to his car, her beloved antique walnut oval made beautiful with her handiwork. It was a lovely low stool she had found years ago, and Daddy had refinished it for her. She had worked on the covering for that stool for months. Once, I went with her to the yarn department in a big store in Des Moines to find just the shade of dusty rose yarn she wanted to go with what she called "Williamsburg Blue," to make the fine design of twined flowers inside the delicate border of the canvas. At night, after the supper dishes were done, she would open up the rolled canvas on which the pattern was emerging, and, with the needle already threaded and stuck into the corner, would pull the gorgeous wool up through the little holes. Her face would soften as she worked, for she was a princess in a green garden, then, an oasis in the parched landscape that stretched outside the palace walls for endless miles. And she was making something clean and colorful and new, full of the flowers she would have loved to walk outside the door to pick.

After a long time, the needlepoint was finished, and she upholstered it over a pad onto the little stool. When she rested her feet on it while she read, which she did every chance she got, so her varicose veins wouldn't hurt, I thought she must have dreamed of walking along a winding path through a beautiful garden.

She just stood there, watching the man carrying it away, the tears running down her face, her hands hanging by her side. He had paid twenty-five cents for a piece of her soul. Bobby and I put our arms around her waist, but she didn't move, didn't even seem to know we were there. She had been crying a lot in the desperate days leading up to this auction sale.

Dad put his arm around her shoulder. "Zee, honey, dry your tears. Just think, when this is all over, you'll have money to buy yourself new clothes, and the kids, too. Maybe your old man'll even get a new shirt when we get to Des Moines, for the trip west."

"I'll try, Merrill," she sniffled. "It's been so long since we could think of having anything, I guess I'm in the *habit* of disappointment. It's been hard for all of us, I know."

The auction went on all day. I wanted to be outside but Mother admonished me, "You stay out of the way, Janie. Too many things are going on out there, and you could get trampled. If you want to watch, keep a safe distance. Stay with Bobby, promise me?"

"I will," I said. She turned to Bobby who had egged me on to get permission.

"Bob, listen to me. Keep close to Jane if you kids want to see what's going on. Take hold of each other's hand if you wander out by the barn."

And so we went out the back steps toward the shed, to peek in there, first. Both of us were surprised to see so many of our things going up for bidding. Our folks must have carted these things out after we'd gone to bed. On the planks were the kerosene lamps whose wicks it had been my job to trim. The three with glass shades over the little balloon wicks like honeycombs were up for sale, the best ones with pretty painted roses and daisies on the glass shades, so fragile I never got to handle those. And the wooden bowl with the cabbage cutter like a metal cradle, a hobnail cake plate we used for birthdays, the glass deviled-egg plate Mother always took full for our Fourth of July picnic with the Kellehers, a demijohn of pickling vinegar, and the Russian tea cozy Auntie Bing had given Mother after their big trip to Europe. And there were some of our own toys, too—the twins' wooden blocks, their Betty Boop celluloid dolls, the Dionne Quintuplets paper dolls, their trike. Bobby's cigar boxes full of his rock collection were open for people to see, and—oh, no! *Not my dolly!!*

"Bobby!" I yelled, "somebody put Clementine out here by mistake!" I grabbed her up and ran to Daddy, who was talking to the auctioneer.

"Daddy, Daddy!" I said, trying to get his attention.

Finally he turned toward me, impatient. He pushed his glasses back up on his nose and ran his hand through his thinning hair. "What do you want, girl?"

I clutched Clementine around her waist, her face and brown braids pressed against my chest. "You can't sell my *dolly*! She's going to Oregon with me!"

"Now you listen to me, young lady. I know you don't want to leave anything behind, but the car has only so much room! If I let you take your doll and Bob his rock collection, and the twins their baby quilts, where do you suppose the rest of us will sit? Sorry, just try to be a good sport about it, will you? There are more dolls in Oregon, and we'll get you another one when we get there."

I began to cry. "I don't *want* any other one! She sleeps with me, and I sewed her new pantaloons. Pleeease, let me keep her, just this one thing, puleeease, Daddy!"

He took hold of my shoulder with one hand, his strong fingers digging into my flesh, and with the other hand he yanked the doll away from me. "Get back in the house with Mother if you're going to bawl and cause a scene," he said, angrily. "The things for sale have already been listed! Now, I'll put this back where it belongs, and I want you to keep your hands off everything, do you hear me?" He turned me around toward the house. "Go back inside if you can't stay out of the way!"

Through my swimming eyes, I watched him put Clementine back on the plank where I had found her. He didn't even pull her skirt down, and one of her arms was trapped underneath her body. I knew her heart was breaking, and I asked God to watch over her and keep her until I came to Heaven to be with her again. Bobby and I had baptized her one day down by the creek, so I knew she'd for sure be gathered up in Jesus' arms.

I whispered, "Maybe you will find a new mother who will love you, Clemmy, but never as much as I do! Remember me always, and I will keep you locked in my heart till I die."

Before the day was over, Dad's harvester, his prize heifers, his corn-husking equipment, our red wagon, the horse harness and saddle, our Flexible Flyer sled, Bobby's fossil collection, and Clementine had gone the way of Mother's footstool. Mother's best wedding dishes, the simple white Wedgewood ones she always handled so carefully were sold, too, but she kept the silverware, insisting that she would carry it all the way to Oregon in her apron if necessary.

As the afternoon wore on, the crowd began to thin. The high bidders put their things into their cars or trucks or baskets and drove away. Our house seemed emptier than ever, but since our neighbor had wanted our mattresses when we left, we still had a place to sleep. The old wood stove still kept the kitchen warm. Our kitchen seemed bigger, now that the pie cupboard with the metal pattern-punched doors was sold. The enamel-topped workbench we planned to ship to Oregon served as a table and Mother'd kept a few things we would need until we moved, things she was then going to give to Mrs. Smith, our neighbor.

"Why Mrs. Smith?" Bob asked. "She's the lady who listens in on the party line and you don't like that, do you?"

"No. I never did like that," Mother said, "because she's a gossip. But she's been a good neighbor to us, too. She's willing to clean up here after we go, so I told her she could have everything we left. She was glad for that because her sister's family is moving in with them and they need extra beds and things."

A pall hung over the days as the year drew down toward Thanksgiving. One day, a truck arrived to pack up the things to ship to Oregon. After Dad and the driver had loaded pieces of furniture, including Mother's corner cupboard, some bedding, and some clothes to ship west that afternoon, we drove into Des Moines. Grandma Chantry had made a delicious dinner of fried chicken and mashed potatoes and gravy, and a cherry chocolate cake to welcome her "beloved nomads," as she called us. We were all going to stay with her awhile before Dad got all his business taken care of. Gango was wonderful. She let us sleep on the floor on some of her best big quilts. She and Mother talked a lot.

Of those few months before we left, I remember little. The city was bustling with noise, in contrast to our small town, and everything smelled like coal smoke, a kind of yellow way up in my nose. Lots of my parents' friends came to say goodbye. Finally, the day came to leave. Grandma took a picture of us by the trunk of our car, Mother in her raccoon-fur coat, Daddy with a billed tweed cap, and the rest of us, awful in our lumpy snowsuits.

"I wish we could stay here in Iowa just a little longer," I confided to Bobby, "I'd like to finish school when the wildflowers are blooming in the pasture."

"I'm gonna miss my stuff," he said.

"Remember our hide-and-seek in the cornfield? And how we'd lie down in the shade of the corn crib where it was cool and make up stories?"

"I'll miss our river...."

"And the little toy towns we built for our cars, down on the riverbank?"

"Are we going to stay with Uncle Howard and Auntie Mae and their kids?"

"Bet they don't have a bed in their attic like we did," I told Bobby.

"My rocks...."

"I never want another dolly...."

"Or a dog. Frieda is all I will ever love when it comes to dogs." We could not forgive Daddy for giving her to Cole Mashur. He already had enough dogs.

"Do you s'pose we'll ever come back to our buried treasure in the woods?" I was starting to cry.

"Don't be sad, Janie. We'll make another secret hiding place when we get to a bigger woods."

We agreed it might be hard to make new friends in a new school halfway through the year, but we promised to be each other's friend, no matter what we found in Oregon.

Without a heater and jabbing each other for the window seats, we crept out of Iowa across the black ice of Missouri, four of us in the back seat of a Chevy. Mother sat in silence in the front, staring out at February.

Leaning up over the front seat, I asked, "Will the groundhog see his shadow, do you think?"

Daddy quipped, "Well, he'll see *our* shadow even if he doesn't see his own!" We had strapped two big wooden boxes on top of the car, and it did make a funny shadow. I'd forgotten what it was like to hear Daddy make a joke. He seemed more like himself again, his new leather-palmed driving gloves steady on the wheel and the open road ahead. Sometimes, he would break into a whistle. He and Mother occasionally sang a song together, usually about trampling on the grapes of wrath or driving six white horses. Once they sang a duet of "Oh my darling, oh my darling, oh my darling Clementine; you are lost and gone forever. . . ." I began to cry, hating them for singing that song. Clementine was probably right then being loved by someone she didn't even know.

Crowded in the back seat, long underwear climbed up our crotches under ribbed and woolen stockings, snaking down despite the garters buttoned onto pantywaists. I pulled and pounded at the ugly lumps along my legs.

My underpinnings snapped from strain, driving into Kansas. Mother told me not to cry. I screamed, "I HATE these long stockings!"

She reached back and slapped my face. Then, she blew her nose, and we all fell quiet. Sitting still we wouldn't spill the warmth out; maybe the twins would sleep.

Bobby and I talked about what we'd left, too, when we weren't quarreling. He was so bossy, and he lied about his turn on the window side. He took half my apple, too, when he said he just wanted one bite. But, we remembered we left our wills in a Mason jar buried near our Raccoon River fort. A nest of mice in our woodpile near the barn had had pink babies with no hair to keep them warm, and we guessed they'd grow up without us.

Our parents talked in the front seat, over the sound of the motor, mostly about those things they'd never forget, over and over again, like prayer beads—the screened-in porch, mosquito-safe; his hybrid seed corn and her hollyhock seeds; the cool root cellar full of parsnips and cracklins for making soap, the strawberry preserves. The things they hated to leave were not just material possessions. They were the memories of their college years in Ames, their friends, their early marriage years, setting up housekeeping, the death of their first baby girl, shared experiences on the land, love of the place where we had all been born, and the dream that burned to a crisp and dried up despite their valiant efforts.

Two old narrow tires wore thin on miles of flatland, so open the wind could bully its way across without a taker, and Dad had to jack up the car and change them. It was cold work, and he would slap his hands together to make them warm again. Mother warmed little Danny's food on the running board over cans of Sterno, burning blue nauseous flames. Big tents of blankets, spread across our knees, became a zoo through seven states to Uncle Howard's house. We played "I spy" and "I went on a trip," in which you had to remember all the items the last person had packed and then add another one. And "states," a game of watching the license plates of other cars on the road, and yelling out "States!" first, when we saw a new one. When night came, and Daddy looked for a motel we could stay in, Mother always had to go in first to inspect the bed for bedbugs.

The diesel smell from a truck we followed up a curvy road made Mother vomit. That's how we knew we would probably have another baby in our family. Bob and I would be more like grownups than children when we got to Oregon, we decided, so we began to call each other Bob and Jane. After all, we were the "big twins," Bob almost fourteen, and I, nearly twelve. We left our little-kid names in Iowa.

LETTING GO

A Quick Reversal

Through the United Airlines gate, brightly lit and teeming with holiday travelers, Bob walked up the ramp, grinning and clutching his carry-on bag. It was December 1992; Christmas was still three weeks away. He had flown out from Washington, D.C., for a month with his siblings and their families, all of us living on the West Coast. He shook hands with my husband, Howard, dropped his shoulder bag and squeezed me long and hard. He felt thinner than I remembered. My arms could encircle his chest and ribs easily. Then, up closer, I saw in the whites of his eyes a kind of opacity that was off-white, maybe tinged with yellow, the way eyes look after an optometrist dilates the pupils with those stinging drops. I couldn't be sure. His facial skin seemed taut and maybe a little sallow. Maybe air travel didn't agree with him. Maybe his winter flight had been an icy nightmare.

"God, it's good to see you!" he sighed, tired I thought. Then, more crisply, "We'll need to talk." In an abrupt change of subject, he asked, "Where's the baggage claim here, upstairs or down?"

"Down," I said, "but we're in no hurry." Still driven by time, I thought, he was more than ready for a vacation.

And so we three, like a sandwich with Bob in the middle, walked toward the escalator down, arm in arm, nearly blocking the wide carpeted corridor, happy to be safe and close and looking forward to the holidays. The drive home down Sandy Boulevard was full of chitchat, about weather, about mutual friends, about his seatmate on the way out who insisted on showing Bob his *Playboy* foldouts.

Home, we caught up on the details of our lives. We were so happy to be together we babbled on, silly in our joy. We laughed about Bob's personally designed birdhouse for wrens, an ungainly attempt to replicate a real tree by nailing bark to the structure around the drilled holes, too large for the birds. No wrens ever nested there! Howard, an architect with a fine eye for style and design, could only imagine what a Rube Goldberg contraption he'd built. He enjoyed being with Bob, his admiration for medicine as strong as Bob's regard for good architecture.

"You probably should have followed the blueprints!" Howard quipped.

"My architect didn't know his ass from a hole in the ground," Bob retorted, loving the chance to laugh at himself.

We told him the hilarious story of my giving a chainsaw to Howard for our anniversary. Fuel shortages were much in the news, and I imagined salvaging wood from downfalls, or, if worse came to worst, the trees on our hillside. Howard was horrified, saying I should know him better than that, that he would NEVER use a chainsaw! Chagrined, I returned it to Sears, bought instead a gift certificate for a haircut, since he has wild and beautiful white curls that are always askew. Hurt because I hadn't known how proud he was of having cut his own hair for over twenty years, he said I could use it, instead. I did. But, up against it for a suitable gift, I finally gave him a huge sack of chicken manure for the garden. That made him happy! We drank good seven-year-old Cuban rum, relaxing into a much-longed-for reunion.

Bob was looking forward to going to California from our house, to spend the remainder of his two weeks with the families of our twin sisters—Merilyn, who lived in Orinda, and MaryLou, who lived in La Jolla. He also planned to see both brothers, Dan and Jess, and their respective wives.

"So how's your health, love?"

"Well," he began, his voice taking on the authority of an examining physician, "my bilirubin count is astronomically high. In fact, all my chemistries are off the wall!"

"Jesus, Bobby, what does all that *mean*? What can we do?" I felt desperate.

"Not much, I'm afraid." He spent a few minutes giving us an anatomy lesson, defining the terms he was so familiar with. Then, he added, somewhat breathlessly, "I may not have the strength or the guts to go on to California. All the way out here I've been thinking. I'm sick, and I know it. I've obsessed over my symptoms and my best self-diagnosis would be that I've got pancreatic cancer. I'm not sure, but my skin has begun to itch badly, and I'm jaundiced and . . ." his eyes filled up with tears, "and that can be a bitch." He rubbed his thumbnail up and down the length of his arm, the way our father used to ease the itch of his eczema.

"Cancer. . . ." I let the word out slowly, not wanting it in my mouth, just wanting to let him know I'd heard. The three of us were silent, the lights outside brighter than usual, the snow on the ground tossing reflections back into the sky. The twinkling lights of the Christmas tree were repeated in the windowpane, then thrown across the room into another double window. Beautiful and festive, but of little consequence now. After awhile the silence became unbearable, for none of us could absorb the enormity of his dark announcement, the terrible certainty, the fear, the hope, without a little time to absorb it.

"Is there anything else it might be, Bobby?" I asked with practiced calm.

"Don't think so."

"I guess you're the expert," Howard said, "being an internist yourself. But. . . ." The longer we talked, the more resolute Bob became. Before we had finished our second drink, he had made some quick and final decisions.

"I've got to get back to Washington immediately, Janie. I shouldn't have flown out just for this, but God, I did so want to see you. It wasn't until I looked in the mirror in the Denver airport that I knew the jig was up."

It was midnight. Regardless of the hour, for emergencies erase time, Bob got up to make some telephone calls. Two of his best friends from Washington, D.C., John and Mal, were vacationing in San Francisco, and he had the number of their host. He let the phone ring for as long as it took. He got John on the line. The conversation was clipped and informative, ending with, "All I know is I am in deep shit!" Then, "Good, call the minute you get back in, will you?"

Then to Merilyn, beloved sister and next hostess down the line, he broke the news tenderly. Yes, he hated to disappoint her. He was equally disappointed, he said, and he'd been foolish to come west at all under the circumstances, but they'd see each other again, soon.

It was after four in the morning on the East Coast, but Bob called Dr. Trujillo. The brevity of their communication sounded like an operating-room exchange. No apology for the late hour, no excess description, just the statistics. Dr. Trujillo said yes, come immediately, he would schedule a CT scan first thing Monday morning. Then Bob hung up, turned to me, took my hands in his. "I'm sorry," he said.

He lived alone in the beautiful home and garden he had created, anticipating eventual retirement. The idea of his going home alone with such a burden was unimaginable. "I'm coming with you," I said, suddenly.

"If you're going, I'm coming, too," Howard said. "I'll see if I can arrange three tickets on the red-eye special for tomorrow. United flies out of L.A. to Dulles. There's a special dispensation for emergencies and I think we can swing it, Christmas be damned." And he did arrange the flight.

Bob began to sob, his shoulders racked and shaking. Then, as we tried to dry each other's tears with our thumbs, our touching each other's face with inexpressible love, our roller-coaster emotions turned to laughter. For a moment, we were jubilant, Three Musketeers confident of the strength to face the future together, to look truth squarely in the face, a bulwark of solidarity against the unknown enemy.

Bob must have known more than he could face alone and had come to get me, his "Numero Uno," as he called me, fondly. A special love had flowed between us all of our lives. We were a matched pair, as Dad called a beautiful team of horses, and I believe he knew before he left home that his time had come. That is my hunch. I never asked him. He never admitted it. But I think he wanted to circle back to our beginnings, to that innocent time we both shared, haloed now by our full adult awareness.

◆

All the way back to Washington, D.C., unable to sleep, we talked, drowsily. Our exchanges were like a vase of wildflowers, gathered on a hike that took a lifetime to walk. Heads of dry grasses. Goldenrod. Wild roses. Mostly we began our sentences with "Do you remember . . ." but, too, we did not skirt the present. He turned to face me, his eyes swimming.

"I'm just sick about this turn of events, Jane. . . ." I put my hand on his knee, for there was little either of us could say. After a pause during which he blew his nose, he said, "I'd so looked forward to going back to Iowa this summer with you. Don't you wonder what Redfield looks like now?" Our heads back against the headrests of the narrow seats, we conjured up what that old town of so many years ago might look like.

In low, tired voices, we tried to remember that old vintage town, wondered about the church where we went to Sunday school, about Diddy's Drugstore, about the Old Settlers' Day carnival, when the band would play in the park. Then he added, "D'ya think you'll go back by yourself?"

"Doubt it. What'd be the point? We were going to let that trip be the start of our book, weren't we? And if the book gets postponed, well, I'll just wait."

"God, that's another thing. All those crazy stories. Can you imagine a rural bucket brigade today, trying to put out a burning barn? And the adventures we had in the brickyard? We could have been burned to a crisp in those kilns. They were still warm sometimes when we set up shop inside, d'ya remember that? And Mother's spirea hedge with the tall, blue delphinium in front? Beautiful, wasn't it?"

"That time we went to get milk from Mrs. Van Deventer and broke the jar?"

"Whad'ya mean *we*? *You* broke the jar," Bob corrected.

"Only because you made *me* carry it." We chuckled at the strange clarity of detail after all these years. We were slipping back into our childhood patterns, the assigning of blame, the defense, the laughter. The stories began to trip over each other.

"Or that time you dared me to walk across the river on the new bridge scaffolding, remember? That was a death-defying dare, those men throwing hot rivets back and forth to each other and me creeping across that skeleton, the moving water below making me dizzy."

"Yeah." He laughed, still relishing his craving for risk.

"What a devil you were, Bob. I was a handy scapegoat, even a willing one. What a fool I was! How old was I, then?"

"Dunno. Maybe four."

And we would drift off, dozing and waking lightly.

But now, caught in the vise of impending loss, both of us began to mull over the inevitable. I would stay with him as long as it was necessary, even if Howard had to return to Portland. Bob's plans pointed in the direction of an untimely end, and I was apprehensive, trying to think through what I would need to do first, on a purely automatic response. Call 9-1-1, probably. I would deal with that if I had to, when the time came.

In Bob's House

Those years of our childhood seem like ancient history. The world has changed so drastically, so fast. And so have we. For over half a century, we lived our separate lives, full of growth and travel, marriages, children, education, professions we found deeply satisfying, and the loss of both our parents. They lie side by side in the Tahoma Cemetery in Yakima, Washington, where they lived their final days, easy with each other and with the means to enjoy themselves, proud of six adult children and twelve grandchildren.

Now, the first two of their brood, we faced the unknown, hurrying back east through the dark. We arrived at Dulles National Airport in Washington, D.C., early in the morning and found a taxi.

Bob's home in Arlington, Virginia, was elegant. He could afford what he needed. In many ways however, he was almost miserly, penurious. He never owned a toaster. For toast, he used the broiler tray beneath his gas oven, turning the bread by hand. He liked it that way, dry, for that was the taste he had grown up with. Mother used to arrange slices of homemade bread on the oven rack of our wood stove. The smell of it browning was bound to bring all of us to the table in time to eat our breakfast—oatmeal with brown sugar and cream, crunchy toast with freshly churned butter and apple butter—before the school bus stopped at the bottom of our driveway.

Although he was instinctively hospitable and admired a good host or hostess inordinately, he hated gadgets. He hated clutter more. He didn't own an iron. Nor, of course, an ironing board. Meticulous to a fault, he hung his clothes up carefully, sent all his shirts to the laundry, picked every shred of lint up off the floor almost before it hit the ground. He was a frugal man who did not use paper products, staying with cloth handkerchiefs and cotton napkins, with napkin rings, using the same one until it was ready to launder. And why spend money for toothpaste when salt and soda, mixed, did a better job? We teased him, saying "You may be a minimalist, Bob, but this is ridiculous."

He used his bath towels until they were ragged-edged and dingy, then he dyed them brown. He saved electricity by shaving with Gillette blades. As much writing as he did, you'd think he'd have a word processor at least. But no, he pounded things out on an old manual typewriter, and prided himself for it. Part of this excessive economy must be genetic, I'm convinced, for our father urged us to eat our apples, core and all, the seeds, the stem, the works!

Bob never raised any children, had been divorced for years after a very brief marriage. He could afford to be persnickety. But it was an adjustment for both Howard and me, newly arrived in his house. He felt compelled, after our first meal there, to explain the dishwashing procedure, which by this time in our lives should have been obvious. Bob raised his voice rather imperiously at Howard, never one given to neatness in the kitchen in the first place, and less than tolerant of being told what to do. "I've told you this already; dirty dishes go in the *left* half of the sink; the *right*-hand sink is for rinsing, ONLY! Can you understand that?"

"Oh, shit, man! What difference does it make? Lighten up, will ya," Howard lashed back. The pitch of their voices was rising, like the first whistle of a teakettle ready to boil. Stony, tight-lipped silence from Bob.

Just like Mother, I thought, whose style of disapproval was the Ice Queen treatment. Howard backed off. "It *is* your house, after all, so I guess you get the last word." Conciliation. Bob rubbed the Bon Ami in a few more circles, cleaning the sink to his clinical standard, and the tension passed over.

This exchange surprised me. He was by nature hugely hospitable. Once, when I was in terrible turmoil over my first, abusive marriage, I called him to heal my hurt. His support was my rock.

"Come live with me, Jane. I have a guest room that is yours. And the two of us could get along better than anyone else I know." I was sorely tempted, but with children I could not accept his invitation.

On the evening of our first tired day in Arlington, as the light lowered over the winter landscape, he walked us through his garden, naming every plant by its botanical name, translating for me their common names, the star lilies he was so proud of, his prize peonies, the rare and delicate irises. This litany of those precious plants he had researched, sought out, planted, and nourished was his obituary for them. I think he could not imagine leaving them after so much love, so much reward. He explained—in much the way I remember our father's style, as if writing a prescription—the value of pine-needle mulch for roses, here; the banked dirt to catch water, there; the way to prune an ornamental shrub; all the advantages of ladybugs in a garden; what to spray, when, with what, and how much. The perfectionism that was a hallmark of his life, professional and personal, was reflected in his meticulous landscape planning. He was a master gardener and he loved the smell of tilled earth, the rarity of hard-to-grow flowers.

Lists were everywhere. I watched his love take care of all the dreams leaking through the sieve of time. Sack after black sack of papers, old clothes, contents of his medicine cabinet, his desk, his storeroom closets went into the big, green garbage can until the lid would no longer close. Newspapers were stacked in the garage for recycling. His mud-caked gardening shoes got tossed. It made me sick. But he was inalterably thorough. In an ironic twist of fate, where we were afraid, he was clear. It was he who helped *us* through the realization of what lay immediately ahead.

◆

Once we had arrived at Bob's home, a short drive over the Potomac from Washington, D.C., the days were filled with excruciating urgency.

Early Monday morning, as arranged by Dr. Nelson Trujillo, we drove downtown to the Washington Radiation Laboratory for Bob's CT scan. The results would dictate his next move. Even with the huge dose of barium required to isolate and diagnose the problem, Bob was witty with the receptionist. She had given him a gown to put on and told him to wait. Out of the dressing room where he had stripped and put on the gown, he came back to sit with me, at ease with the familiar rules. He was so tall the gown barely reached his knees; turning to the woman who told him to wait, he said, "I'll bet you did this on purpose! It barely covers my vital statistics."

She was amused and it didn't take long after that for her to open the door to the inner sanctum and call, "Dr. Belton." He turned to me with the look of a haunted animal, shaking from being so thinly clad, from lack of sleep, and from fear. He went in to face what he perceived already as a death sentence, and he knew I knew. We held each other's eyes in deep grief, hard to disguise. We waited. Time was interminable. Then, it was done.

He was advised to take the pictures to Dr. Trujillo immediately. Professional courtesy. Bob maintained a modicum of composure on the drive to the doctor's office. He was ushered in the minute we reached the waiting room.

Again we waited. We picked through the magazines, unable to concentrate on anything for long. I mostly just sat, looking at my fingernails thinking I should file them, watching the upright antique clock, absurdly out of place in this high-tech office.

The door opened. Bob stood there, very sober. "You come in, now. I want you to meet my doctor, who can explain things a lot better than I can." We went into his office and Dr. Trujillo got up, pulled a third chair up to his desk. The worst was confirmed. Bob had a lemon-sized cancerous tumor on his pancreas and it was growing rapidly. Already the flow of bile from the liver had been constricted. The cancer had invaded his duodenum, had affected the lymph nodes on all adjacent organs, causing his jaundice, loss of appetite, weight loss, everything.

There was nothing to drape over the void. My heart was cracking and I could not imagine what was going on in Bob's own heart or head. How does one's spirit accept the unimaginable end of being alive? The irony of losing this beautiful man when so many lesser men continue to live long and healthy lives was more than heavy and sad. It was unfair. I was wooden, dry-throated. Somewhere in my chest I felt an iron weight that would not lift. I looked at Bob and I let the tears just fall out of my eyes and nose with no attempt to wipe them off. Numb. He thanked Dr. Trujillo with a handshake, and in an attempt to lighten the darkness, said, "For everything, Nelson, thanks. I'll try not to return the favor!"

As we drove home, back across the Potomac, we were quiet, watching the cold sky and the river, gray as granite. Trying to assimilate such catastrophic news, each of us was struggling in a personal way, pulled toward pity and regret and an empathy that is, finally, wordless. Bob began to dictate a list of names. I wrote them on the back of our used airline tickets. He must make a dozen phone calls. "Screw the phone bill," he said, "let my accountant take care of it." Urgency was beginning to sift out what was important, what was not.

And so began his long farewells to family and to friends. He did not spare any of them the clean truth. What courage, what generosity to give each of them his loving voice. Often, after he'd hung up, he would cry with deep, wrenching sobs. Each day I saw more deeply the huge capacity for caring in this man. Still witty and vibrant and handsome, it was nearly impossible to reconcile the visible with the invisible, the way a talented actor so convincingly portrays a character that someone in the audience, engrossed in the plot, cries out to warn of danger.

In a letter he had once written me, an honest and confidential self-revelation, he had said, "I could fool almost anybody." In our family, in the era we grew up in, personal disclosures were hushed and rare, often severely judged. A good appearance was imperative. Bob lived in a secret world when he wore Mother's high-heeled shoes up and down our gravel driveway in Redfield, or when, as lifeguard at the pool in Pendleton, Oregon, he sketched pages of nude divers, arching backwards from the diving board. Only when he cried all the way across the Atlantic on his way to his Fulbright year in Zurich, after saying goodbye to his friend John, did he realize that his deepest friendships lay with men.

His marriage to Livia was a camouflage. It was no good from the beginning, and he knew why. He used her as badly as she used him. For both of them, all that pain—he for Mother's sake, she for a lover's jealousy—led them finally to separate. He had subsequent love affairs, for he was beautiful and witty and kind, generous to his own detriment sometimes. All of his many friends were lucky to have known him.

I ache, now that he can no longer talk with me. I ache for the hunger in him during that long, lonely journey, that immersion in medicine, that study of languages, of botany, of birds. And I ache for the hunger in me, the longing to be inside the fragile man, as I was part of the sensitive boy. He could not admit me totally until the very last, so strong is the habit of withholding. I regret that part of our history more than anything, for the depth of honesty and the tears that were dammed up, waiting to flow at the ragged end of life.

We were tender with each other as the days wore on, allowing tears and touch and the long silences of eyes locked in the unspoken knowledge of how rare and rich our lives together had been. Each moment became, of itself, enlarged. So precious few remained. Each word was listened to. Each shared thought was held awhile, then integrated into a larger whole, linked like the filaments of a spider web, to catch the spirit as it flew.

So many ends are simply splintered fragments of regret. Ours was not. We had time and foreknowledge. We polished each act and each series of acts into a shining whole, honest and true, blessed with an almost complete and voiced recall of our green lives as children, and of our ripened adulthood. Our lifelong affection will always spice my life with sudden reminders—Bob's devilish grin, the tenor of his voice. A pile of snow gear, smelly as a wet dog, recalls the two of us, tumbling with Frieda in an Iowa winter. When I am shopping the Saturday Market, he is beside me in memory, hoeing the rows of beans in the vegetable garden, making a game of it, a race to hasten the task, or shoulder to shoulder, picking up potatoes as Dad forked over the parent plants in the sandy river-bottom soil. The mildewy smell of old burlap bags. Gorging ourselves on cherries or cracklins. Peeling back the husks of an ear of corn, parting the cornsilk to pop the top kernels, testing for freshness. We shared these things.

We grew up in a safe world of earth and sky, weather and waiting, at the slow diurnal pace of earth time, governed by seasons. Together we closed the circle of our love, gently and well. I am deeply grateful for the blessing of being together, for the promise to write down the childhood we remembered, stories that wheeled through our conversation like a flock of homing pigeons. That time speeds up is a frequent cliché, but thinking backwards put our memories into a past that seemed, increasingly as the days wore on, worth preserving. It is a part of American cultural history, now, as rusty as an abandoned hay rake, overgrown with grass. Who understands or cares, much less sees, the bottle of Mrs. Wright's Bluing beside the washboard, or feels the moment of resistance when the paddle in the butter churn separates the curds from the whey?

An Armful of Daisies

Outside the large windows of Bob's house, the huge trees lifted their barren limbs against a cold, blue-gray sky. These many years after our clearly remembered childhood, we sat through the long afternoons, talking. Often we sat at his dining room table, where we could watch the birds. December in Arlington threw a blue shawl over the world, not the gray of an Oregon winter, but the shades of arctic blue that come from dry cold and slanted sunlight.

The grass was stiff, white with rime, crunchy to walk across to fill the bird feeder. It was replenished religiously. The birdbath, always rimmed with ice, was full of mourning doves, sparrows, and starlings in turns. Unlike many people, Bob loved the starlings and their yellow beaks, their jerky nerve, the jet black and greenish sheen, speckled in winter as if by snowflakes. At the back of the garden where scattered seeds, sprouting, would not disturb his plantings, the suet cage hung from a wrought-iron hook driven into the ground.

And there was the wren house of which he had told us with such pride and humor. It was the ugliest thing I think I'd ever seen, all bent and oddly proportioned, a dirty yellow ersatz tree limb with holes in it, sculpted, he was delighted to point out, according to his own custom design. That no wrens had ever nested there seemed not to concern him, for he was sure they would, once the word got around. I never expressed my revulsion at the thing, because it was an irrelevant opinion at this point, but it stuck out in that subdued landscape like a wild Hawaiian shirt at a formal ball. Pigeons the color of slate on the neighbor's garage would hover near the feeder, preening their iridescent purple necks in the sunlight. Bob was as hospitable to the birds as he was to us.

Watching the bird shenanigans, I thought to ask him, "Do you remember your homing pigeons?"

"Oh, my God, I loved those birds! The fat little brown-and-white ones, weren't they funny? I built the chickenwire house on top of the woodshed, and you used to lug the cracked corn up that steep ladder." And we were back on the Ficken farm in Redfield, where we had been born and had lived our first years. Our memories wove together in this way, the myriad episodes timeless symbols of life's affection, and the telling of them lightened our days, drew us down into our hearts.

On December seventeenth, the night before Bob's sixty-ninth birthday, we had a dinner party for eight. All of us a little high on good Scotch, Bob had decided to take his precious antique car, which shared the double garage with his smaller Toyota—a sleek, meticulously restored 1940s Cadillac—out on the road with his friends. Two of the men opted to go on this joy ride, but both Howard and I declined. It was a beautiful car, true, and he had restored it to its original glory, but I thought the whole idea was suicidal. Bob drove the car out onto Route 66, and risking the police and their lives, got the speedometer up to a hundred miles per hour, with his friends goading him to "Gun it, God-damn it! This son of a bitch has more guts than anything on the road!"

I was terribly relieved when the garage door opened and they'd come home, safe in spite of the wild ride. At the back end of the garage, a tennis ball was suspended on a string from the garage rafters, a guide to pulling the car in that far and no further. I heard their drunken laughter as they braked just short of the yellow ball. When they finally came into the living room, they were jubilant.

"By God, I knew she could do it," Bob said, shaking with the thrill of it, loving the risk that had been his hallmark. After a brief recap of the mad escapade, after the buzz of the Scotch had worn off, after sharing a fresh pot of coffee, the guests departed and we got ready for bed.

Just before I climbed into our guest bed, Bob came into the room. He put his hands on my shoulders and looked into my eyes, very deeply. Slowly he said, "Jane, thanks for everything. . . . You're a wonderful hostess, just like Mother." I chalked it up to his decompressing, but knew, too, that it was a sincere good night. I thanked him, kissed him, and wished him happy dreams.

The next morning, I wanted to fix my brother an old-fashioned Iowa breakfast, not just the juice-and-toast snack we usually ate, but several courses—freshly squeezed orange juice, cornbread with honey, bacon, scrambled eggs, real coffee with real cream—all laid out on a pretty table. He needed a little fat on his ribs to carry him through the emotional drain of the last few days. He seemed bent on expending every ounce left to him. Maybe I needed to offer everything I could think of, the morning of his birthday. Mostly for my own sake.

I passed his closed bedroom door, glad that he could sleep so soundly, so late. It was a cold morning and there was no hurry. The cornbread would take about an hour, so why waken either Bob or Howard? Beside the sink where I was filling the coffeemaker, I saw two handkerchiefs Bob had washed out under the faucet the night before, smoothed out on the Formica counter top to dry. Wet with tears and countless nose-blowings, they needed to be washed. Out of habit, to save the washing machine and to avoid the need to iron them, he had smoothed them out to dry, wrinkle-free. So like Bob! His farsightedness, his frugal efficiency made me smile. But, since I was planning to make a birthday breakfast, I folded them up, as squarely as if they'd been ironed, creased and patted and smoothed each one of them with great love and amusement. Then, I put them on the kitchen table next to the cerise cyclamen his old friend from graduate school, Jillian Poole, had brought him a few days earlier. It bloomed its holiday cheer into the whole room. I stood back and looked at that tabletop and thought I would like to paint it, call it "Still Life with Two Handkerchiefs."

For a breakfast centerpiece, I used the adorable miniature Christmas tree our granddaughter, Ellen, had sent out from Portland, replete with shiny red apples hanging on it and tiny make-believe packages underneath, "to keep you from being so lonesome during the holidays," as she put it. I set the dining room table with red and green placemats and got down Bob's crystal wine glasses for our orange juice. I laid out plates, silverware, coffee cups, and saucers in such precise order it could have been readying for a surgical procedure. Fussing over the look of things, I heard a knock at the door. It was Bob's old friend Johnny, here just last night for supper, his arms full of a birthday bouquet, a drift of lovely white daisies, flowers that were among Bob's favorites.

"Come in, John. Oh, how pretty! Here, give them to me, and I'll put them in water."

"Happy birthday to Bob," he said. "Is he up yet?" He seemed loath to let go of the daisies, his strong hands clinging to the delicate stems.

"No, not yet." Then I had an idea. "Maybe you could rouse him with your flowers, you know, waft them over his nose?"

He shook his head and handed them to me, and I put them in a big fruit jar. We would arrange them later. Lighthearted with the prospect of a guest for breakfast and flowers, too, I took them into the living room and set them on an end table.

"Funny, he's always been an early riser," John said.

"We were taught to hear the rooster crow, I guess. Runs in our family, getting up with the first light."

Howard came out of our room in his bathrobe, his white Toscanini hair tousled as usual.

"What's going on?" he asked, still groggy from the night before. He and Bob were just one day apart in age, and Howard would celebrate tomorrow.

John said, "Let's all wake him up together singing 'Happy Birthday,' shall we?"

"Okay by me," Howard chimed in.

I took John's leather jacket and flung it over the back of a chair, closed the front door, and together, we opened Bob's door quietly, tip-toeing to his bed, the more to surprise him.

But he did not move.

I reached over to rock his shoulder. "Bob. Bobby?" I pulled my hand back, stunned, frightened. "Oh, my God." Terribly still, silent, cold, lying on his right side, his arm curled up around his pillow, his handsome face ashen.

John reached over and flung the bedspread back off his body. Bob lay there like a marble sculpture, with only a pair of shorts on, ones he had dyed along with his towels, brown. He'd thought of everything, familiar as he was with the body's final letting go.

"Oh, honey boy," John whispered. To me he said, "Call 9-1-1."

My knees were weak. I felt paralyzed. My heart pounding, it was difficult to breathe. I went out of the room, looking around frantically for somewhere to go. Then, I went into the narrow kitchen pantry, squatted down on the floor beside the washtub and curled up, my eyes closed, my arms tight around my knees. "God," I kept repeating, "God,

God." How long I sat there, paralyzed with shock or fear or sorrow I do not know. Who can ever separate the flood of so much feeling?

The last time I saw Bob, nestled in his bed with one arm under his pillow, his knees drawn up in the fetal position, I wanted to curl up inside that beloved body, to "spoon" as we did when we were children. When it was cold in our separate beds in that drafty Iowa attic, we climbed in with each other to feel the warmth of one another's body. All night, we would turn, hitching up the covers on our side, realign ourselves bottom to belly, or belly to bottom, feet entwined, arms glued to each other like the sticky wings of an emerging cicada. But I could not climb in beside him now.

Too soon, Howard came into my hiding place to lift me up, put his arms around me. "No, no, no, no," I kept saying, not wanting to be comforted, not wanting to be held. I broke away, and went to the telephone. I was so preoccupied with the trauma of Bob's dying that I was thoughtless of Howard. I dialed 9-1-1.

"Please send an ambulance. . . . There has been a death. . . ." I heard myself say into the telephone. To their questions, I responded woodenly. "A suicide. . . . I think."

And then, for a long time, we were silent, each of us trying to acknowledge the truth. We walked into the living room like stick figures and found places to sit down, Howard and I on the couch, John in Bob's favorite leather chair, hardly able to speak. We just waited. Howard locked his fingers together and kept unlocking them, weaving them together again and again, as if to test that they still worked. I kept sweeping the room with my eyes wide open, his library, the mantle, the beautiful rug, his treasures, forcing myself to avoid looking at anything below the surface. John, sunk in Bob's big navy-blue leather chair, his elbows on his knees, his head cradled in his hands, just stared at the floor.

The ambulance and a police van arrived simultaneously, and the men streamed in the door, the paramedics, two uniformed policemen, and one detective.

"How long have you been here?" the chief officer asked us.

"About a week," Howard answered.

"Are you related to the dead man?" Dead man. His words reverberated in the room like doomsday bells.

"Yes," I told them, "I'm his sister, Jane Belton Glazer. This is my husband, Howard Glazer."

While the police and the detective were doing their job, the paramedics were preparing Bob's body to take away. They had brought a collapsible gurney, which they had levered open to make a high, narrow bed, and on it, they put what was left of a beautiful man, wrapped in black plastic. When they wheeled the lift out of his bedroom toward the living-room door, we were too stunned to talk.

It was too sudden. We needed time to absorb the finality of what was happening. They paused, knowing from their experience, I guess, that we needed to be with him for just a little while. We three got up to stand around the awful black bag. John took the bouquet of white flowers from the jar I had stuck them in the hour before, oblivious of the water dripping from the stems, and laid it across the covered chest of his beloved friend.

I had nothing to send with him. Not able to speak, I began to sob those deep, wrenching body-shuddering cries that cannot be contained. Standing beside that cold bier, I realized how brave he had been, knowing the inevitable pain that lay in store for him, for us. How lonely his death would leave me. Forever lost to me was the dear brother who had shared my whole life. With him went my own childhood. Both of our parents were gone. I felt unutterably hollow. My beloved Bobby, my secret-sharer, my nurturer, and my adult confidant, was gone. It was the last time I would ever be known for so long or so well by anyone. I was saying farewell to his whole life, and also farewell to the person I was in Bob's eyes.

I knew, somehow, that what lay ahead would be even more difficult than this sad moment. I bent over the place where his head lay covered and whispered to him, "Goodbye, Bobby," calling his childhood name back from Iowa. Around us, like a velvet cloak, were thoughts of all that would need attention now, his house and garden, his restored antique car, his will, his memorial, and I murmured, "I'll take care of everything for you, love."

That heartfelt whisper recalled to me the last words I had spoken to Daddy as he lay dying, holding his brown eyes with mine. And the awful loneliness of the first suicide I had experienced washed over me again, when my first husband had killed himself, leaving me and our three young children to fend for ourselves. How long ago, now? How deep is the human capacity for grief?

Then, needing to blow my nose, I remembered the handkerchiefs Bob had washed out the night before. I wondered if they were still on the kitchen table, left there to show him how carefully I had folded them. That had been the last thing he had done before he went to sleep last night . . . and forever. I sniffed back up my tears and did not leave his side.

The ambulance people, with quiet courtesy, gradually wheeled the ghastly burden over the threshold and out onto the walk. I stood frozen by the closed door for a long time. What could I have done? I tried to reconstruct the last days, remembered his telling me to pick up his clean shirts at the laundry. Should I bother, now?

From that task of smoothing out the two washed handkerchiefs, Bob had gone to write his farewell note and then, to swallow the fatal pills. The night before his sixty-ninth birthday, Bob took an overdose of Seconal and slept the last, long peaceful night of his life. I know that it saddened him to leave us all so terribly suddenly, to say goodbye to the beloved place he had created. A huge heart spared us all, himself as well, the agony of protracted pain from his incurable pancreatic cancer.

He left his last note to us on his old, black walnut desk where he loved to work, two empty vials anchoring the corners:

> 11:10 PM, 12/17/92
>
> *To all my loved ones—*
>
> *By the time you read this, I will, by my own hand, have passed over into what the religionists are loath to call death. I chose this exit because I knew the grim alternatives. When any one of you were faced with the choice of a peaceful night's sleep at age 69, versus three months of unaleviatable suffering, which would you choose?*
>
> *I have had a fabulously happy life, filled with loving family, loving friends, an exhilarating profession, proud accomplishments, and many passions. The rough spots I've come to, with enormous will, classy professional help, and time, have been largely conquerable. I've got one now that is not.*
>
> *Take from my beloved house and garden any mementoes you want. Remember me fondly, for I have loved you all more deeply than it is in my nature to demonstrate.*
>
> *Peace,*
>
> *As always,*
>
> *Bob*

That note, copied on the back of an envelope because the investigator would not release the original, folded and put in my pocket that sad morning, has been with me all this time. How many times I have read and reread it can never be known. I have shared it with our sorrowing siblings, of course. As the weeks and months and years have passed since that final day, I have been writing our stories, to keep the promise I made to Bob. In this way, I have kept him alive in my memory. That has helped to heal the deep wound of his going.

Ash Roses

February is a trickster. The day before the snow came was warm and spring-like; I had knelt on the foam pad beside my flower beds, beside the winter-bare roses, the withered stubs of iris—the daffodils and tulips peeking up already—to trowel out the weeds and turn the soil. Mother's oriental poppies were up and greening, and the iris corms I'd pirated from Bob's Arlington garden—the Beverly Sills and the Silverado—would take root against the boxwood hedge. It was then, because everything had that tidy look of early spring, before the trees leaf out, before the primroses bloom, that I decided finally to spread my brother's ashes over my rose garden. A day comes when everything shifts in your heart, when you know love's being with you has nothing to do with anything material. This was the day.

We five of the six siblings, who had buried our parents in their turn but who had somehow felt ourselves indivisible, had divided the gray ashes delivered from the crematorium into five plastic baggies. It was the last act, the hardest task. Scooping out equal portions with a measuring cup, we were careful not to spill anything, were silent except for the sudden intake of breath that belies someone's controlled crying. But, rather than leave Bob in Arlington, Virginia, in his garden, so far away from all of us, we agreed to bring him west. Bob's exquisite care, we felt, even in his final form, might insure some horticultural miracles!

I thought of a morning when Bob once visited us. I got up to find my old-fashioned roses drastically pruned and my brother working on the huge old climber that spread across our cedar fence. I went outside, amazed to find him absolutely butchering those graceful canes that arched over and through the mossy trellises. God only knew the age of that rosebush, maybe planted when the house was built in 1925. Its base is an enlarged bole from which, each year, new and aggressive limbs will shoot out and aim for the sky. Now, half of it was hacked away by a madman wielding red clippers and a small saw. How would it ever live up to its name, blazing across the fence by early summer? Bouquets of that twining red rose, prolific enough to pick constantly, looked cheerful on our dining room table. It was one of our favorites, so fat and full and impudent.

To my consternation, Bob assured me that severe pruning called up something hidden in the ichors of old plants. I thought he might be doing some projecting there, since he'd ostensibly beat the odds himself after a near-fatal automobile accident and the year in traction that had followed. Although I was furious, skeptical of his knowledge, I didn't argue, this time.

Having taken as a role model our authoritarian father, Bob was sure-minded. I have often thought the pair of them, strong male presences, created my early definition of manhood, made me, on one hand, dependent on male friendships, having a man as a close companion or for another point of view, even as an adviser; on the other hand, it set me up to rebel against being told what to do. But Bob was a master gardener and had landscaped and planted and pruned countless plots of earth, so I accepted his expertise in my rose garden.

He was the authority, after all. In a talk with Dad just before he died at age ninety, I asked him how he remembered the two of us as children. "You were thick as thieves," he told me. "Of course, Bob was older, and boy, did he lord it over you! But, you never seemed to mind it, just did whatever he said. Yep, you were a pair of pretty close friends. Still are, aren't you?"

Imagine Bob's chagrin when I wrote to report the death of "Blaze." It did not recover that year, seemed dry and dead with its traumatized stumps.

"Wait another year," he said, "it is just taking a much-needed rest. Under no circumstances should you dig it up." So I waited. And sure enough, the rose stretched and rallied, emblazoning our fence as it had never done before. I was forced to forgive him, to see my own stubborn resistance to authority.

I decided this fresh day in late February was the day to honor the memory of Bob. And so, I scattered my share of his ashes among the roses. As I scooped the gritty ashes out with my hand, I felt a hard, metal object, which I examined. It was a staple. For a moment, I held it, looking closely at the stainless steel prong less than an inch wide. Then I remembered. Bob's horrendous motorcycle-car collision of twenty years before had required eleven surgeries, and the bones of his legs and hips had to be stapled in place. Poor love: what bravery his life had required of him, what resilience! And he never complained.

I thought of the little bronze sculpture an artist friend, Una Hanbury, had made especially for Bob, of whom she was so hugely fond, as he was of her. A tentative new-born colt struggling to get to its feet is as leggy and insecure as Bob was after that crushing accident. He cherished that gift, lying on a small but hard ground of gray quartz stone. It now lives with me in my living room where I see it every day. And the metaphor sustains me, for to be human is to struggle. Bob, in his own life, and witnessing the lives of hundreds of patients, knew that truth.

I let the staple fall with the ashes.

The next morning, the snow was falling, laying over him a goose-down comforter, wrapping him up for awhile, then carrying him down deep into the earth he loved so much.

All day the snow fell. Huge, feathery flakes drifted endlessly out of the sky, windless and hushed. It settled on the bare limbs of trees, outlining each one with an inch or two of white. The birdbath rose like an angel food cake, high and straight-sided and fluffy. During the night no air had moved. The landscape stayed that way, utterly silent, a still-life of quiet perfection. No wind disturbed the soft pile of feathers spread over the garden.

For the simple memorial, held in Bob's home, I read excerpts from Wallace Stevens' poem, "Yellow Afternoon." Knowing many of the people in the room that day would never understand the choice, nor even how lines of poetry sometimes stand in for inexpressible grief, I struggled, reading it aloud. But Bob would have understood.

> *It was in the earth only*
> *That he was at the bottom of things*
> *And of himself. There he could say*
> *Of this I am, this is the patriarch,*
> *This it is that answers when I ask,*
> *This is the mute, the final sculpture*
> *Around which silence lies on silence.*

He would know, too, why I spread his ashes, bone meal, and staple on my roses here in Portland, Oregon.

We both loved snow.

Circling Home

Despite the map showing a nearly square state smack in the center of the United States, Iowa is full of a richly textured landscape, rolling farmland for the most part. Gentle hills formed by ancient ice melt are combed with gullies and ravines full of small streams and riverine vegetation, the uplands great whale backs of fertile soil. Rows of corn embroider the landscape like tidy French knots. Soybeans and corn, corn and soybeans under the wide, blue sky. Some fields of alfalfa for winter cattle feed, the hay rolled up in bales like giant curlers on unruly stubble. But to me, visiting in 2000, it smelled the same. I found my nose twitching like a rabbit's. And the quality of light was different from our hemmed-in western skies, more uplifting and expansive. The sky felt like a real presence, overarching the land where no mountains obstructed the view, where the horizon was endless. There was elbow-room, space, and time enough to wave at the man on the roadside mower.

They say you can't go home, again. That bromide clucks from the tongues of the would-be wise, disparaging the dream of starting over, of wanting to pick up the pieces and begin again, of hoping to erase the errors of the past. Time, they are quick to remind us, is a one-way street. *You Can't Go Home Again*, Thomas Wolfe's novel, took its title from folk wisdom grounded in common human experience. We would all "go home again" if we could return to where someone else does the cooking for awhile, puts crisp sheets that smell of sun and air on the bed in your old room, or maybe just sits with you at the warped picnic table under the blooming lilacs of a glowing adolescent summer, talking about life and love and infinite possibilities. Where there is no end to time.

But of course, there is. Houses we live in have a finite duration. Finally, every living thing dies. We trick ourselves into denial, longing to preserve those peak moments that were imbued with such deep meaning, trying to stop time in its tracks. We color our hair. We call our grown-up children "the kids." We try to duplicate our mother's lard piecrust even though home-rendered lard can no longer be found. So, home is not just a function of time. Nor is it quantifiable, being in the realm of feeling. What we would go back to cannot be measured.

Home is a longing, an abstraction, a yearning to be there, among loving hearts who are mystically gathered together, though in reality some are dead, others are scattered over the earth. For me, it is always warm, Indian-summer days, lazy with harvest or the promise of harvest, a pause to reflect on something accomplished—the hay in the barn, the new baby nursed, the pies baked, the heart healed of hurt, the truth confessed and forgiven. It is easy, too, easy speech, easy story, easy laughter, a shared circle of linked experience. Somewhere a whiff of cinnamon or garlic or the sound of a squeaky stair. And there is a dog there, probably on a matted rug by the fire or peering out of his doghouse with soulful eyes, or maybe a fat cat, purring.

What makes it home? Comfort, physical comfort of a ragged overstuffed chair, maybe the wind rustling the pine needles, or the low sun, streaming through the windows, shoes off, arm on the back of the couch, one knee drawn up, no hurry. A bayberry candle burning, rose petals drying on a chest of drawers, the rain outside an open door. Too, comfort in an emotional way, the utter trust of kindred spirits who see the irony of pretense, who laugh at the mistakes we all make, who ask how you feel about such things as using leftovers or getting a haircut or swimming in the river. Home is a place of truth, of complete permissiveness and self-honesty, of joy in nature and despair at the misuse of life, of time. It is a striving to be worthy, of wanting to complete the circle, of a "home" somewhere where hearts meet.

Having left the place of my birth, not by choice but because my father wanted us to move west, having left the haymow, the corncrib, the brickyard, all clustered under wide prairie skies, I cherished the thought that I could walk right back into the same small-town life as if nothing, or practically nothing, had changed all that much. My memory of the home where I grew up—the huge front lawn full of acorns, the German shepherd playmate of our childhood, the root cellar full of rendered cracklings, and the gravel drive leading to a hollow tile garage—all of it has always been so keen that my heart refuses to let it fade.

Probably out of my own curiosity and partly on account of that last promise made to my brother, my husband and I flew into Chicago, rented a car, and drove out to rural Iowa, to my home for the first years of childhood. As I had preserved it, or needed to imagine it, those years were like a continuous Dallas County Fair with booths for hand-pieced quilts, darning samples, contests for the best strawberry preserves or braided rugs, the largest Hubbard squash, baby rabbits in cages, and huge, red-combed roosters. Straw underfoot, certainly, and a pony to ride.

But three-quarters of a century had passed, and the swiftness of change had become almost palpable. Television had brought the wider world into our consciousness. More people on the planet. World hunger. Greed. Squandering of resources. The sea change of a sexual revolution, the advent of technology and modern science, the corporate and governmental dishonesty, the terror of war exploding with the push of a button, all of this had impacted every nook and cranny of America, of the world, really, and I knew it.

Why did the mere saying of the word "home," like the "om" of Zen meditation, conjure up some idealized state of being? Does the sound of the word echo some deep primitive innocence to which no one returns, like the mating voices of whales, foghorn deep, or like low resonant notes of a cello that enter your very bones? Or was it, in fact, a sanctuary, a real place where the traffic of the world could be shut out, our common humanity be invited in? Maybe it meant a sense of completion, like sliding into home plate in the sandlot baseball years. Whatever it meant, I needed to explore some deeper level of my spirit's hunger—for place, for security, identity, love, peace—I was not quite sure. Is the human psyche pulled to its original spawning ground as the salmon are? If so, do we, too, yearn to return to the same stream down which, as young smolt, we first travel toward the wider sea? I wanted to think about these things in the place where I began.

In Redfield, Iowa, the small town of my destination, I hoped to revisit the brickyard, to walk the rails of the train tracks where flatcars would come to load the brick and tile, to see the beehive kilns I remembered so vividly playing in and around with my brother. Would the wild and woolly freedom pastures framed by wild roses, where we staged broad-jump and high-jump contests with George and Rachel Straight, neighborhood kids in cahoots with us, still be there?

Driving southwest out of Des Moines, a much shorter distance than I'd imagined, of course, my husband and I entered the town, bracketed by an old railway station (now museum) and a tall granary for corn storage. My body was tense with anticipation. I began to feel a kinetic reaction to the bend in the road, the color of brick buildings, the railroad tracks. Maybe we pick up the dust, like pollen on the legs of bees, from the ground of our borning and our cells ingest it as some genetic marker.

"Go slowly," I begged Howard as I gawked out the windows, turning this way and that, "Wait . . . wait. I think that's Diddy's Drugstore ahead of us!"

Onto the screen of my mind's eye flashed old Doc Diddy, not a doctor, really, but a pharmacist with that bogus title, also called "Baldy" by his peers, lurking among those tall shelves full of Johnson & Johnson cotton and adhesive tape, aspirin, Iodex, Epsom salts, milk of magnesia, Vick's Vaporub, new tablets of writing paper, and licorice whips. Once I stole a Baby Ruth candy bar from there and, after I'd eaten it, told my brother, wanting to reduce the terrible sense of sin. He told my father, whose punishment, as if the spanking were not enough, was to make me go to Mr. Diddy, confess my crime, and give him the nickel it would have cost. That nickel, like the one I'd earned from not crying out when my foot was lanced, was hard to relinquish. For a long time, I harbored the notion that Bob's tattling had been the greater sin.

And it was Diddy's Drugstore for sure, although now some lawyer's office, the same old corner building, red brick, a diagonal front door with two skinny cast-iron posts on either side, narrow windows on the floor above. The same bank building was across the street. And the restaurant, called simply "Restaurant," still had an old wood stove with blue Ball jars full of dried beans on the black top, just for effect, the same kind of stove out of whose oven Mother would produce baking-powder biscuits or eight loaves of honey-brown bread, or, for company dinners, pecan rolls and mincemeat pies. The walls in this eatery were hung with washboards and shelves with an odd collection of salt and pepper shakers in the shape of cows' udders or the front and back of an old Model T, a wooden-paddled butter churn, candle molds, and kerosene lamps, all objects from a bygone era. In an oak highchair exactly like the one I remember feeding the younger children in, all turned spools and galleried tray, sat a stuffed dummy in overalls, simulating a satisfied customer.

The Old Settlers' Park was on the left of the main street where it had always been, carnival or no carnival, First Street being only four or five blocks long. Next to it, the library in a prime location at the end of the road, spiffed up substantially in recent years, said something of the values that still exist, there. On the edge of the old street, thrown toward the curb by car tires, lay the flattened carcass of a garter snake, its elegant diamond skin stiffened by the heat. The slight decline in the concrete roadway jogged a clear memory of walking down to the river, and sure enough, there was the bridge! It was smaller than I thought it would be, but it was there, as was the weir I had once thought a giant dam.

It was the same. Only the ice house was gone, that palace of moisture and the heady reek of sawdust. The water of the mighty Raccoon River was but a trickle! The lime-green algae of "dog days" stagnated in the backwater of the banks, now, although the river is capable of being unruly and destructive, the flood damage of a few years ago frightening. Iowa is no sissy, as my father used to say. He had lived through the terrifying dust storms, the drought, lightning storms that could crack a great tree right down the middle as tidily as an axe could split straight grain.

The road runs west out of Redfield, past the Old Settlers' Park, across the narrow bridge that spans the middle fork of the Raccoon River. Once across the water, across eddies that form in the rocks below a small spillway, the road branches. The small town ends and the country opens up. The road that veers abruptly left was gravel, once. Now it is paved.

"Go slowly," I said again, hardly able to bear the rush of familiarity.

"Ye gods, Jane, if we go any slower, we'll have to camp out!" Howard quipped, sensing at the same time my deep excitement. But the car slowed.

"Across the river, turn left," I directed him. The rental car we'd picked up in Chicago responded like a well-trained horse. I gave directions as crisply as my father had always given them. "And just after the curve, turn right into a gravel driveway. Go in as far as the garage."

He did turn in. The driveway into the house, still grass and gravel, turned off the county road and led directly to the garage, exactly as I remembered it. We drove the hundred or so yards to stop in front of that seedy old red garage, now a "bit down at the heels," as my mother might have described it. He turned off the ignition and parked to my almost inaudible chant, "Yes, yes, yes," for I had begun to breathe the seductive air of memory. An addition had been tacked onto the garage to accommodate the half century of changing car design, but the *feel* of the driveway, the *sound* of it, the tall tree on the left by the neighbor's pasture fence—open wire with old, weatherbeaten posts, leaning now and lichen-covered—had not changed. The hospitable crunch of tires on gravel, the gracious and welcoming verge of grass where no barrier separated us from the front lawn—all of that was absolutely, almost spookily, familiar. When I was small enough to stand up in the back seat, I remember my head not quite touching the ceiling of Dad's 1930s Chevrolet, parked exactly where Howard had stopped our car.

There it stood, my beloved white farmhouse, a bit less romantic than I had expected, but recognizable. I *had* come home again, and I was mesmerized by the moment. Seemingly interminable years had passed. Yet I felt, as if in the soles of my feet, in a strange kinetic memory of the landscape, just how to find what had been our childhood home. Once the grounds were dotted with huge American elms and tall, furrowed oaks. They were all gone now, all but two. The Dallas County road crews had cut down the spirea hedge that once edged our front lawn, separating the road from the front yard and the house. That hedge was Mother's pride, loving as she did the sense of privacy it gave her in what must have seemed to her, a city girl, a vast expanse of land.

"Bobby," I thought to myself in a flash of longing, "we are here, just the way we planned it." For a few minutes, I just sat there in the car, unable to breathe deeply, my heart racing, dumb to all but the rush of recall. My eyes scanned everything, indiscriminately—the big oak trees, the screened-in porch, the wooden roof shingles, uneven and warped, outlined in moss.

It was the same tile garage, the shingles curled up like dried orange rinds. The hollow rectangular tiles, textured by combed grooves on the long sides, mortared horizontally, were badly in need of pointing, but that was an unlikely repair, given its vintage. I rubbed my thumb across the other fingers of my hands, remembering how we wiped the lime of our mudpie frosting off on that rough surface. A narrow opening, one-third of it hinged as a separate door made of diagonal boards, would scrape on the grass as it was pulled open to admit the old, skinny car. And the big square window on the side. Yes. It was still there, its sill, bricks laid on end lengthwise, side by side. This had been our oven, putting our cakes of coconut straw, chocolate mud, or acorn nut up there to bake in the oven of Iowa summer sun.

Deeper than I could have imagined, my emotions churned, like crossing the bar of a turbulent river mouth, and tears swam in my eyes. How much a part of that was loving Mother and Daddy and the life they had given us, how much of it was missing Bob, and how much was a wash of feeling for my own years of childhood, I could not know.

It was a moment full of mystery and longing.

After a few moments of a noisy nose blow, I leaned toward Howard. "Wait here awhile, love. I'll see if anyone is home."

"Fine." He put his right arm around my shoulder. "Take it easy," he said.

I opened the car door and stepped down onto the land. The first moon landing could not have been more moving. My stepping out onto the ground was a physical and emotional sensation, but it was also metaphoric, a chance to go back to square one or ground zero. I realized, then and now, how few people ever come full circle like this, that it was a rare and special experience, almost holy, to use the word of wonder from my childhood. That feeling is round, is whole, like an expanding cup that will hold whatever is poured into it. I was ready to fill it with whatever came back to me, whatever memories would be resurrected just by retracing the landscape of their origin. One thing I knew; I would not be alone. As in our childhood, Bobby and I were one person. He was here, walking with me, now.

Once on the ground, I stood still, marshaling composure. Up through my shoes, I felt the land and the power of place. Was that part of the home I sought? Up past the deep basement window well where our fat Frieda had whelped her eight cuddly puppies, to the screen door, I walked slowly, nervously. Then, I knocked on the screen porch door. A man inside, in a faded red sweatshirt, sat on a woven plastic chair.

"Come on in," he said, unperturbed. As I opened the door, the rarely used little brass hook inside hanging there like a bell clapper, out bounded a large German shepherd, the spitting image of Frieda! Unbelievable! I was stunned. Along the inside of my arm was the warm fur feel of my child's self, lifting up my arms around her patient, soft neck. I found my voice.

"Can she go out?" I asked the man.

Taken by surprise, he said, "Well, sure," as if the question were absurd. My eyes followed the big dog, incredulous, as she ran toward the car, curious and watchful.

I stepped inside, walked over to where he sat, and introduced myself. I told him my name, my mission, my parents' names. "My father was a veterinarian in Redfield, once. We used to live here," I said. He sat there, laconic, not getting up, not taking off his crushed felt hat, looking me up and down.

"Yeah," he said, finally, "I knew yer dad. Old Doc Belton, wasn't it? I come out here with my dad, once, to get the vet. Hog cholera I think it was we had. I was just a little shaver, then, ya know, but I remember him. Tall man, was he?"

"Yes, he was," I answered, remembering how I used to stand on his boot toes and arch my neck back to see his face.

My father, Dr. Merrill J. Belton, was a young veterinarian just out of Iowa State Agricultural College, as it was called in those days, who had settled in Redfield, Iowa, to set up his first large-animal practice. To this house he brought his pedigreed dog and his city-born wife. He and Mother had five children here, the first one dead within the first heartbreaking twenty-four hours, her little metal grave marker still corroding in the Redfield cemetery.

I had a sudden memory that made me smile, the happy laughter in our family when Daddy would play with us children, tease us with puzzles, and make us guess, meeting our creative attempts to solve them with sparkle and delight, a bit like Grandma Chantry and her eternal riddles. He taught us a lot about anatomy, explaining things as he took care of our sprained ankles, cut veins, bruised elbows. As if living among animals weren't lesson enough.

The man got up out of his chair. His wife came out to see who he was talking to. I cracked open the screen door to motion to Howard, who came to join us. Together then, we went from room to room. I remembered how the iceman used to bring a square of ice balanced on his burlap-sack-covered shoulder, swing it into the top of the icebox with his tongs. It had stood there in the kitchen, its thick door with the lift-up handle, in that corner, yes! And the bedroom where the twins were born, a built-in dresser drawer pressed into service as a bassinet, since they'd expected only one baby. The rooms, the house and grounds, all seemed so much smaller than they used to be, but that is another phenomenon. What we once perceived as mountains of ice where we scooped out our winter caves were mere snowdrifts once we grew tall enough to use a shovel.

I had come home again, after all, at least back to Redfield, to the farmhouse of my first memories. But I was such a different person, I had to ponder what it was that so deeply affected me. Surely, it was more than the incredible coincidence of another German shepherd living in the same house. I think it had to do more with trust or generosity, with the man who sat on his screen porch with nothing but goodwill, still lodged in the sweet remembered time when doors were left open for the friendly neighbor or the weary traveler. Home may be a larger metaphor for openness, for a heart or a hearth meant to be communal, for a time when, all fear and deadbolt locks aside, we care for each other.

Perhaps my longing to go home had to do with wanting to live simply again, viscerally as children do, full of wonder. Maybe it was missing my brother who had been my first playmate. Maybe I was wanting to inhabit a place that does not change with time, a place with frogs and spiders, where groundhogs dig their holes in the cutbank, where acorns ripen and fall off the trees with their little brown caps still on, where tall grain, trampled down in a circle and smelling like warm bread, makes a hideaway in the field where children share stolen oatmeal cookies.

To my amazement, the screw holes that held up the chains of our beloved porch swing were still visible in the wooden ceiling of that screened-in summer porch. I could hear our Gango singing "Abide With Me" as she rocked us there.